WATCHING MEN DANCE

MARCIA CEBULSKA

Flint Hills Publishing

Watching Men Dance
© Marcia Cebulska 2020
All rights reserved.

Original cover paintings by Barbara Waterman-Peters
barbarawatermanpeters.com

Photos by T.J. Prasch and J.T. Hansen

Cover Design by Amy Albright

stonypointgraphics.weebly.com

Flint Hills Publishing

Topeka, Kansas
www.flinthillspublishing.com

Printed in the U.S.A.

ISBN: 978-1-7332035-6-2

Library of Congress Control Number application pending.

For Tom, Inge, and Judah—

treasured family and
fellow adventurers.

PROLOGUE

Chile
New Year's Eve Day, 1969

She thinks she may have taken the wrong path. The grass has given way to hard-packed dirt. The barren boulders surrounding her are increasing in size. Her rented stable horse is slowing down, trying to find his footing. What happened to the village that was supposed to be here? Where are the happy natives, dressed in yellow, festooning the streets? And the children carrying empty suitcases, ready to start the adventure of the new year? Where are the copper vats of chicha, the intoxicating grape beer she's heard so much about? The animal masks, the drumming, the jumping twelve times at midnight? It was all in the guidebook!

Ava tries to comfort herself with how snugly she sits cradled in the Chilean saddle. It's really just a pile of hand-woven blankets cinched with a wide belt, but it makes her feel safe. And her horse, she reminds herself, is a corralero, a sturdy Chilean breed, built strong and low to the ground. Worse comes to worst, she could give him free rein. Horses always know their way home, don't they? Her right knee scrapes against the rock face of the narrowing canyon. No turning back now.

Just when she thinks she is hopelessly lost in a stony maze, Ava sees a widening space between the rocks ahead. An opening. A beach. The Pacific Ocean lapping gently on the shore. As far as the eye can see, there is sand and turquoise water. The view is awesome! Here she is, in a picture-postcard world, riding a horse on the wet sand of a stunning beach. She wishes she had a camera. She really must buy a camera. Taking her feet out of the stirrups, she sinks into a comfortable slump, whispering thanks to the gods for leading her to this quiet peace. Not bad for a girl who grew up above a Greek restaurant in Chicago.

Chicago. Where, right about now, her father is reaching into ovens for the holiday legs of lamb, fragrant with garlic and rosemary. Where, right about now, he is lifting a wineglass to toast before the busy night. And, right about now, he balances the wineglass on his head, practicing for tonight's entertainment. Ava pictures her mother laughing and applauding her Greek husband, his showmanship. Ava's parents didn't like the idea of her leaving home for the holidays, but they would be happy to see her on this beautiful beach, rocking lazily in the saddle, the sun

7

warming her skin. The lazy gait of the horse rocking her gently. The peace of it all.

The rhythm of the waves is drowsily soothing, so she is surprised when she sees the gelding's ears twitch. And then, a sound. A distant pounding. The sky is clear yet there is this deep loudening, like muffled thunder. She slips her feet back into the stirrups, looks over her shoulder and sees horse heads bobbing among the boulders. Riderless horses—wild horses?—making their way onto the sand behind her. Her horse picks up speed. The herd thunders forward, gains ground behind her, approaching fast.

Blankets are all that are holding her in place. A pile of blankets. Holy crap!

Finding themselves on open ground, the wild horses work up to a canter, then a gallop, their manes like flags in the wind. They pound the ground alongside her.

A guttural sound emanates from her depths. The voice of fear. A scream of terror drowned out by hoofbeats. As the wild horses pass her, kicked-up sand bites her lips, her nose, her forehead. Instinct takes over and she lifts herself off the saddle. Leaning her head down close to the gelding's neck, she stands up in her stirrups like a jockey. Her long dark hair streams behind her like a flag in the wind. She is in the middle of the pack now. Ava gives up and gives in. She joins the herd.

The herd has its own heartbeat and she becomes a part of it, the larger rhythm of the swarm, the flock, the hive, the tribe, the living moving earth, the chorus, the crowd, the flood, the unanimity, the all-ness and togetherness of beings. Standing high now in her stirrups, she seems to split open inside, losing any trace of fear. She is light and powerful.

She is flying.

The wild horses pass her, then turn into the rocky hills, leaving Ava and the stable horse behind. She returns to sitting in the saddle. Her sweaty hair is plastered to her face. Her face is covered in grit. Her nose is skinned; her hands are cut raw from clinging to the reins. Her eyes blink wildly. The lathered corralero slows to a trot, a walk.

The sea laps gently at the gelding's hooves. The sky is clear.

She is safe.

She is throbbing.

She wants it to happen again.

PART ONE

Chicago
Spring 1971

"No! I forbid it! First you go to some country with a name like some canned American food. . ." Giorgos Paputsakis strikes his knife down on an eggplant for emphasis.

"Chile. The name of the country is Chile. Not chili, like a can of Hormel."

Ava and her father are standing in the fragrant kitchen of her father's restaurant where most of the important conversations of her life have taken place. Her father chops with purpose.

"Now you want to go to the end of the earth. . ."

"Seattle. The West Coast. I've got a job. You should be proud. My teacher, my professor, Dr. Baines, is hiring me, paying me for my knowledge and expertise." Even she realizes that she sounds a bit haughty.

"Wild West, you go to. Drunken cowboys, arrows flying through the air."

"No, Daddy, Seattle is a city, like Chicago. And the Indians we'll be interviewing are urban Indians. They work in banks and restaurants." Ava is guessing here.

"Don't bring home no stray savages. You were always bringing home stray puppies and kittens."

"I promise. No strays."

In between rants, Giorgos Papatsakis lifts lids, inhales, adjusts spices, tastes. Ava is almost dizzy with hunger, but her dignity does not allow her to grab a spoon. "Daddy, I have a good job, an excellent job. I'll be training and supervising interviewers. It's very unusual for an undergraduate to have such an important job and work with a distinguished urban anthropologist like Dr. Baines."

"You send your child to school. Good School. University of Chicago no less, and they come home and talk so you don't understand." He chops a handful of fresh oregano, sniffs it deeply, and tosses it into a red sauce.

"C'mon, Daddy, you and I have discussed this a thousand times. It's a summer job. It'll look good on my resume. I'm twenty years old, not five!"

"Summer. You should be home. Here, home."

He grabs a small onion from a basket. He looks up and meets her eye. "So soon after your mother, she die."

"I know." Ava softens here. This is her father's ace-in-the-hole. Ava chokes up. "I know." She hugs her father from behind. "It'll be hard for you. But she wanted me to go. Try to be proud of me. I'll be back before you know it."

He puts down his knife, shrugs his shoulders, and tosses the whole onion into the sauce.

"Last time you go, you don't even take pictures. Couldn't even show your mama and papa where you been."

"Sorry, Daddy. I should have brought a camera."

"A camera?" Her father repeats this in a louder voice. "A CAMERA?" And in through the swinging door strides her Aunt Dena, dressed to entertain customers in a turquoise-spangled gown, carrying a tray of sparkling wine. Behind her strolls her cousin Julie from the Polish side of the family, in jeans, T-shirt, and a tomato-stained apron, carrying a box wrapped in white tissue and tied with blue ribbons.

Ava examines the faces of these, her closest relatives, their proud, long-suffering faces. Their faces tell her they know she is doing the right thing and at the same time they already feel the pain of her absence.

Her Aunt Dena speaks up in her deep throaty Melina Mercouri voice, "We miss you."

"I haven't even left yet."

Her cousin hands her the box, "But this time, take some pictures, okay? Open! Open schmopen."

And, of course, she knows what's inside. A camera. A Minolta Hi-Matic, a definite step up from the Brownie of her childhood.

"Thank you. I promise you pictures."

Her father squeezes a twig off of a rosemary plant.

"Or, you could change your mind, stay in town, meet a nice Greek boy to take over the business when I'm too old. . ."

"You'll never be too old."

He pulls off a handful of rosemary leaves to stuff into legs of lamb with the cloves of fresh garlic waiting on the counter. He lifts off a particularly tender sprig and holds it out in the palm of his hand, like an offering.

"You'll recognize the right man for you because, behind his ear, you'll see a sprig of rosemary. Like this." And, of course, he demonstrates, tucking rosemary next to his graying hair.

"Okay, Daddy. I'll know what to look for."

Aunt Dena, a singer and dancer herself, adds, "And make sure he can dance." She hands Ava a glass of sparkling wine while sneaking a $50 bill into her front pocket. She winks with both eyes.

"*Ya mas,*" Julie, the cousin from the Polish side, intones in her best Greek. And together they all raise their glasses and say in perfect unison, "*Ya mas.*" To us. They drink as one. Ava wonders why she is leaving this warmth, this love, this cocoon, in order to study Indians. She's never even met an Indian.

Seattle
Summer 1971

She finds herself in an abandoned part of town. Trying to cheer herself on, Ava makes up a wish list for her summer in Seattle: eat some salmon, smoke a cigar, see a totem pole, climb a mountain, sail on the sea, look for mermaids, take tons of pictures. On this, her very first night, she's recording the journey of a piece of cellophane being carried by the breeze. Remembering the French movie, *The Red Balloon*, Ava is photographing what turns out to be a potato chip bag as it tumbles along the sidewalk and sails through the air. And although recession-hit Seattle is not Paris, and what she's following is just a crumpled bag, she trails it as if it were Fate itself. It leads her through a forgotten park, past a cigar-store Indian poised outside a Chinese restaurant, past a boarded-up shop called The Grand Map Emporium. The bag somersaults and sails until it plasters itself against the window of a mirror store where Ava's image confronts her by the dozen. Seeing her travel-weary eyes and her hair frizzled like a clown wig, she spits on her hands and uselessly pats down the top of her head.

Unceremoniously, the bag falls to the ground. Ava looks up at the sky, "Hey, You-Up-There! Really? Can't you send me something with a little life?" A gust of wind picks up the red and white bag again and Ava sprints, trying to capture the fluttering cellophane in motion as it flies around the corner.

And that's when she sees him, the Boy in Feathers. He stands in profile, poised in concentration, waiting, just beyond a mural of a mermaid painted on a brick wall. Bared arms and legs, adorned in feathers and bells, he holds himself perfectly still. She thinks, Omigod, he's so. . . when the sound begins, the loud, wonderful beating. Her attention moves sharply to the right where three, four, five men, all wearing jeans, T-shirts, and red bandanas strike a large drum in the middle of the street where a crowd is starting to gather. How lucky she is. She barely got off the plane and finds this happening.

The drummers start singing. To Ava's unfamiliar ears, they seem to wail, to cry out in a language she doesn't recognize but thinks she can understand, can't possibly understand though she desperately wants to. Voices call and respond. Drumbeats resound. The sound is strong. It makes her forget hunger, fatigue, homesickness. She is in Seattle, listening to a band of Native drummers. Indians. Real live Indians. Men beating out a rhythm, voicing a lament. Ava becomes absorbed into the sound. She feels herself reverberating, as if she herself is a drum.

Now the ankle- and wrist-bells of the Boy in Feathers add to the rhythm. He begins to dance. She wants to see this up close. She is eager to see this. She must see this. Ava edges forward between T-shirts and handbags to get a better view. She watches the dancer strike the pavement with bare feet. Bells jangle, the fan of feathers on his back vibrates. Shiny black hair moves in waves across shoulders that are strong, graceful, and stately. Body lithe and young, he can't be much older than she is. He is beautiful.

Ava Odesza Paputsakis is twenty and she believes she is hearing an ancient song about the pettiness of humans and the wrath of gods. She is young so she thinks she can right grave wrongs if she just really listens. She photographs the five singers, sitting in a circle, striking the large drum, and the single dancer. She snaps pictures quickly, hungrily. She wants to capture the fleeting movement, record the vision as if it were about to evaporate.

The rhythm shifts to single, unison beats. The tempo increases, volume rises. Feathers whirl; sweat gleams; the dancer stomps. She leans forward, watching with her whole body. Now she can see him up close. Two stripes of color paint each cheek. His eyes are a captivating sea green.

Really? She lowers her camera. He dances in place. If she didn't know better, she'd say he was dancing just for her. Her cheeks flush.

As the song ends, Ava tries to assemble herself into some kind of dignity, walks toward the drummers and drops change in the donation box for the Indian Cultural Center. She watches the next dance and the next. The crowd thins. The air cools. The singers pack up and leave. She sees this from the corner of her eye, knows this is happening, but she is watching this beautiful being who is still dancing. She is the only audience left. He starts to sing now; he is his own accompaniment. *Aya-waya-haya* is what she thinks she hears. She wonders what it means; she doesn't care what it means; she very much wants to know what it means.

The evening darkens. The street empties. They stay: she, watching; he, dancing, ever more slowly. She bites her lip; his foot bleeds. She drops her backpack; he stops singing. She steps closer; he leans forward. She closes her eyes, feels warmth. Was that a kiss or a feather?

He speaks. "Y'oughta come with us to Portland for the big powwow next weekend. It'll be good."

She steps on the potato chip bag that has been floating around the square, arrests it in its journey. She thinks: Just got here. Portland far away. Can't possibly. But then, again: a chance to hear the beat of the drum, the jangle of the bells, to feel that tremble in the bones.

She says, "Sure."

He watches her walk into her building. She turns back to wave, her slight frame topped by an impressive mass of spirals, like the wild manes of those English women in Pre-Raphaelite paintings with their tousled dignity and intense gaze. Her eyes look like they're listening.

Walking past the peeling boat-tour company mural with its wavy sea and long-haired mermaid, he thinks: She must not be from around here. He itches to get out of his regalia and back into his jeans. He picks up the potato chip bag and impales it on a wrought-iron fence.

The next morning Ava Odesza Paputsakis wakes at dawn, the victim of sunshine blasting between the slats of blinds. She crawls out of bed and onto the fire escape, camera in hand, and yawns with gusto. Red clouds streak the sky. "Red sky at morning; sailors, take warning." She is careless about where she steps and her foot lands on the tail of a roaming cat. The stray screeches and Ava jolts, dropping the camera on her foot. This could be an omen.

Ava crawls back inside and examines the rosy swelling on her foot—she'll live—and the little black box that created it, her Minolta—intact, with four shots left. She vows to finish the roll before breakfast. She crawls back into bed, hoping to ignore the ache, fall into a doze, and start the day again minus the cat screech. She flips over three times, too eager to get the photos printed to laze about. She wants evidence. She wants to see printed images of the drummers and yes, the dancer, the Boy in Feathers, to know it wasn't all some misleading dream.

Holding an ice cube to her foot, Ava dials her cousin Julie back in Chicago. They grew up together. She can ask Julie anything.

"What's a powwow?"

"Um, a gathering, a meeting for deciding something, like 'President Nixon powwowed with his Chiefs of Staff to decide how best to escalate the Vietnam War and wreak further destruction on unsuspecting civilians.'"

The cat sits calmly, looking Egyptian and noble, Cleopatra of the fire escape. "Yeah, except not so much the evil-white-person co-opting of the word but maybe the real thing, an Indian powwow to which a hopefully not-so-evil white person has been invited?"

"Invited by. . ."

"I mean, how can I know what 'hegemony' means and not know what a powwow is?"

"Omigod, you've met a boy. One night in Seattle and you've met a boy."

"We're asking them to not call us 'girls' anymore, so the least we can do is not call them 'boys.' " She grimaces in self-recrimination.

"You met a boy. And he's taking you to a powwow. Aha, an Indian boy. Is he cute?"

"I'm in love."

"Does he have long black hair and high cheekbones? What color are his eyes?"

"Sea green. Impossible, right? I probably dreamt it."

16

"You scamp. But an Indian, hmmm. Your dad will kill you."

"I haven't even said two words to this guy. In fact, I only said one word to him."

"Which was?"

"Sure."

Julie is laughing so hard that Ava's sorry she told her. She wants to indulge herself in preteen-style daydreaming, wants to replay the brief encounter over and over in her mind, maybe dress herself as a princess with flowers woven into her hair, riding in a carved boat pulled by a pair of unicorns. After too long a silence, Julie asks, with a tad more seriousness in her voice, "Ava, are you all right?"

"Fine. Great. Smashing." Having recently buried her mother, Ava has been handling her grief through escape and relentless cheerfulness.

She decides to plead hunger. Having been raised in a Greek restaurant by a Polish mother and Greek father, food is always a priority. She can eat her way through anything. Ava opens the refrigerator in this all-too-beige apartment. "My last meal involved fish sticks and marshmallow cream. The only food I have in my refrigerator is a jar of foggy-looking olives left by a previous tenant. Gotta find myself some bacon."

⁂

Ava walks down the hill, toward her first day at work and, hopefully, breakfast. She immediately likes the name of the street, Yesler Way, the idea that Yes is part of Yesler. No one has told her yet that this street was also called Skid Row, named for the skidding of logs down to the waterfront on the very path she is walking. No one has told her yet about Henry Yesler, whose sawmills sent the logs rolling down. No one has yet said a word to her about the rascally Yesler's free-love marriage to Sarah, who was as tolerant of his dalliances with other women as he was tolerant of Sarah's dalliances, also with women. Not a word has yet been spoken to her about the nineteenth-century prayers uttered in Seattle's churches for that "God-forsaken couple" whose wild investments helped create this City on the Sound.

Carrying the optimism of morning, Ava tries to concentrate on the excitement of starting her internship and her class on field research. She is twenty and believes that urban anthropology is the path to human understanding. Anthropology and maybe a boy, one certain dancing guy. A Boy in . . . a Man in Feathers. What is it about guys who dance? And those who don't? Don't they know that dancing is the most seductive thing the male of the species can do?

Ava walks through the square where the drumming was the night before and finds the potato chip bag impaled on a wrought iron fence. She looks inside, thinks better of eating the chip crumbs, and replaces the bag where she found it.

Ava continues down Yesler Way, heading, she hopes, toward platters of bacon and pancakes, fried eggs with melted cheese, mounds of buttered toast. But there, in her path, is a totem pole. Awkwardly, it stands surrounded by five-story buildings, some sandblasted in an attempt at urban renewal, others falling into abandoned decay. Nearby, a red neon flophouse sign announces beds for 75 cents. On the ground, nearly a dozen dozing men wrapped in ragged blankets try to block the sun out of a day that, for them, is starting too early. Middle-aged white men, young hippies, and old Indians, all of them wearing worn jeans and several days' growth of beard. Seattle has been in a deep economic depression, the Boeing Bust.

Ava's seen totem poles in books, of course. She even attempted a replica of one for a fifth-grade class project. She carved balsa wood discarded by her brother Mickey, frustrated in his attempts at making a model airplane. But her clumsy childhood whittling did nothing to prepare her for the real thing. Sure, there's the sixty-foot tall, neck-stretching majesty of its elegantly carved wood, but there's also the turquoise and black and white and red of it, the encircled eyes, the protruding beak and wings of it, the feeling of life in this be-carved tree. She raises her camera but feels a presence at her elbow.

"Far-fucking-out, right? Except for the fact that white invaders stole it from the Tlingit."

"Pardon?"

"White business guys hacked it down and carted it here to Pioneer Square. As a tourist attraction. Back in Seattle's heyday." The speaker is one of the blanketed white hippies, now awake and standing at full height. "Hey, I'm Gary." He lights a joint, offers it to her.

She shakes her head.

Gary indicates the totem pole. "It's a beauty, right? Raven stealing the moon, Frog, Mink. Whale with a seal in his mouth, not that they really eat seals." Gary positions the doobie in the gap between his front teeth. Ava is impressed by the feat but tries not to stare. Hands now free for gesturing, he continues, "Memorial pole, carved by a Tlingit in memory of his mother-in-law."

"Really?"

"A lady called 'The Chief of All Women.' She was pretty cool, I guess, back in the day. Traveled all over, up and down the coast." Ava nods as Gary draws deeply on his tooth-propped doobie. "White guys stole the pole. Had a great big party when they put it up. The Tlingit were mad, of course."

"Of course." Ava is interested, immensely interested, but can't seem to manage anything more intelligent on an empty stomach.

"Let's face it. White folks, we got some big-ass sins to make up for."

"Yeah, right." Ava spies a coffee shop down the street. *Bacon.* Though she appreciates the history tour and, despite herself, is enjoying the secondhand pot smoke, Ava searches for an exit line. She pulls a dollar out of her backpack, hands it to Gary, then makes a quick V-sign with her right hand. "Peace." Gary answers with a V of his own, hands her a circular, and stumbles away. Ava stuffs the paper in her pocket.

Edward Curtis paid Chief Seattle's aging daughter Princess Angeline a dollar to take her photograph. Ava reaches into her backpack and fishes out the other dollar bills her Aunt Dena gave her for pocket money. She hands them out to the other men and points to her camera. Some turn their backs, others smile. She kneels, she focuses, she shoots.

⁕

The small diner has a sign in the window: "Salmon and Eggs $1.99." She orders the special, adding a side of bacon, pancakes, orange juice. From the window, she has a view of vessels advertising passage to Alaska. She grew up in a restaurant where pictures of Greek Islands adorned the walls, but she'd never actually gone to one. What would it be like to take a sea voyage?

Her food arrives and she can't wait to delight in the salty crunch. Who doesn't love bacon? And then, there's the salmon dish that melts in her mouth. As she consumes the tasty bits, she surveys the row of vessels and notices a small boat propped up on land, as if it had walked there. A whale's tail is carved into one end and its interior is painted red. Turquoise, red, and white stylized animals are carved and painted on the outside. A raven's head and wings. The boat has wings. She likes this idea, feels a kinship to it. After all, her name, Ava, after all, means wings.

She catches sight of a small group of people walking toward the carved boat. And then she sees him, the Man in Feathers. Only now he is wearing a blue work shirt and jeans, his hair braided like Willie Nelson's and bound with rawhide and cowry shells. He wears a beaded cuff on his left wrist. He is beautiful. He walks around the boat, surveying it with obvious pleasure. He points out its features to his friends, a tall white man with a warm smile and a striking woman with straight black hair. He pauses to tuck an escaped strand of hair behind his ear. Ava wants to lick that ear.

Ava leaves the pancakes behind and hurries in the direction of the Man Who Used to Be in Feathers. She sees him emerge onto the sidewalk, one of his friends running to catch up with him. The striking woman with the straight black hair embraces him. He kisses her on the forehead with obvious affection.

Ava sighs. Oh. A girlfriend. Of course. An Indian girlfriend. What was I thinking?

He catches a glimpse of the mane of spiraled hair and her backpack bobbing away. He wants to run after her, but he is with friends, reminiscing about the good old days.

"Remember the time Jesse spit out an apricot pit and Kaya caught it? In her teeth?" Jesse nods but it is as if he is hearing voices in an echo chamber. His eyes are following the Girl with the Pre-Raphaelite Hair.

Noting his friend's distraction, Carlo turns, sees the abundant tresses. "Yeah, Rosetti would have loved that."

"What?"

"That girl's hair. Dante Gabriel Rosetti. He would have painted it."

"It's your fault I even know what you're talking about, Dweeb. You made me take that damn art history class."

"You needed a civilizing influence."

"Only a slightly racist thing to say."

"Hey, I took it, too. We both needed civilizing."

Kaya chimes in, "You still do, both of you. And Jess, really? A white girl, no less?"

He flinches but continues to observe the Girl with the Pre-Raphaelite Hair. No one around here walks with that much hope. Midwestern. Undoubtedly lives in a tidy white suburb. She turns a corner and is gone. The three friends enter the diner, take a seat by the window, keeping the small boat in sight.

He'll see her on the weekend. She did say, "Sure."

★

Ava finds the Urban Research Center in a recently sandblasted building perched on Elliott Bay. Whatever kind of fishery or whorehouse it was before, no matter; she is instantly fond of the place, its proximity to ferry boats and bowls of clam chowder. The offices are on the second floor. She is never late. She is five minutes late.

Framed Edward S. Curtis prints grace the exposed brick walls. His portrait of the Nez Perce Indian leader Chief Joseph. The Sia Buffalo Mask. Sepia tones. Formal poses. Curtis's photographic studio was just a few blocks from where she now stands.

With its high ceilings and brick walls, the narrow room could be a trendy restaurant except for its desks and phones, one of which is ringing. Ava picks it up and announces, "Urban Research Center." She is in charge. Her boss had put an ad in the Seattle paper for staff, but his arrival was delayed, so Ava will hand out applications. The reality that she will start the ball rolling crashes down on her. She's too young to be in charge. Whoever was on the other end of the line hangs up.

The space is open and airy, unlike the cramped airshaft-facing office at the University of Chicago where she'd last worked for Dr. Henry Baines. She had taken her part-time student job on his study of homelessness seriously. She wore suits and dresses while other students wore jeans; worked devotedly while others did crossword puzzles. On her breaks, she argued theory with Dr. Baines. Her diligence paid off. He offered her this summer internship on his study, "When the Natives are Homeless: Urban Indian Culture in Seattle."

Dr. Henry Baines wanted to hire local Indian interviewers to give him an entrée into the difficult-to-reach Native community. Ava suspects it might also have something to do with his religion. Aren't Mormons always looking for the lost tribe of Israel?

On the far wall, a door opens to a smaller office. Ava ventures in and seats herself in the executive leather chair. She swivels around and looks out the tall window. Below, ships are moving toward open waters and odysseys unknown. She thinks of the small carved boat and the Man in Feathers.

Ava senses a new presence in the room. She slowly turns and finds herself surrounded by five young Indian men, all wearing intense expressions and red bandanas. One of them speaks in as forceful a tone as he can muster. "What tribe are you?"

Nothing. A freezing of the brain.

And then she spouts out, "*Polska.* And *Elenika.* Half and half. My grandparents on my mother's side? They come from Poland. That's the *Polska* side. My dad's side come from Greece. I'm Polish-slash-Greek-American." She chides herself for rambling.

The young Indian turns quizzical. "So, your family, back in the old days, they weren't with Custer?"

"Custer? Like Custer's Last Stand? Well, they hadn't come to America yet, but. . ."

"But they killed Indians? Made bad treaties."

Ava thinks about her grandparents who were sweatshop workers in tenement buildings and peddlers, pushing carts around, selling fruits and vegetables. "They came to Chicago just before the First World War and never left, so I doubt it." Even to her own ears, it sounds inadequate. She puts Vine Deloria's book *Custer Died for Your Sins* on her mental reading list.

Another Indian chimes in, "At least she's not saying that she's 1/20th Cherokee." The others laugh. "Every white person West of the Mississippi claims to be 1/20th Cherokee."

She tries to sound professional. "My name is Ava Paputsakis. I'm a student intern. What can I do for you?"

One of the red-kerchiefed young men reaches into his pocket and pulls out a local newspaper with a circled want ad. They are University of

Washington students looking for summer jobs. She asks about the bandanas. They belong to a Red Power group, United Indians of All Tribes.

"We occupied Fort Lawton? Resurrection City? Jane Fonda talked about it on TV?" Ava looks mystified so he continues, "The government stopped using the army base, so we tried to reclaim the land for a cultural center." He goes on to tell her about how they threw blankets over the barbed wire to get in. How men, women, and children put up tipis and organized drum circles. How they went to jail. Ava wonders how she could have missed these events, if they were even covered in the Chicago papers.

Ava likes the idea of hiring revolutionaries. She asks routine questions about their backgrounds and hires them all on the spot, crossing her fingers that Dr. Baines will approve.

He will not.

The young urban Indians leave behind the local paper. Ava reads a headline: 85,000 JOBS LOST AT BOEING. Vietnam War and space program money dry up. Flocks of citizens leave the city. Ava recalls a billboard near the airport: "Will the last person leaving SEATTLE—turn out the lights!" She considers herself lucky to have a job. There's a smaller article about fishing rights being lost by local tribes. Nisqually. Makah. Tlingit.

Tlingit! From her pocket, she pulls out Pioneer Square Gary's flier, printed on red paper.

IMPERIALISM!!! CULTURAL THEFT!!

On September 3, 1899 at the dedication of the so-called Pioneer Square Totem Pole, William J. Lampton read a poem about how the Tlingit pole would delight in its new status as a Seattle monument. Having the nerve to speak not only ABOUT but FOR the totem pole, he said:

> *'I am the only civilized totem pole on earth. . .*
> *Here in Seattle's surging scenes*
> *So, here's farewell to all my past*
> *And welcome to the things that are:*
> *With you henceforth my die is cast,*
> *I've hitched my wagon to a star.*
> *And by the Sacred Frog that hops.*
> *And by the Bird that flies,*
> *And by the Whale and by the Bear,*
> *I'll sunder all the ties*
> *That bound me to the ancient creed*
> *which holds my people flat*
> *And I will be a Totem pole*
> *That knows where it is at.'*

RETURN THE TOTEM POLE NOW!

To Portland

She waits outside, having been taught by her protective father that she should never let a man into her room until she knows him as well as a cousin. Her father also told her never get into a car with a stranger, but she is about to do just that. Ava pictures her widowed dad pacing dark wooden floors, worried. Nah. Most likely he spent last night serving up stuffed grape leaves, setting cheese aflame, and crying out "Opa!"

Having borrowed a car so he wouldn't have to pick her up in his truck, he drives toward her building, thoughts spinning through his brain. It's hopeless. Her dad is an accountant, her mom makes bologna sandwiches on white bread. Wall-to-wall carpeting. A swing set. He sees her hair flying in the breeze.

Observing that this guy still has the same disquieting green eyes, Ava makes a less than dainty entrance, banging into the car door with her camera, dropping her tape recorder on the street, half-sliding, half-falling into the sedan. He tells her that the three teenagers occupying the backseat—he borrowed the children when he borrowed the car—needed a ride and will catch up with their parents at the powwow.

One of the impatient youths complains, "Hey, Chief, I got myself a mighty big taste for fry bread!"

Mmmmmm, food. If nothing else, she thinks, it'll be a culinary adventure. Did that kid just say, 'Chief?' What she says, though, is, "Thank you for inviting me," and arranges her tape recorder on her lap.

Having eased onto the interstate, he nods toward her tape recorder, "So, Margaret Mead, I see you brought your equipment."

She laughs at what she hopes was a joke and says, "I'm taking a fieldwork class. Anthro."

"On the reservation, they used to say that every Indian family had a husband, a wife, two children, and an anthropologist."

With a smile, she clarifies, "Urban anthro, actually."

"Ah. Anthropologists are done examining Rez Indians like bugs under a microscope, now they're going to start in on City Indians dancing on cement?" Maybe this isn't the best way to start a conversation with a stunning-looking woman.

"If you don't like people watching you dance, why do you do it?" She wants to swallow her words. Oh, no, I sound like my brother.

"Okay, Elsie Clews Parsons, turn on the machine." She presses ON with pronounced force. He says, "Dancing in the street is a political act."

She raises her voice ever so slightly to let him know she enjoys a good debate. "Political? How so?"

"For a hundred years, the U.S. government forbade us to speak our own languages or practice our traditions, so we did it in secret." He steals a quick glance over at her as she tries in vain to tuck her tumultuous hair behind the shell of her ear. The car swerves briefly across the line. "Secret potlatches, secret rituals. We tried to keep them alive, but we lost a lot." Out of the corner of his eye, he can see her furrowing her brow. "Now we're doing it in the open. On the city streets." He waxes with enthusiasm. "We're letting the world know we're not a vanishing people. We're here. We're alive." He catches himself preaching. Damn.

One of the teenagers saves him, "Can we please turn on the radio?"

Ava, picturing what it would be like if her parents weren't allowed to speak Greek or carve butter lambs for Polish Easter, wants the conversation to continue. "With the beads and the feathers, maybe some people might get the impression you're enacting a stereotype of an Indian?"

"I AM an Indian. Would you stop an Italian from dancing the tarantella BECAUSE he's Italian?"

In a quieter voice, she asks the question she rehearsed all morning. "So, um, what tribe are you?"

She expects him to laugh at her clumsy attempt, but he doesn't. "Makah. On my mother's side."

From the teens in the back, "Klamath."

"Nez Perce."

"Ogalala."

The boy who said Nez Perce counters, "You are not Ogalala."

"Yeah, well, Nisqually could get me in trouble."

An explanation comes from "Chief" in the front seat. "Roger is

Nisqually, from Frank's Landing. Where the police have been raiding the fish-ins?"

As if on cue, a siren sounds and red lights flash in the mirror. "Chief" pulls over.

The officer reads aloud the name on the driver's license: Joseph Weaver Lightfoot. He orders everyone out of the car, shines a flashlight into their eyes, then examines the interior and the trunk. The Indians stand still, heads bowed. When Chief Joseph—is he really named Chief Joseph?—starts up the car again, Roger starts singing Floyd Westerman's "B. I. A., I'm Not Your Indian Any More" and the other Indians join in.

BIA, you can't change me, don't you try
We don't want your white man rules no more
We can live our own way
Way ah hah, Hah, yoh
Way ah hah, Hah, yoh

At the fairgrounds, the teens eject themselves from the backseat and run. Indian men take turns slapping "Chief Joseph" on the back. A group of young women watch. Ava plops down on a grassy mound and checks her batteries for the third time.

The men fell three slender trees from a stand of red cedars and strip them of branches. "Chief Joseph" lingers over one of the trunks, carving carefully and leaving a twig with greenery intact. The men hoist and triangulate the tall thin logs, add other tree trunks and animal hides. They're putting up a tipi. *A TIPI!* Ava snaps photos as fast as she can. Then realizes: tipi, tent, sleeping over. No toothbrush. No jammies. Sleeping over? Sleeping with? Papa would have steam coming out of his ears.

When the other men leave, she exclaims. "So! A tipi!"

"Not the usual for these parts." He shrugs. "But Pan-Indian is what we do here. Blame it on Bernie Whitebear."

"Bernie Who-who?"

"Whitebear. Y'know, founded the Indian Health Center, started the U.I.A.T?"

Ah. United Indians of All Tribes. Like the revolutionaries who surprised her in the office.

She can't bring herself to inquire about sleeping arrangements, so she asks, "Why did you leave one branch with leaves still on it?"

"Y'know how Indians are about Nature." A trace of irony followed by a wink. "I have to change. One o'clock, come watch me dance?"

Looking around her, Ava realizes that she is the only white person in sight. Indians are setting up booths and tipis. She raises her camera but a hand falls in front of her lens, blocking her shot.

"Your permit?" A stern-looking woman gives her a look.

"Sorry. I didn't know."

Another voice chimes in. "Miss, you can take all the pictures you like. Never mind Helma Rabbit here."

Helma persists. "This is sacred ground. Our great fathers and mothers were slain here."

"She's carrying a camera, not a gun. This is a powwow, not a religious ceremony. Besides, she's a friend of Joseph Lightfoot."

"Worse. Young lady, we don't cotton to white girls taking our men."

"Cotton to? Hell, Helma, your daddy was white. You were raised Presbyterian."

Feeling like she is the ball in a tennis match, Ava finally speaks, "I'm sorry. First time at a powwow."

"Helma's forgotten that we are supposed to be hospitable. My name is Meg Standingwater."

Ava tries not to stare at the African American-looking woman.

"Never seen a black Indian before?" Meg notices that Ava is looking at her hair. "These? Beaver wraps. I can do yours, if you want." At her stand displaying whalebone carvings and beaded necklaces, Meg Standingwater braids Ava's unruly crest, then wraps strips of beaver fur around the plaits, finishing up with rawhide and cowrie shells. When she finishes, she hands Ava a moose-hide dress with elaborate beading and nods toward a nearby curtained area. "Try it on."

The beading is gorgeous, and she likes how soft the moose skin feels. Meg assures her, "It looks real good on you."

"It's just. Well, my anthro teacher is always warning us not to 'go native.'"

Meg laughs loudly. "And what exactly are you doing here, girl? Spending the night with Chief Studmuffin isn't 'going native,' but wearing a prairie dress is? Don't worry, it's not sacred or ceremonial, just something I made. And that moose-hide will last a lifetime. You'll be wearing it when you're a grandma with papooses on your knee." She laughs at Ava's shocked face over her use of "papoose." Ava's teacher instructed her never to say "squaw" or "papoose."

Ava spends her first week's paycheck on the dress. When she hears the thump of a drum, she runs, camera bouncing against her side, cassette player awkward in her hand.

A voice wails and others join in. Six male dancers, including Joseph, high-step around the drummers. Feathers whirl; sweat gleams; dancers stomp. Ava scrambles to take notes.

With the beginning of a new song, women replace the men. Ava writes in her notebook: "Some in black dresses adorned with cowry shells, others in jeans, they take small steps, dignified and sedate." As an anthropology student, she wants to record the cultural moment. As a newly-hatched feminist, she wants the women to break out of the restrained movement, to move and leap like the men. Among the dancers, she notices Helma Rabbit dancing with her head held high and holding a wing-like fan in her hand.

When the dance ends, Ava asks her about the difference between the male and female dances. Helma smiles, "The men, they have to show off for us. We get to be dignified."

"Chief Joseph," aka "Chief Studmuffin," leans against a railing. Ava is not the only young woman looking his way. He pauses a second, takes in the sight of her. "Nice dress."

"Thanks." In her best interviewer voice, she asks, "Can you tell me what the songs are saying, translate some lyrics for me?"

"We don't really know. Could be goodbye, or I love you, la la la, or abracadabra. Remember when I said our languages had been outlawed for like, a hundred years? One of these days, we'll find a way to reclaim the language."

"And the dances. Do you think the movements replicate any from your people's work world like hunting or sowing seeds?"

He grins. "Did you get these questions from some old anthro textbook?"

"*Fieldwork 101 Handbook.* I'm not doing a very good job at this, am I?"

"And what questions do you really want to ask?"

She does not hesitate, "When you're dancing like that, with the feathers and the leaps, do you feel as joyful as you look?"

"Lucky. Blessed. Proud. Sometimes achy. Tired. But then, something happens, and I feel taken over. Inhabited. I lose myself in it."

"And does dancing make you feel connected somehow to your community, your history?"

"Why did you want to be an anthropologist anyway?"

"I grew up in Chicago, where there are all these ethnic neighborhoods, like villages. I loved seeing the dances, hearing the music, seeing tradition in action. I still love things hand-painted and hand-carved."

He touches her hair. "Just watch, Raven. Watch and believe."

She ponders for a second. Raven. He called me Raven. What's that about?

When it's Joseph's turn for a solo, he is costumed as a deer. He runs and leaps. Occasionally, he moves his head jerkily, from side to side, watchful. Two other dancers costumed as hunters enter with bows and arrows to pursue him. The deer leaps but can't outrun the hunters. He takes an arrow, staggers and falls.

Ava walks from table to table until she sees a large poster with a photo of a well-worn canoe about the same size and shape as the one she saw in Seattle.

"Ozette." The young man speaking could pass for Joseph's brother.

"Some people call it, 'The American Pompei.' "

"Pardon me?"

"Last year a storm washed away a lot of dirt and uncovered a 4,000-year old Makah village. Our history came spilling out of the ground. Like that canoe." He smiles and adds, "I'm Charlie. Charlie Weaver. I work at the Ozette Archeological Site with my cousin Joseph Weaver Lightfoot."

She can't help but wonder, Does everybody know who I came with? Ava, however, is delighted to hear that her date works with archeologists. Someone she might, maybe, be able to introduce to her family? Nah. Self-conscious, she looks down at the table. Fliers with photographs of tools, ancient baskets.

"Jesse and I are carving replicas of some of the old cedar artifacts to help the archeologists see how they worked."

Ava recalls the painted canoe Joseph Lightfoot was showing off in Seattle. "You mean, like canoes?"

"Exactly! We've carved replicas and now we're going to row them to British Columbia and back to prove they made the journey."

"How glorious!" she says and means it.

✻

When the sky has turned dark, Ava returns to Meg Standingwater's booth and hesitantly asks where Chief Joseph Weaver Lightfoot might be. Amused, Meg answers, "Jesse—that's what his old buddies call him— Jesse is off with my brother Bird and the rest of the guys. You know how they are about the bone game." Ava's face contorts in confusion. Meg adds, "Slahal? It's like dice except they use the knuckle bones of dead white women." When Meg sees Ava's face, she can't help sniggling. "Anthropology 101. If you ask an Indian a question, we'll answer with a joke. Not to worry, nobody uses white-woman bones. Lately."

"Oh."

"It's a betting game. He's pretty good at it. He could win large."

"So, I might get a really BIG stuffed animal?"

"Ha!" Meg likes it that Ava can take a joke and give it back. Covering her wares with a tarp, Meg says, "C'mon. I'm tired of eagle feathers. Helma makes a mean posole."

Meg leads her to a little camper where she pulls out a couple of cans

31

of soda. Helma Rabbit joins them, indicating lawn chairs, and hands out bowls of fragrant posole.

Helma pointedly asks Ava, "What tribe are you?"

"Ummmm. My dad's restaurant serves spanakopita." She feels a sudden wish to be at home, eating babaganoush.

"Greek! And your mother?"

"Polish-American. She used to make pierogi. Polish dumplings? Little pillows of deliciousness with chopped mushrooms and bacon inside. She was the best cook in the world."

Meg looks genuinely curious. "Was?"

"We lost her."

"So sorry. Moms are important."

The bottom of her stomach drops, but Ava smiles and says, "Anyway, I'm out here because I'm a student. Anthropology."

Helma shrieks. "The people who dig up the bones of our grandfathers?"

"No, no. I pester living people. Today, I've been recording music, watching dancers."

"You're not going to learn nothing here. At powwows we all dance like we're from South Dakota."

Meg tries to clarify. "Helma thinks we should maintain more tribal identity."

"Damn right. We're Northwest Coast Indians. Where are the Raven masks? Thunderbird? Wolf?"

Ava's mind stopped at Raven masks.

Meg intervenes. "Powwows are Pan Indian. No sacred dances. We can't do those in front of. . ."

Ava finishes, "White people. Maybe I shouldn't be here."

Meg is quick to reply. "Of course, you should be here. Northwest Coast people pride ourselves on hospitality."

"And look where that got us."

Meg strikes back, "Helma Rabbit, you're here selling frybread and making a good buck at it."

Helma defends, "It's all Bernie Whitebear's fault. He had the big idea that if we went Pan Indian, we could attract the attention of white people, and they would come and save us. I don't want to be saved."

"Saved?"

"Missionaries, BIA government agents, somebody is always trying to save us. Anthropologists were the worst. They stole our bones, our masks. They had a shitload of nostalgia for the very things they were destroying."

In the pause, Ava stares out to the middle distance, looking for an escape route.

Meg adds, "Helma's joking about Bernie Whitebear. He's our hero." Then, she downshifts to the more personal. "Now, your friend Mr. Lightfoot, he knows dances from a lot of tribes even though he grew up back east, in Kansas."

Kansas? She thinks: Big skies, puffy clouds, and buffalo. The home there's no place like. "How'd he get here?"

"His mom was Makah. They'd come out here in the summers to see his grandma. Now, he works for Ozette."

Helma, being one of those people who don't believe one should talk and eat at the same time, declares, "Time to shut the pieholes and eat. Posole's getting cold."

Full of spicy posole and sitting on frayed lawn chairs made of aluminum tubing and braided strips of colored cloth, the women pass around their last cigarette. Helma makes a recommendation. "You oughta try salmon cooked Northwest-coast style. Local specialty."

Meg adds, "Yeah, go to one of them salmon bakes organized by Bernie Whitebear."

Helma laughs, mellow after eating.

Ava recalls, "I think I remember something about salmon and Marlon Brando."

Meg points to Helma, "This girl here, she was on the front line, got beat up good by those Fish and Games cops."

Ava looks at Helma in a new light. "What happened?"

Helma says to Meg, "Shut up, you." Then turns to Ava. "I'm fine. We don't want you thinking all we do is fish and sew beads on deerskin."

Meg agrees. "True. I like my dried halibut but I'm not against a washing machine or nail polish."

"Or even a white boyfriend with a job."

Ava dares to ask, "Does Joseph Lightfoot have a girlfriend?"

Cause for conspiratorial looks. Meg says, "Used to" at the same time Helma says, "Kaya? Off and on." Helma adds, "He's a good guy if you like his type."

"His type?"

Meg warns Helma, "Watch it."

Helma says, "He's a good carver. Works well with his hands." And giggles.

Meg says, "He's funny. Smart. Not too hard on the eyes."

Helma, with a devilish look in her eye, adds, "Chief Studmuffin."

When the evening grows chilly, Meg hands around blankets. They sing along to Floyd Westerman songs on Ava's cassette player until Joseph arrives with a fistful of bills and a big grin. He deposits most of the money in the U.I.A.T. donation box. When "Chief Joseph" picks up her backpack, Helma winks.

❦

He leads her away from the powwow grounds.

"We're not sleeping in the tipi?"

"I like sky more than smoke." She feels relieved.

When they're out of earshot, she says, "They call you 'Chief Studmuffin,' you know."

He finds that funny. "Meg and Helma? What does that even mean, 'studmuffin?' Am I getting soft in the middle and ready to be put out to pasture?"

"I'm guessing it means a good-looking guy who also has a sweet, soft side."

"Don't believe a word they say. They like to mess with tourists." He pauses to look around at their surroundings. "Look at the pattern the moon is making on the water. I'd like to try to paint that. Except if I did it, I'd use bright orange and lots of animal heads would be involved."

"You paint?"

"Only canoes and totem poles." He pauses. "But listen. I've been hauling trees and dancing. I'm so stinky, even my sweat is sweating."

"Not a problem. I'm Greek. Partly."

"Please turn around for a minute?"

She stays turned until she hears a splash and then whips back to see

34

the moon's reflection broken up into shards by a body thrashing around and yelping. "It's freezing in here. Wanna join me?" Silence. A shaking of the head he can't possibly see. "I didn't think so. Please turn around again. I'm awfully shy."

She waits until he says "Okay" and she turns to see him, wearing pants but still barefoot and shirtless, shaking his head like a puppy, spraying her with drops of water. "Oops."

But she enjoys the coolness of the water on her face, her arms. "Kinda refreshing, actually."

He takes a deep breath. "I'm sorry I gave you such a hard time about studying anthropology. I guess I was wondering why you chose the field."

"I read too many *National Geographics* as a kid. But urban anthro involves some social issues, too. I hope I can do some good. If I can survive in the field."

"Why wouldn't you?"

"I've already broken several rules about hanging out with the people I am supposed to be studying."

"God forbid you should get to know them."

"We're supposed to maintain a critical distance."

"'Critical?' Why?"

"I think they mean essential or appropriate."

"But they say, 'critical.' Why not non-judgmental or embracing or warm? And why distance at all?" He's walking closer to her to demonstrate. Drops of water are falling from his hair onto his bare shoulders. He reaches over and runs his finger down her nose.

She wants to get clear. "You have a girlfriend, right?"

"If I had a girlfriend, why would I have invited you here? What kind of guy does that?"

"Exactly."

"And everybody here knows me."

"They kept you busy, all right."

"I was avoiding you. Like I said, I'm kinda shy. And you are so. . . spectacular. Look at this hair. And your mouth." He runs his finger over her lips. "You look like one of those pre-Raphaelite women. Jane Morris, only prettier."

"I have no idea what you're talking about."

"I'm talking about you. And beauty. Sorry. I was trying to impress you with my tiny bit of knowledge about European art history." As he talks, he runs his fingers over her face, memorizing its features.

"It worked. I'm impressed." She instantly regrets never having taken an art history class.

"I love that era. Arts and Crafts. The emphasis on working with one's hands, on craftsmanship, on the handmade, the individual design. And I fell a little in love with the women in those paintings. Hair like yours. Lips like yours." He again runs his finger over her lips, and she captures his finger in her mouth for a second.

He makes a sound like a low hum. "Mmmm."

Afraid that she might be giving the wrong idea, she lets go.

"I love this dress, too. The beadwork." He traces his fingers over the beads that run over her shoulder, down her chest. He leans in to kiss her and she responds. All too suddenly, he stops.

She finds her voice. "Aren't we going to um—continue?" but then wonders: Who is this brazen hussy who's inhabited my body?

"Here?" He indicates the hard gravel.

She looks around at the stony path where anyone could walk past.

He touches her shoulders ever so softly. "Besides, we've already made love."

Ava thinks: Okay, that's kind of a sweet thing to say, but really, who is this guy?

He takes her hand and guides her to a patch of grass near the water. "I apologize. I don't have another minute left in me." He calumphs onto the ground and closes his eyes. "But tomorrow. . . 'My course is set for an. . .'"

Maybe there was more to the quote but Chief Joseph, Chief Studmuffin, Joseph Weaver Lightfoot has fallen asleep.

Lying down next to him, Ava stares at the stars. She never was a girl scout, doesn't know the names of constellations. She is uncomfortable on the hard ground but afraid to move, to waken him, so she lies awake, thinking of all the things she didn't say to him, like:

I feel like a fish out of water.

I don't know the rules.

I never met an Indian until I met you.

I've never been to a powwow before.

I look like a tourist playing dress-up.

I've violated every rule of where I came from.

My teachers would be disappointed.

My father would be furious.

Tears well up in her eyes. She slows herself down and watches this lovely man breathe. She tries to calm herself by observing that his body is firmer, smoother, stronger than her bookish classmates in college, boys with Che Guevara posters on their walls who argued from the safety of seminar rooms. He reminds her more of the men in her family. Her Polish uncle who is the world's reigning polka champion. Her Greek cousins who dance sirtaki every Saturday night at the Café Athena. Guys who laugh, tease, and sing easily. Unselfconsciously. And this guy knows something about art. He carves, he paints. He dances.

Her breathing slows down.

She leans over him to tuck his hair behind his ear.

He turns, in his sleep, so that he's lying on his back.

She puts her head on his chest and listens for his heartbeat.

Just after dawn, she is awakened by the pungent smell of horse sweat, quickly followed by the muffled sound of hooves on wet sand. Ava sits bolt upright to see five riders along the edge of the water. Rubbing curdled sleep out of his eyes, Joseph looks toward the horizon, "I've always wanted to do that. My dad has horses, but I've never ridden by the water." He looks at her face and recognizes that a memory is flicking across the screen of her mind. "You have, haven't you?"

"Most exciting thing I've ever done."

"You're not going to tell me about it?"

"I was riding peacefully along a quiet beach at the sea." She stops short.

"Don't be a tease."

Look who's the tease, she thinks.

"And?"

"From out of nowhere, or actually from between two giant boulders, a herd of—you're not going to believe this—wild horses dashed down from the hills right onto the sand."

"You're kidding."

"Those mustangs were kicking up sand right behind me like they were running for their lives and I ended up in the middle of the herd. I put my head down along my horse's mane and stood in the stirrups like a jockey."

"You weren't scared?"

"Terrified. But then I went beyond fear into some kind of altered state. Had the ride of my life."

"Damn. I'm surprised you're still alive." He thinks that maybe it's the hunger for adventure that makes her eyes so eager. He scrutinizes her as she watches the horses go by until the last tail is out of sight.

Ava pats her tummy. "I am SO hungry."

"I like a woman with a good appetite."

"I like a man who likes a woman with a good appetite." She adds, "Doesn't hurt if he also has high cheekbones."

"Ukrainian grandmother."

"Ukrainian grandmother? So that's where you got your pale-face coloring."

"Hey, look." He puts his arm next to hers. Her skin is darker than his.

"Greek dad. My Polish-American mom married him even though her father forbade it. My mother wasn't exactly the obedient type."

She has the same deep chocolate-brown eyes his mother had. He says, "Apple doesn't fall far from the tree?"

"I could use an apple about now."

He laughs. "I'll get you an apple. Even if I have to dance for it."

"Is that what you were doing yesterday, dancing for apples?"

"I'm one-quarter Ukrainian, one-quarter Anglo, and one-half Indian. So, only half of me was dancing." He smiles wryly. She never knows if he's joking.

"But the kids called you 'Chief.' 'Chief Joseph?'"

His laugh is nothing short of boisterous. "'Chief' is one of those names white men call Indians. Same with 'Tonto' and 'Cochise.'"

"So, it was a joke?"

"A good joke."

"But your name is Joseph Lightfoot?"

"Named after my father, who was named after Joseph Lightfoot the Intrepid, who came from Liverpool."

"You're kidding me. A Liverpudlian, like the Beatles?"

"Yeah, don't I look exactly like Paul?"

This Joseph Lightfoot, far more striking to her eyes than Paul McCartney, takes her hand and pulls her up. Her moose-hide dress is dusty and creased. She looks less like a tourist and more like a hippie now. She's never had the luxury of being a hippie before.

"I'll follow you in any direction as long as it involves food."

"And I thought you anthropologists weren't supposed to consort with your subjects."

"Consort? There's a nice nineteenth-century word. I think I'll regard breakfast as 'participant observation.'"

"You're going to participantly observe me eating a tamale?"

"I get one, too, right? Maybe three or four?"

"Makah is a Klallam word meaning, 'people who are generous with food.'"

Over breakfast, Ava tells the story of her seven-year-old self on her first visit to a Mexican restaurant, when she surprised her family by eating three tamales slathered in superhot chili sauce. She'd read in the *World Book Encyclopedia* that the Mayans invented them and, curious, she pushed aside her burger and fries and grabbed her brother's plate of tamales. Mickey was grateful for the trade. When she finished the first plate of tamales, she asked for seconds. Ava slips her camera out of her backpack. "And while I was waiting for my thirds, I took out my little Brownie camera and took pictures of this huge tree growing in the middle of the restaurant." She snaps his picture, fork in hand.

"You ate them all, didn't you?"

"Licked the plate."

He likes this hungry girl. He likes seeing her unabashedly enjoy the spicy breakfast. "I better get you more to eat."

"Do they have bacon?"

Taking notes later that morning, Ava tries to be professional, asking herself anthropology-of-dance questions: Is he duplicating motions used in the culture's work? Is his regalia made from elements naturally found in the vicinity? But she gets lost in the moment, his movement, passion, and grace. She experiences something like pride, even though she's done nothing to deserve it.

When the tipi comes down, Ava asks if she can have the leafy green twig off the pole. She wraps it in damp Kleenex and puts it in her backpack. The teenagers yawn their way into the car. After twenty miles or so, they stop at a drive-in and Joseph treats to burgers and shakes. When they are about to leave the parking lot, a police car pulls up. The trunk is opened, the feathered and quilled regalia tossed to the ground. Ava decides what she will record in her notebook: The Indians are cooperative even when Native regalia is treated with disrespect.

When the police are finished with their search, Joseph thanks them politely with a nod of his head. In the car, Roger speaks up, "Driving while Indian."

Rebekkah nods her head fiercely. "I've been in juvie so many times, I could puke."

But they fall asleep until the next siren sounds and red lights flash on the interstate.

"Watch out, Chief, here they come!"

The state trooper glares his flashlight in their eyes but doesn't ask for ID. He gives them some advice. "You've got a bad rear left tire. Take the next exit. There's a gas station there—Lucky's—they can help you. We'll ride alongside you, make sure everything goes okay."

The trooper goes back to the car with its whirling lights. Ava, relieved that there's one good cop in the world, says, "There you go. Not all policemen are bad." She wants the young teenagers to believe. They tap their feet impatiently.

When they drive into Lucky's, the state trooper takes off and a local police car drives up. The officer instructs everyone out of the car. "Do you know what time it is?

"10:35 p.m., sir."

"And how old are these children?"

Joseph indicates each of them in turn. "Fourteen, thirteen, fifteen."

"Are you their father?"

"No, sir, I am not. Their parents were vendors at the powwow and their cars are full. They asked me to drive."

"Been to the powwow, have you?"

"Yessir."

"Minors unaccompanied by their parents are subject to a 10 p.m. curfew in this town. Officer Kane will accompany the children to the juvenile facility. I'll be escorting you and your squaw over to the county jail. It'll be in your interest to cooperate, Cochise."

Squaw? Jail? Cochise? She can't be silent. "Sir, with all due respect, you can't do this. We're not in town, we're on the highway, led here by one of your own."

Handcuffs.

They've been pushed in front of a large counter. The officer who rode shotgun addresses the one behind the desk. "Got us a couple of Injuns."

Joseph Lightfoot looks around for the second Indian. When he realizes they are talking about Ava Puputsakis in her moose-hide dress, he can't help but laugh.

"Somethin' funny, Tonto?"

Joseph makes a mask of his face and remains silent as they take his wallet and her backpack.

"Contributing to the delinquency of a minor." Another officer hands over a wanted poster. "Ah, yes. We've had a rash of murders committed by a Redskin couple bearing a remarkable resemblance to the two of you. I'm adding 'suspicion of homicide' to the charge."

Ava cries out "NO!" Joseph is taken roughly and quickly away. Ava is pushed past a heavy door into a small cell where five women lounge like odalisques on thin mattresses.

"We're clean out of beds." The uniformed man at the door tosses her a blanket and shuts the door. Ka-chunk. The sound is final.

"Whatcha in for, Sweetie?"

"Contributing to the delinquency of a minor."

The prostitutes find this hilarious.

"Several minors."

Even louder throatier laughs fill the room. They are not going to be her friends. Ava finds a small square of unoccupied floor near the lidless, seatless toilet and spreads out the navy, moth-eaten blanket. She has always hated peeing in front of others and waits until the other women are asleep and her bladder is bursting before going to sit on the cold porcelain. Her great surge of relief is short-lived when she notices movement in the corner. Shiny-eyed rats scour the floor for crumbs. Ava wraps herself in the holey blanket, sits back on the toilet, and pulls up her feet. She stays this way most of the night until she is too tired to care about rat bites and returns to the floor.

❧

At 6 a.m., breakfast is pushed through a slot in the door, one tray at a time. Ava yells through the slot, demanding her rights. In the movies, the accused always get one phone call.

"You can have all the phone calls you want." She is led down a hall to a pay phone.

"But my change is all in my backpack and it was taken away last night."

"It was seized as evidence."

She is returned to the jail room. One of the older women speaks up, "Flash a little titty. He'll give you a quarter."

Ava waits until the lunch trays have been picked up and asks for the phone call again. She won't expose herself, but she is willing to lie. "I know my rights. My father is a judge. Now, give me my coins from my backpack so I can call for bail."

"Don't worry, little girl. It may look like a pay phone, but you don't need no coins to call with that contraption."

❧

Dr. Baines, a tidy, suit-wearing Mormon, bails her out. Ava feels like a teenager being picked up by a parent. She is self-conscious about her moose-hide dress, which is even more rumpled and dirtied by the jail floor. On the way to Seattle, Dr. Baines says that her hiring of the United Indians of All Tribes boys was not quite what he had in mind. Neither is getting jailed. He suggests she take a couple of days off to recover. She searches her backpack. Cedar twig yes, camera yes, tape recorder, no. It's missing.

Seattle

Instead of going to class, she holes up and reads *Bury My Heart at Wounded Knee*. She eats nothing but tangerines and potato chips. Her only excursions are to drop off and pick up film from the Fast Foto booth. She wants to see "Chief Joseph" again, if only in photographs.

❧

He paces outside her building, walks around the block three times. He's sure she'll slam the door in his face. He knocks on two other doors with no answer before he finds hers.

❧

Back at her apartment, Ava throws away all her matching sweater sets and neatly pressed skirts. From now on, she will only wear this single moose-hide dress in solidarity with the oppressed Indians of the small tribes of western Washington. She'll quit school and do something meaningful. But what? From her backpack, she pulls out the small red cedar tipi branch, puts it in a plastic cup full of water on the windowsill. Despite all it's been through, it's still green.

❧

Except for the Fast Foto guy, it's been four days and three hours since she has spoken to another human being. She looks through the peephole before she cracks open the door. Joseph Weaver Lightfoot stands there, holding out her cassette recorder, a peace offering.

43

She cries out when she sees it, "My tape recorder! The tapes—did they come out?"

"Perfect, except for the interview with that idiot dancer." She laughs and he continues, "Sorry. I shouldn't have listened to your tapes."

"Damn right you shouldn't have." She grabs the recorder and pretends to start closing the door.

"Please don't shut the door. I've come to apologize."

"For listening to my tapes? Bad form, but I'll get over it." She pretend-almost-closes the door.

"I got you arrested."

She opens the door wide and lets him in. "The most important experience of my life."

"We got booked as a rampaging homicidal Indian couple." He walks in.

She goes for offhand and ironic. "Oh, that."

"Yeah, maybe we'll laugh about that someday."

"They're going to drag us to court and throw us back in the slammer again, aren't they?" She enjoys the sound of the word "slammer," reminds her of Bonnie and Clyde.

"They were just trying to hassle us. It's all about the salmon."

"We got thrown in jail because of a fish?"

"We got thrown in jail because we're Indians." He takes a deep breath. "The tribes here believe they have the right to fish in the rivers where their grandfathers did. White guys disagree."

"May I remind you that I'm not an Indian."

"Your dress tells a different story. Anyway, charges have been dropped."

"Why?"

"Why? Were you looking forward to going to prison?"

"Good point, but still."

"Your boss told them you worked for the Urban Research Center—cool, by the way—and it'd look like bad publicity."

She puts her hands together, as if in prayer. "Thank you, Dr. Baines."

When he laughs, crinkles break out near the corners of his eyes. He bears no resemblance to the Edward S. Curtis sepia prints she's been poring over in books. Instead, he looks alive and delicious. She wants to reach out and take hold of him, but he wanders further into her apartment.

He takes in the books on the floor with their scraps of paper stuck in as place keepers. He walks to the table where her own photos are spread out. He picks them up one by one, studies them slowly. She waits, biting her lower lip and craving marshmallow cream. Or maybe even a BLT without the lettuce. Or, considering the occasion, salmon.

"People are always taking pictures of us looking posed and solemn. You caught movement. Life." His face grows serious and his eyes find hers. "I'm in love with these."

"Oh," is all she can manage.

His eyes don't leave her face. "Before we had this crazy little weekend together. . ." He pauses, trying to find his words.

"Before? There wasn't much before that." She notices how his hair, when it catches the sun, reflects blue-black, like that of a comic-book hero.

"That first time I saw you. When you were standing out there," he gestures vaguely toward her open window, "watching me dancing, your eyes were so wide open."

"I'd never seen anything like it. For a city girl, I'm pretty naïve when you get to know me."

"I want to get to know you." And then he steps closer to her. He takes a piece of her hair between his fingers. "For one thing, you've got these spirals for hair."

"Yeah, it's like having a thousand springs on my head." She says, "Boing" and regrets it.

He coils some of her hair around his finger. He's standing so close she can feel the warmth of his chest. She can't stand it anymore. She grabs hold of his shoulders and kisses him hard. After the long kiss, during which she's melted into a puddle of chocolate in the sun, he moves his hands up and down her arms. When their mouths meet again, they both go a little dizzy. They believe that no one has ever felt this way before. And, of course, no one has. He lifts her dress. They explore each other's bodies like continents.

※

In the morning, he offers her a ride to work. She explains how she's not going to work these days. School, either. How she's educating herself on the plight of indigenous people.

"Are you nuts? Do you know how many indigenous people would die to have a job like yours? Have a job at all?" He commands, "Get dressed."

She explains how she threw away her work clothes in favor of wearing her moose-hide dress in solidarity with Native Americans. Her moose-hide dress which is now creased with dirt, smelling of sweat, and none too pretty.

"When do they pick up your trash? C'mon, maybe we can still fish your stuff out of the bin. And hey, if you don't want to wear your good clothes, there are plenty of Native women who do. We'll put it in the donation box outside the Indian Cultural Center."

"I didn't think of that."

After dumpster-diving for her clothes, he sorts and sniffs through them and hands her a clean outfit. Fortunately, she had put everything in a heavy plastic bag before throwing it in the bin.

"I think you should put it on."

"Are you telling me what to wear?"

"You're not going to keep a job in this town in a dirty hippie prairie dress." He carries the clothes into her building's basement and puts them in a washing machine.

He takes a second shower to get the garbage stink off and then opens her refrigerator to see if there's anything for breakfast. Two tangerines. A half jar of marshmallow cream. Nothing.

"C'mon. I know a little place with great salmon and eggs."

"You're mad at me."

"Yes, I'm mad at you. But no use talking about it until we've had something to eat."

Outside, he opens the passenger-side door of his truck. A turquoise truck. She steps up into it. "Where's your car?"

"Wasn't mine. I borrowed it to impress you."

She laughs. "I like the truck better."

"Yeah, well, sure, all us Indians just love the color turquoise." He pauses, then, "I borrowed the kids, too."

"Lotta good that did us."

She's got him there. His anger is quelled by the memory of his own senseless posing.

❧

She chooses the same booth she sat in on her first day in Seattle. When she looks out the window, she sees the ferry boats, but not the frog- and raven-carved canoe. Once they've ordered, she says, "I saw you once outside this window. You were showing a painted boat to a couple of people. Your girlfriend, I think."

"Ex-girlfriend. Visiting from Kansas."

"She was so affectionate with you, I got up and ran away."

He recalls the sight of her Pre-Raphaelite hair, her backpack bobbing away. He says nothing until they've eaten. "I appreciate your passion over the plight of Native people. But you're doing nothing by staying away from work and school, wearing a beaded dress and pigtails."

"You made that clear."

"If you want to do something, come to the fish-in next weekend. You're good with a camera and we can use documentation."

"It's on my calendar."

"I have to go to Ozette for the rest of the week."

"I heard that you're doing some cool stuff there."

"As much as I'd love to be cool, this is about setting precedent. We've found some old whaling and fishing gear: harpoons, fishhooks. Similar to what we use today. I'm hoping that the local archeology will prove what the traditional fishing techniques were for the Northwest Coast tribes. Makah need to be able to fish in the traditional ways."

"It's all about the salmon?"

"Yup, it's all about the salmon."

She points to her dish with her fork. "And this here is some mighty tasty salmon."

He laughs, in spite of himself.

☙

Talk of food makes Ava miss her father. She dials the number to the Café Athena. "Hi, Daddy!"

"Ava, you know this is a place of business."

"You didn't answer the home phone."

"I don't like to talk on the phone, you know that. What's wrong?"

"Nothing's wrong."

"Why would you call if nothing's wrong?"

"Just to hear the sound of your voice. To tell you I'm all right."

"Good. Done."

"They eat a lot of salmon here."

"Hmm. Grilling or boiling?"

"Who would boil salmon?"

"Icelanders."

"Oh. No. I'm not in Iceland. And I'm just fine."

"Okay. Customers come. *Kalynichta,* sweetheart."

A group carpools to the fish-in protest at Frank's Landing. Ava is surprised there are so many white people, on both sides of the Puyullap River. She also notices, on the Indian side of the river, several dark-skinned people wearing Black Power T-shirts. When the Indians drop a net into the river, the police attack with billy clubs and tear gas. Amid the constant motion, Ava photographs quickly. She tries to keep her distance with her camera, but eventually she is pushed to the ground and called a "squaw whore." Along with the others, she is dragged into a police van. Once inside, the Indians start singing. They are elated. Joseph smiles broadly. The act of civil disobedience was successful. The press was there. When they sing, "B.I.A., I'm Not Your Indian Anymore," Ava hums along while she snaps photos. No official press inside the van. Only her to record what's going on. She is revved up and confused.

When Dr. Baines bails her out for the second time, he is not pleased. "You can't interfere with local politics."

"It's not politics, it's food. It's what they eat, what they've always eaten. What they've always done to live."

"You're missing a lot of work and so are the boys."

"We'll make up for it, I promise."

"Y'know, Ava, our study could help these people. Think strategy, not passion. And, in the name of science, stop getting thrown in jail!"

The passion for politics is tinder for other passions. Ava and Jesse spend the night together, hungry for each other. When he's asleep and breathing evenly and peacefully, he reminds her of the word *home*. But when he wakes, he starts chewing on his lower lip. "I need to tell you something. This is temporary."

She lies, "I wasn't expecting anything. Summer romance. . ."

"I mean I don't live here. I have to go back to Kansas at the end of the summer."

She mentally surveys her fall plans: go somewhere, find a job, earn enough money so she can go back to school. "Kansas, huh?"

"It's different from here."

"Yellow brick road and all that."

"Farms and ranches, small towns."

"Big skies?"

"Puffy clouds."

"And you live in a very small tipi?"

He appreciates her joke. "Big old farmhouse with creaky floors."

"The kind with tall windows and a porch?" She's hoping for Victorian.

"Drafty, creaky, spooky."

"Have you been listening to my dreams? I've had some very vivid ones about a big old spooky house. There's no place like home."

"But for you, home is the big city, Chicago."

"I knew Al Capone personally, you know."

He laughs. "That explains a lot."

"Ever been? To my hometown?"

"Saw a statue of some Polish hero there who fought in the American Revolution. Went to Greek Town. Had some lamb kebaby thingies."

"Kosciuszko. And I happen to have a noisy family that makes those lamb keboby thingies."

"Mmmmm."

"Now that we know we have so much in common…"

"Girl, we are as unalike as Raven and Whale. But I can't resist you."

⁂

Ava and her co-workers return to the homelessness project vowing to work long hours and weekends. The interviewers report to her on the life-history segment of the study. A guy named Hal who used to get seasonal work with a lumbering company that isn't hiring any more. A fourteen-year-old girl named Janet who lost her parents and has lived in four different foster families. An elderly woman named Mae who has outlived her family and has nowhere to go.

A few of the interviewees have slid down due to alcoholism or other addictions. More left their reservations due to poverty or because their tribes had been dissolved in negotiations with the government. Some moved to the city in the hopes of finding work. Ava listens, takes notes, gives interviewing tips.

Two interviewers who went to take a census at a homeless shelter report that, when handing over the files, a member of the shelter staff said, "These smell as bad as our clients." Ava tries to control her righteous anger.

Between spoonsful of carryout clam chowder, Ava pours her heart out to Jesse. They talk about what needs to be done, what is possible beyond gathering data and charting graphs, writing scholarly articles. They are faced in the same direction. She feels a surge of commonality and affection.

Weeks pass with more protesting, lovemaking. They hang out with friends from work, hold hands in the movies. He dances in the street to raise money for the Indian Cultural Center and she takes pictures.

When he goes off to work at Ozette, she calls her Aunt Dena. "I'm in love."

"Me, too." Athena Paputsakis is always falling in love. People say she should be called Aphrodite instead of Athena. Not that Athena is even her real name. She was christened Constantina and called Dena most of her life. But when she and her brother opened Café Athena, everybody started calling her Athena. Dena lives in a mobile home situated on an urban island surrounded by freeways, festooned inside and out with strings of tiny Christmas lights all year long and furnished with turquoise couches. Fifty-year-old Athena is now in love with a thirty-year-old black man. "Mine's called John Henry Cullen. How about yours?"

"Joseph Lightfoot. He's an Indian. A dancer."

"Dancers make good lovers. And an Indian! You always did go for the exotic."

"He's more American than I am. He's Native American."

"When're you bringing him home?"

"I've really only known him a short while but. . ."

Dena finishes her sentence "You feel like you've known him your whole life. You're a smart girl. Trust your inner Greek." Ava wonders if she has an inner Greek. Dena continues with an invitation, "*Ela, ela.* C'mon, c'mon. Bring the boy home so I can pinch his cheeks."

"I can't. You know Daddy. And Mickey."

"Yeah, they'll probably call him a savage and ask him if he knows how to use silverware. He does know how to use silverware, doesn't he?"

"Never heard of it."

Dena laughs. "And he carries a tomahawk, right?"

"Only for trimming his toenails." Ava hears the chuckle but still, she is trembling with negative anticipation over her father's ire.

"So, what's your father gonna do, disown you? Anyway, you can always elope."

"I'm not ready to get married. I haven't even fed him yet."

"What? Did I hear you right? What would your mother say? Are you Polish? Are you Greek?"

"I know, I know. I need you to tell me how to make the lamb with the lemon and garlic. And some nice tartufi, maybe."

"You haven't fed him?"

The next day, armed with recipes and instructions on how to avoid the evil eye, Ava runs down the hill from her apartment to look for a butcher, a place to buy grape leaves, and some good honey.

Back in her apartment, she regards the leg of lamb like a stranger, as if she'd never seen her father prepare this a thousand times. At first, she is shy with the knife, but eventually she makes the piercings and stuffs 40 slivers of garlic and 10 sprigs of rosemary into them. She squeezes dozens of lemons over the meat and sets it to roasting in a pan with water. She peels and cuts up potatoes, gives up on squeezing more lemons, and pours juice straight out of a Real Lemon bottle over them, adding salt and pepper. She bastes for hours, in between stuffing grape leaves and struggling with layers of sticky phyllo dough. It's hot and she's sweating like a racehorse. She despairs. Shouldn't the cooking instinct be in her blood?

Opening the freezer to cool herself off, she eyes the bottle of ouzo, lying there frosty and content. She stands there for a full three minutes to relieve her sweating and anxious head. When she turns around, she sees how puddles of olive oil have muddied up with spilled flour on the counter, how crusted pans and dirty mixing bowls cover every surface. A disaster zone.

She goes for a quick walk around the block to gain perspective. Tells herself all the things she's heard growing up: Cooking is an honor. Eating a pleasure. Hospitality is the first rule. She also realizes: Cooking is hard work. But then again, I can always order Chinese take-out.

When she returns to the apartment, she detects the distinctive odor of burning potatoes. She yanks open the oven door and pulls out the smoking pan. The edges are burnt and black. She dials. "Auntie Dena?"

"What's burning?"

"Potatoes."

"Good. Something should always be a little off to remind us we're not perfect. The old Greek weavers would always work a mistake into the rug so it wouldn't look like they were trying to compete with the gods."

"Well, since I pissed off the gods by waiting so long to feed him, maybe this'll help."

✻

The kitchen table is covered with Ava's carefully pressed top sheet. No chance at perfection or angering gods here. The doorbell rings.

Joseph is at the door with a bottle of wine. He reaches for her with a kiss but quickly comes up for air.

"Something smells good. Really, really good."

"I did a terrible thing. A bad horrible terrible thing."

"You invited Officer Kane for dinner?"

"Where I come from, what I did is a sin."

"First, I don't believe in sin. Second, I don't think anything that smells this good could be a sin."

"Weeks have passed and I haven't fed you. The gods are going to smite me."

"The gods."

"Someday, I'll be punished. Out of the blue, I'll be shipwrecked on some desert island for seven years. I'll have to listen to the wild screams of mermaids and a one-eyed ogre will gorge on my friends."

"Been reading your Cliff Notes, I see."

Ah, the man knows his classics. "Please, not another word until we eat." She pours ouzo over ice in jars once full of marshmallow cream. She stuffs a flaky square of spanakopita into his mouth. Then, a hand-wrapped moist stuffed grape leaf. Some olives. Ava worries she might be choking him with the large chunks of feta she's stuffing down his throat. They eat the tender bites, the tangy pieces, the juicy bits.

Now she can raise her glass. "*Ya mas!*"

"*Ya mas.* Did I just agree to avenge some evil deed by murdering your brother's wife?"

"It'd take a lot more syllables to say that. *Ya mas.* To us."

"I can drink to that." And they do.

She sprinkles oregano over the Greek salad, wondering if she cut the tomato pieces too big. She carves the lamb, scoops out the less-burned layers of potatoes. With clenched-teeth bravery, she shovels a spoonful into his mouth. He beams.

Ava cuts off a small slice of lamb and places it out on her fire escape.

"Don't tell me. For the gods."

"Or the stray tabby. I named her Cleopatra."

✦

The lamb is damn succulent. He eats third helpings. "Where'd you learn to cook like that?"

"I did grow up in a Greek restaurant."

"With food like that, why did you leave?"

She can't wait any longer. The wine has emboldened her to flirtatiousness. "Dessert later?"

✦

On her sheetless bed, he tastes of lemon, lamb, and mint. Home.

An hour later, she brings him dessert. The baklava is sweet. The coffee, bitter. After he swallows the greater part of the thick, brown liquid, he looks up and asks, "And now you're going to read my fortune in the coffee grounds?"

Assuming the voice of a wise fortune teller, she peers into the bottom of his cup. "I see a house with tall windows and a porch. Six children."

"Six?"

"And a dog named Homer."

"Are you proposing?"

"Oh, no. Sorry! I was telling your fortune, not mine. I really don't think I even want to get married."

He finds himself feeling a bit disappointed but says, "Fair enough."

"And we haven't even said the words."

"The words?

"Yeah, y'know, the words."

"If you're talking about love, I think I fell in love with you the first time I saw you."

"You've had too much wine. You believe in love at first sight?"

"Definitely. And, listen, you fed me Greek food. I think it's time I take you to Ozette."

He lifts a sprig of rosemary to his nose and then tucks it behind his ear. Just like her father. Uh-oh.

Ozette

Combs carved out of whale bone, oars, fish nets, blankets, clothing made out of cedar bark, objects encrusted with sea mammal teeth whose purpose no one has figured out yet. At the Ozette lab, Joseph excitedly tells her of how some objects match the tales the old people tell about their ancestors. How a large box of seagull wings puzzled the archeologists until a woman recalled how her grandmother cleaned the house with seagull wings, used them for dusters and brooms.

They hike down to the Ozette site itself, four miles over slippery rocks and muddy terrain. Joseph tells how the Federal Government denied the Makah the right to net fishing but now, with the traditional nets found at Ozette, tribal members can argue for net fishing as a customary practice. He glows with enthusiasm.

At the site, he introduces her to the rest of the staff, who are measuring artifacts, taking notes. The principal investigator, Doc Daugherty, talks about a recent discovery, "See that island? We've uncovered some blankets made of woven dog fur and cattail fluff. This meshes with accounts from a couple hundred years ago of Makah keeping a herd of Samoyed-like dogs out on an island so they wouldn't interbreed with their domestic dogs. Turns out they kept them like sheep for their fuzzy fur which they used in weaving blankets!"

"Wow. Dog fleece instead of sheep!"

"Sorry, I get so enthused sometimes I forget my manners. I'm Doc Daugherty. Joseph's an invaluable member of the team. Someone like him who comes from a long line of carvers is enormously helpful."

"He loves Ozette."

"And he thinks the world of you, you know."

When they are back in the forest, Joseph points up to the trees. There are old canoes in the branches. "They used to put people to their rest up there."

Neah Bay

He tells her to wait outside in the yard and she does, impatiently pacing.

An older woman approaches on Joseph's arm. She wears a black dress decorated with tiny shell animals, miniature versions of the ones Ava's seen on totem poles. The cowrie shells show up brightly against the dark cloth. In her hair is a piece of something that Ava guesses is whalebone carved into a comb. His grandmother. Rather than looking wizened as Ava had expected, Joseph's grandmother is robust, smiling. Ava puzzles over the possible relationship between the words "wise" and "wizened." Joseph leaves them alone.

"So, this is you," the grandmother nods.

"In the flesh," Ava says and then regrets her reference to bodily matters.

"The most beautiful woman in the world, my grandson tells me."

"Very kind of him but I hardly think so."

"You have stunning hair."

"All spirally and a bit wild, I'm afraid." Flesh. Spirally. Wild. Ava can't seem to say anything that sheds a good light on herself but then adds, "Thank you." One can never go wrong with a thank you.

Calling on her childhood manners, Ava compliments the grandmother on her dress.

"Jesse told me you were interested in the old ways, so I put on my old dancing dress. But I can't wait to change back into my sweatshirt and jeans."

"The dress is amazing."

"It looks old-timey, right? But I'm not sure anybody actually wore a dress like this in the old days. My grandparents dressed in woven cedar bark to keep the rain off. We get 100 inches a year, you know. But that photographer man Curtis came here a long time ago with a box of wigs and clothes and he dressed up people like he thought Indians should look."

"Edward S. Curtis? I had no idea." Ava thinks of the sepia pictures that Curtis took, Indian faces with piercing gazes. But yes, she remembers a Makah whaler among them, dressed in a wild wig and bearskin. A photographer trying to capture some imagined past.

"His pictures did bring us some tourist money, so people started dressing like he dressed us. Maybe we wouldn't be trying to revive our language or dig up Ozette if it wasn't for somebody else being interested."

"Well, I'm interested! I want to know everything and see everything! It's gorgeous here."

Seattle

Ava has missed a lot of work. And school. She tells herself she's learned so much more than she would have in a classroom with an old white man trying to teach her about Indians. Ava steps out of her dress and puts on her shirt and pants. She locates Joseph's single tie and adjusts it loosely around her neck, trying for an urban unisex look. She walks down to One Yesler Way and stares up at the building. She puts her hand on the doorknob and hesitates. She walks around the back of the building and paces near the waterfront. When she looks up at Dr. Baines' office window, she sees him sitting at his desk, his head in his hands. Good. She walks around to the front again. One of the interviewers she hired is coming out through the door. He greets her with a smile. "Haven't seen you for a while!"

"Hey!" Embarrassment propels her up the stairs when financial necessity had not. She straightens her shoulders. "Nothing ventured, nothing gained," her father used to say. She knocks on Dr. Baines's office door and walks in.

"Ah! Ava!"

"Morning, Dr. Baines." She is gratified to see large stacks of papers on his desk, untranscribed tapes crowding the IN box waiting for her to sort.

"I have an apology to make to you, Ava."

"No, you don't, Dr. Baines. It was a difficult moment there, after you bailed us out."

"No, I meant about the young interviewers. They do have the trust of the community. They're working out quite well."

This is her opening. "I know I've been gone a lot, but I promise you I can catch up." The pause is too long.

"I'm sorry, Ava. While you were gone, I hired someone else."

He is speaking but she isn't comprehending. Something about how he's hired a young Yakima man. Qualified resume, master's degree. Ava knows hiring a Yakima for her old job is better for the project, but she tastes sour fear rising from the pit of her stomach. Anxiety plugs up her ears. She doesn't have a job. She will become a homeless woman starving on Skid Row. There is a silence. Dr. Baines is looking at her with a question in his eyes. He is repeating. "So, you'll do it?"

"Do what?"

"Ask Joseph to come in. We're short of interviewers?"

She doesn't answer for a minute, her mind computing, trying to make sense of the situation. Dr. Baines wants Joseph to work as an interviewer. Here. On her old project.

"Joseph is working on the Ozette dig."

"This way he'd be in Seattle more. I thought you'd like that."

She wants to say: You just fired me, asshole, but instead she says, "It's totally up to him."

Joseph would be home more. They'd grill salmon out on the fire escape. It's only for the summer. Damn it.

Back in the apartment, she removes Joseph's tie, the traitorous outfit, and puts on a summer dress. When she answers the ringing phone, a woman identifying herself as Kaya asks for Joseph.

Ava hurls books at the wall. Paces the apartment. Standing by the open fridge, she shovels leftover fish scraps into her mouth. A spoon of marshmallow cream. She almost gags. She needs to do something. Go back to the summer class which she's only occasionally attended. Where is the damn syllabus? Somewhere among the tossed books behind the armchair? She scrambles to uncover it. A page of driving instructions. A bus schedule. The elusive syllabus.

If she hurries, she can get to class today. She can meet with her professor, write a paper, take the final. At least she wouldn't get a failing grade. She could hold her head up.

On her way to the bus stop, she passes the Fast Foto booth with its faded "Help Wanted" sign in the window. No sign of the bus, so she hurriedly picks up the packet of protest pics. Still no sign of the bus, so she sits down on the bench and splits the tape with her fingernail. She looks at each photo as if it were from someone else's life. When she reaches the photo of two zealous young U.I.A.T. Indians in their red kerchiefs raising their fists, looking for all the world like a Native Che and Fidel, she looks up just in time to see the back of the bus leaving without her.

Ava promises herself she WILL go tomorrow, but right this job-hungry minute, she walks back to the Fast Foto booth and asks if the bleached-out "Help Wanted" sign is for real. She can hear her father say, "Never think you're too good for a job." She tells the acne-faced boy several years her junior that she knows how to run a cash register and learned to give change when she was five. He tells her that the job is down the street at the lab. She runs down the street and offers herself for the job. She starts immediately.

Joseph comes home from the fish market, a paper-wrapped salmon filet in his hand but a flicker of anger in his eyes. He ran into Dr. Baines on his way home. Why didn't she tell him about the job? She explains that it just happened. She was going to tell him tonight, for sure. He wonders aloud if there's anything else she's not telling him.

She tells him there was a phone call from his ex-girlfriend Kaya. "Why is she calling?"

"She helps take care of my dad. You should have told me. Anything else?"

She confesses that she's taken a job at the Fast Foto booth. He laughs but she tells him it's not a joke. She wants to save up money for the trip home. She doesn't want to sleep on the dirt. She wants to be able to stay in an occasional motel so she can wash her hair once in a while. He says, "Yeah, like one of those cement tipi places? Sorry."

"I'm sorry, too." Deep breath. "So, you're going to interview for Dr. Baines?"

"You gotta be kidding. I couldn't work for someone who fired you."

She thinks he is a much better person than she is. That night, when he goes to a meeting, she goes to the Fast Foto lab for an evening shift. She takes her camera with her, snapping pictures around Pioneer Square, its totem pole and homeless men. Once at her job, she is taught how to develop the rolls of negatives into snapshots, how to change tone and adjust color. On her break, she experiments with her own negatives, turning up intensity and contrast, cropping and blowing up images. She prints a photo of a panhandling elderly Indian that turns out looking like a miniature psychedelic Avedon print. Another, of Joseph, with his intelligent face and kind eyes.

Walking home, she sees a woman wearing an outfit that used to be hers, one of those that Jesse rescued from the trash bin. Is it the woman with the shiny black hair?

⁂

Ava is supposed to meet Joseph at the ferry dock. He says, "Let's celebrate Monday and just ride the ferry back and forth all night like in that Millay poem."

We were very tired, we were very merry,
We had gone back and forth all night on the ferry;
And you ate an apple, and I ate a pear,

From a dozen of each we had bought somewhere.

She loves that he quotes poetry to her. She says, "An apple sounds good."

⁂

Seeing the shore retreating, they have the sense of going on a journey. Foghorn blasts. Heavy ropes pulled off the pier. She feels like she is leaving all troubles behind.

At the mid-point of their return, seated at a fake-leather settee, they share a lemonade. He reaches for her hand. He kisses each finger, then looks up. "Marry me?"

Her mind is reeling. It was supposed to be a summer romance. They don't have real jobs. Her father would be furious. Deliberately echoing her first word to him, she says, "Sure!"

He slides his hand beneath the Formica table and under her dress. She looks around to make sure no one can see his hand roving over her, concentrating its efforts. After a few minutes, she pulls away his hand. She motions to the deck, where they make out like teenagers.

They barely make it up the stairs to the apartment. As his mouth moves down her body, his long blue-black hair fans out across her thighs. She knows he enjoys giving her pleasure. She utters encouragement, then loses her mind.

⁂

Ava calls her father to tell him the news of her engagement. He doesn't answer until the twenty-fifth ring.

"It's me, Daddy."

"You go out to the West and what happens?! You get yourself mixed up with some savage, I hear."

"You'll like him."

"I'll have no part of this, Ava. Call me back when you're my daughter again." And he hangs up.

60

The Edge of the World

When the day comes, Jesse drives them in his pickup, following the eastern border of the Olympic Peninsula, alongside waterways of pale aquamarine. They pass vacation cabins and long, groaning logging trucks that give off the scent of freshly cut cedar. When they eat their picnic on a narrow sandy strip, Jesse points up. A white-headed eagle sits atop the barren tree like the knob of a cane.

At Sappho's Corner, they turn onto an even smaller, rougher road. A sign says, "loose gravel" but it doesn't warn of the hairpin turns. Ava almost says, "Are we there yet?" but then sees hundreds of delphinium-like spired lavender blossoms along the roadside and she says, "Stop!" She picks a dozen for her bouquet. In her teen-aged daydreams, she'd wanted long-stem roses, but these are wild and wonderful.

Jesse takes a sudden turn onto an unpaved road through a landscape as unfamiliar as the moon. Primeval. The trees are so towering, the ferns so immense and sprawling, she expects to see Bigfoot, elves, and gnomes dancing.

"Ready?" he asks.

"No," she answers, "but that's never stopped me before. We're eloping."

"Close your eyes."

"I always thought of it as romantic, eloping." She closes her eyes and automatically holds her breath.

He leads her away from the truck. When he stops, she inhales deeply. The scent is mushroomy, redolent of wet wood and wild vegetation. Disrupted animals and birds chatter and shriek. "Okay, now open them."

Mosses grow like tiny forests on bark. A stand of white birch. Her Polish grandmother told her stories of the white birch forests of her homeland, of the wild mushrooms.

In a small cedar hut, Meg Standingwater fusses with Ava's hair, adding a few fern fronds to her crown. She takes what looks like raffia and binds the stems of the flowers into a tidier bouquet. She leads Ava down a cedar plank path into deeper woods with taller and more tangled trees, wider and taller ferns. They reach an opening. A cathedral of ancient trees surrounds them. Birds hover. Joseph awaits her wearing a cape of woven cedar bark. He smells wonderful.

Joseph's cousin Charlie chants solemnly, then smiles. Words. A song. A kiss. On the third finger of her left hand, a smooth wooden ring. They didn't bother with a marriage license. Like in the Joni Mitchell song, they don't need no piece of paper. Ava gives a quick thought to her childhood dreams of her dad walking her down the aisle, but this is stunningly beautiful and far more adventurous, isn't it? She is terrified and ecstatic.

Meg throws wild rice.

Joseph embraces Ava so tightly, he crushes a few blossoms.

Hobuck Beach

She walks out onto sand. Before her is the Pacific. She moves through a stand of dune grass toward the sea and tears tumble from her eyes as if her body remembers what her mind cannot. She looks out over the water and sees a line of white on the horizon. Her legs swish through the tall grasses, continuing toward the water, watching the line on the horizon advance toward her, lined now with white and black and red. The line becomes dots, becomes dabs, becomes sails.

The sails emerge with white clarity against the blue. Canoes with sails. Sails painted and canoes carved with Wolf and Raven and Whale. His family and friends in canoes, paddling to greet her and Jesse.

The loudening sound begins. From down the beach, people come, banging the bottoms of pots and bowls with spoons, drums with sticks. Others come from the woods. A young man declares himself to be a messenger and states a demand, "If Ava and Jesse wanted to run off and get hitched, that was up to them, but now that that's done, the couple owes it to us to have a party!" Joseph smiles his crooked smile. Laughter surrounds Ava and eyes appraise her.

Ava and Joseph follow the group to an area where driftwood logs have been arranged in the sand. Meg Standingwater brings Ava a mug of clam broth. She breathes in the warm steam, detects the aromas of burning wood and roasting salmon. She turns to see butterflied fish pinned with strips of wood to cedar planks, roasting over an open fire. Joseph notices her interest, leaves her side for a moment, returns with a furtively acquired bit of fish. So delicious, she'll forgive him his secret plans.

Ava surveys the faces, expecting her brother, her father, her cousins to magically appear.

"It's my job to welcome you to the family." Joseph's grandmother pronounces a greeting in Makah, then continues in English, "You are my granddaughter now, so I made you something." She places a small, carved red cedar box into the palm of Ava's hand, where it fits just so.

Ava opens the box to see what's inside but then realizes, with a blush of embarrassment, that the box itself is the gift. With its scent of these forests. With its scent of Joseph's cedar cape. She has married into a family of wood carvers. A little timid about the next steps, Ava tentatively reaches out her arms in gratitude and the embrace is returned. The young man who served as messenger announces Ava's name and something in Makah. A series of young people come forward and place gifts at Ava's feet: blankets, dishes, silverware, an envelope of cash.

After profuse thank yous from Ava, the grandmother's face looks pensive. "C'mon, let's go smoke some cigars." A somewhat flabbergasted Ava follows to a couple of outdoor chairs.

"I know you two have to leave and go to Kansas. I'll be heartbroken to say good bye, but it'll be good for you to get away from the salmon wars and the seals."

"But I love the seals!" Ava coughs up some cigar smoke and the old woman laughs. Ava wonders if everything the Makah say is a joke.

"Come back. You and Jesse come back with my great-grandchildren."

Jesse. Ava moves the name around in her mouth.

Grandmother nods at the cigar. "Good, isn't it? I rolled it myself."

The guests feast on salmon, wild onions, berries, and white wedding cake. Ava tunes in to tidbits of conversation. Bernie Whitebear. United Indians. Who got arrested at the last fishing-rights scuffle. People come up to her and tell her how fond they are of Jesse, how much help he's been to them, what a good carver he is, like his grandfathers before him. They wish the young couple well. Ava is dizzy from tobacco and attention.

When the elders leave, guitars come out. The young men sing Beatles's songs around the fire.

"Ah, we're honoring all of your ancestors, I see," says Ava.

"I don't know any Ukrainian dances but at least the Liverpudlians are represented."

Ava thinks about the Greek and Polish weddings she attended in her childhood. Ava loved weddings. The against-all-odds hope of them. The turning of the beloved into family.

Charlie calls Joseph away. Left alone, she fingers the ring on her finger, made from the root of a red cedar tree. Northwest Coast Indians aren't called "People of the Red Cedar" for nothing.

The atmosphere changes. An energy shift. A presence added. Ava slowly turns and sees four young men, all wearing intense expressions and red bandanas, each holding a hand drum. The sound begins, the loud, wonderful beating. Work buddies and friends from United Tribes begin to chant a mixture of Makah and English. When the song ends, there is a sudden stillness. Eyes are turned toward Ava. She tries to quiet herself, to assemble herself into a kind of dignity. She reminds herself about her father's poise. How calm he can be in a crowd. How her dad can balance a glass on the top of his head. Ava straightens herself. She looks up.

And then she sees him. Joseph. His body poised in concentration, waiting. But instead of feathers, he is wearing ferns, the fronds curling over his head like a feathered headdress. Ferns gathered and tied around his body with strips of inner cedar bark and sea grass. He leans forward, waiting. A drumbeat starts. The young men sing. A foot moves.

He strikes the ground with percussive steps. The shells on his ankles and wrists jangle, accentuating each drumbeat. His legs are bare and brown. The fan of fronds on his back vibrates. Shiny black hair moves across his shoulders. He is beautiful.

After dancing around the circle, he faces her. The drumbeats increase in pace. And stop. He sings and dances just for her, as he did that first night. Joseph reaches out for her hand and pulls her away. Everyone claps. Ava's cheeks redden.

Joseph leads her through the forest. The noise of the party grows distant. Soon, there's only the sounds of their feet on twigs and the rustle of their clothes. When they reach a long wooden building, Joseph lights a lamp.

Huge posts hold up the ceiling. Benches and colorful carvings furnish the empty spaces. Wood shavings litter the floor. The scent of cedar is intense, intoxicating.

With a kind of reverence, Jesse removes his regalia slowly, placing the shell bracelets and ankle circlets into a wooden box. He turns toward her and touches her shoulder. She loosens the cedar ties that hold the ferns tightly to his body.

Her dress falls to the ground.

This is the moment he has been waiting for.

This is the moment she has been waiting for. She leans toward him, eyes closed, waiting. Was that a kiss or a feather grazing her lips? She senses more than sees that she is being lifted into a boat lined with cedar mats and feather pillows. She is resting on cushions but doesn't care whether where she lies is hard or soft, on land or sea.

They ride the boat till morning.

Neah Bay

The next evening, Ava and Jesse take their seats in the Longhouse Community Center.

"You're not dancing?" Ava asks.

"We're guests of honor."

Two elderly men string up a curtain painted with Northwest Coast-style figures. Four women wearing capes over their street clothes stand before it. Four men carry small drums painted with Wolf and Bear. A singer announces, "This dance belongs to the Weaver family, one of the

Weaver men received it in a dream." He shakes a rattle made of scallop shells, setting a rhythm, and begins a refrain. The drummers beat on their hand drums, repeating the lines of the lead singer. The women dance in place.

On the lead dancer's head is a two-foot-long carved wooden bird mask, painted in red, black, and white. He wears a black dance cape with wide borders of red, the back covered in a large design of a double-headed Raven. His bare feet move in figure eight patterns on the floor. He cocks his head from side to side. The wooden mask opens and closes its beak, making clacking noises. Bits of white fluff—feather down—fly out and waft to the ground. Raven.

Another dancer enters, walking backward and extending his arms out. On the back of his cape is a depiction of Whale. He seems to move like a wave breaking on the beach, a whale coming up for air. Raven and Whale dance around each other twice as the song continues. The drumming grows louder, the dancers' steps more lively, as they move quickly around each other. The music stops. The dancers show their backs. Their capes have been interchanged. When did that happen? Whale is Raven. Raven is Whale.

Seattle

When she hears the clatter of empty cans on the pavement, she looks out the window to see the "Just Married" sign on the back of Joseph's truck. They should really take it off, but they enjoy the shouts of encouragement as they drive around town, the beribboned tin cans bouncing, making a racket, announcing their new status. But today he is driving off alone in the turquoise pickup, trying to get back to Ozette after the wedding weekend off. The truck rounds the corner and she feels an ache of left-behindedness. He'll be gone for two weeks.

Ava inhales deeply, filling her mouth with scalding American-style coffee, which she spits out immediately, wondering how Joseph could possibly drink this stuff. She pulls on one of his many plain white T-shirts and looks around for something to wear on her bottom half. Joseph's neatly folded jeans look homeless on her bookshelves. He actually irons his jeans. She tries on a pair. A little long but they'll do for the moment. She cuffs them like 1950s dungarees and heads for the phone. She takes another mouthful of the coffee and forces herself to swallow it for courage. She is going to call her brother.

Instead, she walks into the bathroom. She should at least be showered. As if Mickey could smell the sweat of lovemaking over the phone. Hanging from the shower rod is her moose-hide dress that she laundered in the bathtub, now stiff as a board. Maybe it needs to be washed in a salmon stream and pounded on rocks. She shakes the dress, rolls it and unrolls it repeatedly, trying to soften the texture. She is stalling.

Ava takes a shower. Washes her hair. Looks forlornly into her closet. Only the shirt and pants Joseph dug out of the trash for her. She puts Joseph's clothes back on instead. For courage.

She dials and waits while it rings for what seems several eternities. She hangs up and dials again.

"Hell-oh."

Ava pauses, picturing her brother, wearing his diamond pinkie ring, sitting in an elaborate brocade chair. She hangs up, changes into her moose-hide dress. Dials again.

"This is Mike Powers."

Mike Powers is five years older than Ava Papatsakis. He has Americanized his name to "fit in." No more Michalis Odesza Papatsakis for him. He sells something. Stationery. Works for the business mogul whose daughter he married. Ava looks over at the red cedar twig, reminding herself that she should really get that thing some dirt.

"It's Ava, Mickey."

"Ayyyyy-vee!" He is the only one who calls her Avie. She is the only one who still calls him Mickey.

"I got married."

"You're shittin' me. Don't tell me. You went to Vegas." Mickey's own wedding had been at Chicago's Drake Hotel with fifteen WASP bridesmaids wearing plum-colored satin and fifteen Greek- and Polish-American groomsmen in penguin suits. His blonde bride wore a seed-pearl-covered gown with a train ten feet long. Ava had to help the maid-of-honor heft it from place to place. Mickey wore a top hat and a striped cravat. She remembers his carefully pronouncing the word. Cra-vat. His clothes matched those of his father-in-law, who was clearly the model for the guy on the Monopoly board.

"Congratulations, Kiddo! You can finally get rid of that moniker."

Ava did not want to be called "Mrs. Lightfoot." She had heard of some women defiantly keeping their maiden names. "Maiden name." The expression itself sounded medieval. "I like Paputsakis. Reminds me of Daddy."

"So, what happened, ya get knocked up?" A number of cousins from the gum-chewing-and-working-at-Woolworth's side of the family "had to get married."

"No, I'm boring. Fell in love."

"Love at first sight? Like the 'fairy-tale crap' you used to make fun of?"

"I've always been one to live up to my principles."

"Still studying the uh, anthrophilophology?"

Ava pictures a falafel. She doesn't bother to correct the endearing mistake. She recalls when, as a freshman, she had declared a major in philosophy, puzzling everyone in her community except the priest, who told her mother it was "great preparation for anything she might want to pursue." She changed her major the next day. Here she is again, changing her mind, her field. "I might wanna try out a class in photography."

"Good. You could get a job at JCPenney's or somethin'. Everybody wants to have pictures of their brats."

"You should know." He has three.

"When do I get to meet the sucker?"

"Auntie Dena wants to have a party at the café."

"Does Dad know?"

"No."

"He's gonna kill you."

"I know." Ava taps her foot on the ground repeatedly. She can smell her own anxiety.

"You can always get it annulled."

"Nothing will get annulled. I just wanted to tell you about it. And the party."

He snickers devilishly before responding. "The Polacks and Greeks, they love all that dancing and eating that ethnic crap. Just make sure I get a big steak, a nice baked potato."

"No garlicky cucumbers for you."

He emits a deep hearty laugh and all the things she likes about her brother flood into her bloodstream. "I wish you all the best, Nugget. I'll send you a nice check."

Ava tries her dad again. She waits for what seems like forever and he answers.

"Daddy, please don't hang up."

He does.

PART 2

The Turquoise Truck

Outside the apartment building, Ava and Jesse load boxes into the truck bed. Jobs have been quit, furniture tag-saled or given away, exams taken, adieus bidden. Ava has even handed in her hastily but passionately written final project for her fieldwork class, "Watching Men Dance: A Study of Intertribal Convergence in Male Dance Styles among the Small Tribes of Western Washington," complete with cassette tapes, photographs, and an addendum on "The Racist Arrest Practices of the White Male Police Officers of Western Washington." She couldn't help herself.

In the truck bed are three boxes of books, two suitcases of clothes, one box of photos, his tent, and her hibachi grill. A tall and spindly red-cedar sapling sloshes in a Rubbermaid pail until Joseph scoops up some dirt from the yard near the trashcans. "So it won't spill."

She is anxious to get going. She loves road food, adores eating hot-turkey sandwiches smothered in gravy soaking into slices of white bread and mashed potatoes. Such white and soft food, so different from the colorful and potent fare of her childhood, seems exotic and forbidden, like having Thanksgiving on a Monday. And then there are the sights, the changing vistas. She thinks of family road trips to Yellowstone and the Grand Canyon.

Ava suggests they travel first down to San Francisco before heading East. The honeymoon they didn't have. She may never have the chance again. She grabs a flower from a neighbor's vine growing over the fence and tucks it behind her ear. Joseph starts singing about going to San Francisco, wearing flowers in her hair. He sings and dances so easily, so unselfconsciously.

A feather falls. From out of nowhere. No bird flies overhead, no cat spits, no hat sheds. Ava reaches for it. Just as she is about to grab it, a swirling wind picks up the feather, carrying it out of reach. It's then she notices Joseph's be-feathered and be-quilled dance regalia shut up in a plastic bag, hanging from a tree limb. She reaches for it.

"Don't touch it!"

"Why?"

"We'll drop it off at Meg's before we leave town. She can give it to her brother, Bird."

"But you love dancing."

"I'm done with all that."

"Done?"

"Remember when I said only half of me was dancing? Well, I want to be the other half now. I don't want to be some poor Indian living on the dole. I want my children to have good teeth. I don't want to end up drunk and panhandling under a totem pole." He gestures in the general direction of Pioneer Square, the world's original Skid Row.

"You know that's not going to happen." She pauses, thinking he would respond. He does not, so she continues, "All that work you've been doing, at Ozette, on the reservation. . ."

"Reservations are home to the poorest people in the country."

"But you could help change that."

"I did what I could to help. I'm done demonstrating at fish-ins and digging up old whale bones. I'm not gonna be some aging revolutionary. I'm starting fresh. I've got a wife and a life now."

"Am I part of this this now-I-am-a-white-guy plan? So that's why you married me. I'm a white woman." His face fills with stricken disbelief and she knows she's said a very bad thing.

"And you married yourself an Indian to be different? To find out what it's like to be with someone exotic. Have I disappointed you?"

"No, never."

"Or maybe you want to keep me as your pet Indian. Maybe you'd make a good anthropologist after all. I'm going for a walk." He tosses her the keys and he is gone. Just cooling off, she hopes. She'll find a way to make him see her point of view. She'll argue that the regalia is a cultural artifact. They'll keep it in storage. And then, someday, he'll change his mind. She climbs into the cab of the truck, waits, worried about their harsh words.

A tense hour later, he opens the cab of the truck, hands her a bouquet of creamy-colored roses, and turns the ignition key. His hair has been barbered short. He turns to her. "I have to do this. I have to go home to my white father in the middle of Kansas. Yes, there's a part of me that doesn't want to leave. That wants to keep up the work at the Ozette dig, to honor my Makah mother."

"Maybe. . . "

"No. Don't even try. You don't understand. This is something you can't understand."

⚜

They drive silent hours through endless green forests. She didn't know there were so many conifers in the world. When they pause at the coast, and sight the dark roiling ocean, she tries to lighten the mood.

"There once was a sea so wine-darkish. . . "

"Blankity-blank-blankity-blank fish?"

⚜

They drive through a redwood, stop in old gold-rush towns, stand on boulders, look out at crashing waves. The Pacific is not pacific. When they see a sign announcing the presence of elephant seals, they know they have happened upon mythological beasts. They stop at Fort Ross on the Russian River, imagining their distant cousins, early nineteenth-century Russians and Poles and Ukrainians, on this ground. But when they read a guidepost saying how smallpox killed all the Indians in Mendocino and Sonoma counties, Joseph turns away without a word.

⚜

At a beachside campground, he cooks hot dogs over a driftwood fire. She has the first s'mores of her life and curses her parents for never having sent her to camp. They build a sandcastle.

He studies her fine-boned face, her wild hair.

"Did I really marry myself a mustang?"

"You knew that."

"On that wild-horse riding trip, how'dja get all the way down to Chile?"

"Flew." He doesn't laugh, so she goes on. "School friend from Santiago invited me, then had the nerve to get sick on New Year's Eve. So I rented myself a horse and went exploring. Someday, you and I'll fly down there together, stay with my friends, ride on that beach."

"I don't fly."

"You don't fly?" She can't believe she didn't know this about him.

"But I did think of a place for us to stay in San Francisco." When they unpack the back of the truck, Ava sees the powwow regalia under the tarp.

In the morning, Ava snaps a picture of their sandcastle being lapped by waves, its edges now rounded and flattened. Joseph scoops his hands into the flattened sandcastle and empties them into the tree pail. Red cedar likes a little sand.

Thrilled to be going to Haight-Ashbury, Ava is wearing her moose-hide dress and all the beads she owns. She fashions a wreath out of the surviving bouquet blossoms and wildflowers picked near the beach. This might be her chance to be a hippie, if only for a day.

San Francisco

Joseph parks in front of a recently remodeled Victorian. Ava tries to put the flowery tiara on her head, but her hair is so rambunctiously wild from sun and saltwater the wreath teeters and falls off. Joseph finds this funny, so she plops it on his head in revenge. When he catches himself in the rearview mirror, he leaves it on as he marches to the doorbell.

Carlo, blond and dressed like Joseph in jeans and cowboy boots, greets them. One look at Jesse and Carlo says, "What are you doin' with that fucking bird's nest on your head, man?" Carlo grabs it and throws it like a frisbee, but Joseph catches it on the fly. Carlo says, "Saw you in the papers, Tonto, storming the barricades."

"Beats hangin' out with you." Ava registers the easy friendship between them. She recognizes Carlo as the friend she had seen Joseph with on her first day in Seattle, admiring the painted canoe.

As Carlo leads them up a flight of stairs, he narrates how he and his wife Paulette, a real estate agent, bought the place for a song and rehabbed it. When they reach the landing, Ava can see Paulette posed on a settee, a vision of *Vogue*-magazine fashion in brocade breeches and lacy shirt, like a latter-day Louis XIV. Her porcelain skin is powdered to a near-white. In comparison, Ava is a waif. Her spiraled mophead is like a white 'fro from the musical *Hair*. Her beads weigh on her neck like albatrosses. Her pores are growing coarser by the second. Everyone assembles in the living room, where carved Asian furniture is tastefully arranged.

"I gotta tell ya, Jess, when we moved in, there was three feet of dogshit piled up in here. We filled up fifteen dumpsters with crap."

"Looks great now."

"Yeah, we got ourselves a Painted Lady. I gotta credit Paulette with the décor."

Joseph pulls out an envelope with the first photos Ava took of him, dancing. She had no idea he carried these with him. He hands them to Paulette who studies them.

"You have a good eye, but you need a better camera."

Paulette leads Ava into her office and tells her how she'd recently gifted herself with a Nikon F2. She hands Ava her old Olympus.

"Thanks, but I can't really take this."

"Believe me, it's just going to collect dust here, so you're doing me a favor."

Ava pets the used Olympus as if it's a Pomeranian. She loves the gift camera from her dad but this one is real-deal professional. From the other room, she can overhear Carlo's strong voice. "What the hell is Kaya gonna do now that you're hitched, man? That girl followed you around like a puppy."

When the women return to the living room, the conversation quickly shifts to dinner plans. Ava has one burning request. "I would love love love to go to Ferlinghetti's bookstore."

When she walks into City Lights, Ava knows she's entered a temple. Joseph hands her a copy of Kerouac's *On the Road*, for reading, yes, on the road.

Carlo leads them down the block to a small Italian restaurant where the waiters greet him familiarly. The crowded place quickly produces a table, white napkins, fresh flowers. When they're seated, an ancient woman with a tomato-stained towel pinned to the front of her dress emerges from the kitchen. Gina kisses Carlo on both cheeks. "Why you not call me?"

"Your line is always busy!"

They switch to Italian, accompanied by much gesturing. To Ava, this feels familiar, like the restaurant in Chicago. She can't imagine how Carlo and Joseph had become friends.

"This guy—Jesse—I wouldn't have made it through college without him."

"Well, this guy—Carlo—speaks like what, seven languages? So it had nothing to do with me."

At the University of Kansas, Carlo had breezed through Japanese, Chinese, and Korean, but had a pile of requirements to get through in a hurry. He was eager to move to San Francisco, to expand the Asian import business that he had been running from his student apartment. Counter-culture kids craved the Asian stuff, inexpensive and exotic. Joseph was putting himself through school tutoring. English literature. Art history. After one semester, they decided to share a small house with a big garage for Carlo's stock.

⚜

After dinner, Paulette suggests they go for a nightcap at Finocchio's where female impersonators do husky-voiced versions of Sophie Tucker and Carmen Miranda. Watching the performers, Ava thinks about how the drag queens wear make-up like no woman she has ever met, but then she looks over at Paulette, with her lacquered hair and powdered face. The Evettes lift their legs in a unison chorus line, wearing size-12 stilettos, and an enthralled Ava wonders how they pull off the convincing cleavage.

At 3 a.m., Carlo insists they have to see his office, so they squeeze into the car and take a freight elevator up to a loft-style warehouse stocked with inexpensive Asian imports: fans, fountains, and paper umbrellas.

Carlo leads them into his office, where there is a solitary, striking, contemporary piece of wooden furniture. "You DO know who made my desk." Joseph lowers his head shyly. "Those Makah sure know how to whittle." Ava squeezes Jesse's hand. Through the huge windows, she can see the city lights scatter over hillsides.

Almost stumbling in his intoxication, Carlo leads the way around the

78

warehouse to an area of planting pots. "Jess, I think it's totally hilarious that you're growing your own lumber in a Rubbermaid bucket, but that runty twig needs a bigger home." Since red is the Chinese color for happiness, he chooses a huge terra-cotta item. He and Jesse heave the gigantic container onto the truck.

Once back at their house, Carlo hauls several bags of potting soil from his backyard, pouring dirt sloppily into the new pot, spilling clumps of soil over the bed of the truck. Paulette, doubled over in laughter, puts the garden hose between her legs and waters the plant as if she were a man peeing. Ava picks up her camera. Carlo, Joseph, and Paulette form an impromptu chorus line and raise their legs like the Evettes. A drunken Carlo calls out to her. "C'mon, Kaya, get over here."

Ava reddens as she swallows his use of the wrong name, especially that wrong name, and hides behind her camera. That night, they sleep in their clothes, their teeth unbrushed.

On the Road

"Never drinking again. Not a single drop. Ever." They take turns saying this as Joseph drives the turquoise Ford F-100 toward mountains. When they pass a chainsaw sculpture rendition of a totem pole shellacked to a glow, he doubles over.

Snow. They stop to wash their faces in it. Ava drops a snowball into the red cedar's pot.

When they start moving again, Ava asks him the question that has been burning in her mind all morning. "Um. . . Kaya?"

"What an idiot Carlo is. Drunk as a skunk."

"What tribe is she?" She knows this will get his attention, require an answer. He tells her Kaya is part Hopi, part Makah.

"Did Kaya's grandmother come to our wedding?"

"No."

"Because she wanted you and Kaya to get married?"

"I married you."

He wants this to be the end of the conversation, but her hangover emboldens her. "What does Kaya do these days?"

"Kaya Sutter helps takes care of my father's place. Cooks and cleans. I've known her all my life. Makah are expected to help each other out."

Ava fingers the instruction booklet for her new camera, but the directions about f-stops and aperture blur on the page. She wishes she had an instruction booklet for life.

Joseph repeats, "I married you."

Ava breathes in the reassurance as if it were pure oxygen. "Yeah, you married me, a girl whose name you barely knew."

"Hey, my mom and dad barely knew each other and it worked out great. They had me, so you know it was a match made in heaven."

"A love story? Tell me!"

His parents met when his mom was a student at Haskell, back when it was a boarding school, training the Indian out of Indians. Boys were in machine shop and girls learned cooking and sewing.

"They were trained as menial laborers?"

"They wore uniforms and had to march to breakfast and learn to serve but, along the way, they also met Indians from other tribes. Those old guys who were drumming the night we met? They know each other from Haskell. It was a different kinda school by the time I got there, but still, most of my closest friends I know from Haskell."

"You went to Haskell Indian School?"

"The two years before K.U."

She wonders if Kaya went to Haskell. "Back to the love story!"

Joseph's dad, also named Joseph Lightfoot, was a curious white guy, so he snuck onto the Haskell campus. Winona, known as "Winnie," had learned the craft of jewelry making, and was making stuff as if she were some Navajo chick instead of Makah. "Bad enough she had a name as if she were a Lakota girl."

"You sound like such an Indian."

"Gotta work on that."

"The love story!"

"Love at first sight. He bought a ring from her, put it on her finger. End of story."

"So, you do believe in love at first sight?"

"I believe in Fate and the Tooth Fairy, too. I like stories with happy endings and homecomings."

"Are you sure you're a boy?"

"I guess I didn't tell you the part where my parents were separated for seven years and met up by accident when she came back to Kansas for a visit. He'd been carrying the ring in his pocket all that time. He'd never forgotten her. He'd never gotten married."

"So he bought the ring but there was a seven-year gap before he put it on her finger?"

"Yup. Love at first sight."

⁂

When they stop for gas, Ava calls her cousin Julie so she can find out what it takes to get married, legally, in Chicago. License, witnesses. She wants to be legal before they get to Kansas.

Ava jumps up and down when she hears Julie's voice. She catches Julie up on the trip, asks for help with the party. Before she gets to the legal business, the operator interrupts, demanding more coins.

Winnemucca, Nevada

The mountains have gentled into soft mounds, sheep-grazing hills. Ava rolls the name of this town around in her mouth. "Winnemucca. Winnemucca. Sign up here to win a mucka!" Joseph stops in front of a small Basque hotel with a battered sign. They walk into the mouth-watering aroma of Basque food. Ava says, "I think we did win a mucka."

Platters covered with lamb chops are passed around the oilcloth-covered table. Bowls of beans and potatoes. Salad. Pitchers of red wine. Grizzled men, wearing berets, smile at them through deeply-lined faces. Joseph explains that this hotel used to house roving Basque shepherds and there are few of the old bachelors left. Ava and Joseph eat ravenously, drink gratefully. A rivulet of lamb juice courses down Ava's chin.

One of the Basque men starts singing. Others join in. Five men keen ancient words. A foot moves. Another. The men can't sit still but dance in their seats, moving their feet to the old songs. A clarinet appears. An old accordion. The men pass around a sweet liqueur made from a wildflower

81

in the Pyrenees.

A man named Andoni points to the bar. Joseph admires the intricate carving from another century. The shepherd says whittling helps pass the time. He tells how the men used to carve their marks into tree bark to guide them, back when there were millions of sheep on these hills.

Andoni studies Joseph's face and announces, "We Basques are the original people, the Indians of Europe! And the Basque language is the oldest in Europe."

Ava challenges him. "Nope. The oldest is Greek!" She loves arguing about such things, especially when there are no books around to confirm anyone's claim.

"Greek is a baby language compared to Basque. Older than Greek, older than Latin."

Joseph speaks up, "What are you gonna do, she's Greek."

The discussion is interrupted by voices growing ever louder at end of the bar. The Basque men are challenging a bereted man to give them a poem. Andoni explains that Xabier is known as a bersolari, someone who can compose rhymes on the spot. Andoni asks them what kind of car they are driving. Joseph points to the turquoise pickup outside the window. Even though they don't know Basque, Ava and Joseph sense the rhythm and rhyme. When Xabier incorporates the English words "pickup" and "stickup" into his song, the bar explodes into laughter. When the bartender announces last call, Andoni warns them to watch out for the cranky hermit up in the cave and blows them a kiss.

Walking up into the hills under the bright Nevada moon, they easily find the markings on the trees. Joseph takes out his own pocketknife and, on an unmarked tree, carves the simple yet clear image of a boat with wings. Ava knows he is marking their first married night together back in the Makah village.

When they step on a fallen log to cross a stream, Ava turns around, like Lot's wife, to get a possible sighting of the hermit's cave. She hears a loud crack and is forced to dance on the log to keep her balance. "I think that's a sign not to bother the hermit."

Jesse picks up a handful of rounded river pebbles. At the truck, he deposits them into the terra cotta pot.

Provo, Utah

When they reach the salt flats, Joseph pulls over to a side road. She thinks he is going to pull her toward him, but instead he asks her if she wants to take a turn at the wheel. She likes the look of her hands on the turquoise steering wheel. When she starts up the truck, Joseph starts reading aloud to her in a cool hepcat voice from *On the Road,* alternating with sung lines from *On Top of Old Smokey.* She likes this man who makes her laugh.

They swore they were going to sleep in the truck bed or look for a motel so cheap all the flowers were dead but, since here they are in Utah, Ava suggests a call to Dr. Baines. "He did say, when we left town, 'If you're ever in Provo. . .'"

"And you know, as a Mormon, he'd love the chance to try to convert one of us Redskins."

At the next gas station, Joseph fills the tank near a giant green dinosaur. In the restroom mirror, Ava startles at the sight of her freakishly unruly mop. She struggles with clips and rubber bands. In desperation, she plunges her head in the rust-stained sink, gets her hair soaking wet under the small faucet, and forces it into braids.

Joseph laughs to see her hair. "If only Officer Kane could see you now, you homicidal squaw, you."

"Does 'squaw' really mean a woman's, y'know, lady parts? A white guy told me that."

"A white guy told me that, too."

The trickster smile appears on his face.

She continues to think about words like *squaw, squash*, and *squat*, as they drive through treeless suburban neighborhoods. They spot Dr.

Baines's address on a country-style mailbox in front of a huge house sided with aluminum and Permastone. Ava recalls that they have nine children, but Baines was aiming for an even dozen. Doc Baines and Rachel greet them at the door as if they were all the very best of friends. Ava finds herself interested in observing this long-term Mormon marriage; perhaps there's something to be learned from this coupledom so different from her own.

The living room is large, beige, plain. No art on the walls except for a single picture of a dreamy-eyed Jesus above the dining room table and some family photos in the hallway. On the coffee table: Cheetos and Lay's potato chips with clam dip. Cubes of cheddar. Glasses of Grapeade are passed around. Ava worries about her tendency to spill.

Doc Baines invites them to call him Henry. He shows them where they can put their gear, in a room with a double bed and a crib. Rachel explains that they have a system by which the oldest child sleeps in the same room as the youngest, the next oldest with the second youngest, etc. Ava takes mental notes should it happen that she and Joseph end up with many children. She's always wanted to have six. Rachel makes a comment on how one child or another is always sick or breaking a bone or needing stitches. Ava mentally dials down her wish list.

Henry invites Joseph to help grill burgers while Rachel takes Ava on a tour. As they stroll through numerous tidy rooms with cribs and bunkbeds, Ava can feel her hair falling out of braids and into disarray. In the basement, Rachel displays a gigantic locker full of canned and packaged food. It's a requirement of Mormonhood that there always be a year's supply of food in the house. Ava recalls something about an invasion of crickets and seagulls. Rachel, as a good wife, is supposed to rotate the food stock, but she doesn't. She's writing her Ph.D. dissertation and doesn't have time to move cans around. Ava might just like Rachel Baines.

"It's hard for the good local Mormon women to be friends with me since I'm getting what they see as a useless education for someone who should be paying full-time attention to raising her kids. When we lived in Seattle and I was in school, it was hard for me to have friends there, too, because, let's face it, no hip young woman wants to be friends with a Mormon lady with eight kids and a big pregnant belly."

Ava wants to jump in and say she would, she'd be her friend, but instead confesses that she has some questions about stuff she'd always wanted to know about Mormons but was afraid to ask. "Like ummmmmm, okay, about Mormon underwear. . . ?"

"Is mine showing?" Rachel tugs at her sleeve in a half-hearted attempt to cover up. "We order it out of catalogues. It's got symbols on it to remind you of your marital vows."

Ava tries to picture Rachel in the hungry clutches of a man resembling Jesus, and, in full passion, changing her mind at the last minute because of hieroglyphics on her underwear. "And polygamy, dead issue?"

"I wish. We are asked regularly about polygamy as a test of faith. If it should come back, we would need to welcome sister wives."

Ava knows she could never embrace sister wives, but she thinks Rachel Baines could use some help around the house. When they reach the menfolk—and yes, Ava finds herself thinking the word *menfolk*—Ava sees Joseph with one toddler on his shoulders and another tugging on his pants leg. Just looking at babies makes her uterus ache to conceive. She revises her offspring wish list again.

Henry hands them a copy of *Meet the Mormons* and invites them to Sunday services. Joseph and Ava cannot refuse.

The walls of the church are painted with more depictions of Jesus resembling the long-haired muscular men seen on the dustjackets of bodice rippers. Henry stands to tell the congregation that they have with them today Ava and Joseph, friends visiting from afar. Ava reprimands herself for unchristian thoughts. The music begins and a flood of memories come to her of the elaborate services of her childhood: the costumed processions, the sweet, heavy smell of incense. Her parents, of different ethnic backgrounds, had ignored the reprimands of priests and taken her to both Catholic and Greek Orthodox churches. She realizes now how much closer those services were to each other than either was to this.

When the choir starts singing, she is lifted from her stream of thought. Rachel is at the organ; Henry and some of the older children in the choir. They know how to sing a cantata, that's for sure. When it is time for communion, Henry nods that they should join in. As she consumes the squares of Wonder Bread and tiny Dixie Cups of Welch's grape juice, she knows she could never be a Mormon.

Indian Country

The speed limit is high, the mountains a blurred purple majesty. On the paper placemat of the Denny's where they stop, a map reads: "Wyoming!!! Home to Wind River Indian Reservation!!! 2.2 million acres!!!" Joseph quickly covers the map with his bowl of chili.

Billboards tell them they are in "Indian Country." Trading posts with Minnetonka moccasins and kid-sized war bonnets beckon from the highway. Joseph does not stop. Tomahawks bedecked with neon-bright feathers and "genuine" Indian blankets are heaped on tables alongside beads and rings. He keeps driving at top speed. Suddenly, Joseph exits quickly. She opens her mouth, but he says, "Not now."

He pulls off onto a small gravel road. The landscape is breathtaking, but Joseph clearly is not interested in scenery. Gravel gives way to dirt. Dirt to dust. He brakes, slams the door, and starts walking. Something like a cross stands up from the ground in the middle distance. Except it's not just a cross, it's a propeller, the kind you might see on an old-fashioned plane, whirring in the wind. Joseph stops short in front of the propeller-cross. His shoulders are shuddering.

He curses, "Damn him!"

Ava spies a rectangle set in the ground, carved with letters. She makes out the faded name of Winona Lightfoot. His mother.

"Local guy took her up in a crop duster. Her first and only plane ride. It'll be fun, he said. Maybe her only chance to fly."

"I'm sorry."

"We were driving out to my grandma's. I didn't go with her up in the plane. I was a snotty-nosed punk with a new rifle who wanted to take pot shots at prairie dogs instead."

Ava doesn't like the direction his story is taking but Joseph keeps talking.

"I've read every book there is on survival guilt, so don't even start. I was 11, she was 35. 35! Goddam pilot, flying drunk. Damn him, drunkin' skunkin' goddam no-good sonofabitch!"

Anger spent, Joseph starts to shed tears. Ava's never seen him cry before. He looks innocent and eleven years old again. She lets him weep for a while, and then, from god knows where, she speaks softly to him in Greek, *"Ela, "* as if a language so ancient might have better effect. *Ela,* which means "Come." And he does. He crumbles onto her shoulders. She holds him firmly. No pats, no rubs. She embraces his body as familial. *"Ela, agapi mou."* "Come, my love." She finds herself weeping for her own lost mother.

They stand like that, letting the minutes pass and the tears dry. Dust flies into their eyes and mouths. The propeller stops and starts again. Joseph breaks away from the embrace, kneels on the ground, kisses it. He gets up, crosses himself and walks away, without looking back.

In the truck, Ava picks up her camera. She pauses, thinking maybe he will stop her, but he doesn't. She walks back, crouches low to photograph the propeller cross.

Ava pulls into a parking lot with a large number of trucks outside, maybe a place with comforting hot-turkey sandwiches, mashed potatoes and gravy. The tables are full, so she takes a seat at the counter. Joseph walks over to the juke box. A waitress elbows another. Ava catches herself in the mirror above the milkshake machine. Her usual olive-toned skin is tanned dark from the sun, her wild hair is parted and barretted up. One of the waitresses nudges a man with pocked reddish skin. He looks Ava up and down, then strides over and points to a sign: "WE RESERVE THE RIGHT TO REFUSE SERVICE." The eyes of the other patrons are focused on her. The man points again, as if just the gesture is enough. She looks down to make sure she is not barefoot or shirtless. He points, "Get it, nigger?"

She answers quickly and loudly. "I ain't no nigger, asshole. I'm Greek. Y'know, like Zorba!" She breaks into a dance with a grapevine pattern, waving a paper napkin in one hand and la-la-la-ing the movie theme song. Her body, her voice come from some place she does not recognize.

The ruddy-faced man adds, "And take goddam Tonto with you." In the background, Johnny Cash wails.

Joseph is behind her now. He puts his hand firmly on her shoulder, then gently edges her out of the restaurant.

"Don't push me! Don't you ever push me!" Her bottom lip trembles. Although she is yelling at him, she feels like she is the one who has done something terribly wrong. Once in the car she says, "Why did I do that? Why didn't I shout, 'SAY IT LOUD, I'M BLACK AND I'M PROUD!'"

"You're allowed to have a survival instinct."

She thinks of Meg Standingwater, half-black, half-Indian. She faces West and silently apologizes to her. Joseph skids out of the parking lot, flipping the bird over his shoulder and adding, "I dropped three quarters in the damn jukebox."

"Yeah, we could use some quarters. I need to call my family." She registers the loss of the hot-turkey sandwich. "I didn't even get to tell them about my Polish side. And let me tell you, I am one hungry Polack."

⁂

As they drive into night, taking turns at the wheel and eating drive-through French fries, Ava thinks about all the different nationalities she has been taken for in her 21 years of life: Lebanese, Jewish, Portuguese, Italian, Spanish. Now that they are out of danger of a possible lynching, she's pleased to add African to the list.

Ava tells Joseph about herself at fourteen when she became livid when a visitor to their house used the word "nigger." She could not apply the word to Johnny and Alice, the nice, smiling people who did clean-up work in the restaurant kitchen. The next day, she got on a CTA bus to return library books. She stomped down the aisle to the rear section and sat down next to a middle-aged Black woman who moved her shopping bags to make room for her. Young Ava had heard about White people not being willing to sit next to Black people. Even though she paid a lot more attention to *American Bandstand* than the news, she had heard of "sit-ins" and wondered if what she was doing qualified. Joseph can't resist an affectionate smile.

The bus wasn't air-conditioned and it was sweltering hot, but she rode on. Her usual stop at the public library came and went, but she rode on. The bus continued to the South side of Chicago, into what her family would have called "a colored neighborhood." She rode on. She rode on while the bus emptied, until the only people left were the woman with the shopping bags and her fourteen-year-old self. "I rode on until the Black woman next to me turned and said, 'Would you mind moving to another seat? It's awful hot in here.'"

Joseph laughs and Ava congratulates herself on turning the mood of the evening around.

The next time Ava takes her turn at the wheel, Joseph pages through *Meet the Mormons.*

"Looks like my ancestors were called 'Lamanites,' an Israelite group who were descendants of Joseph of Egypt." He reads further, then tosses the book to the floor of the cab. He picks up *On the Road.* "I heard a great laugh, the greatest laugh in the world, and here came this rawhide oldtimer Nebraska farmer with a bunch of other boys into the diner. Everybody else laughed with him. He didn't have a care in the world."

Nebraska

They stop at an old hotel in Western Nebraska and pay $2 for a room with tall ceilings up two flights of stairs. A gigantic bathroom down the hall has a clawfoot tub about nine feet long. Ava fills it and adds a capful of jasmine-scented bubble bath from the shelf above the sink. She sheds her clothes, climbs over the edge, and sinks herself into the water. Her body sheds the day. She is sailing on a boat without a destination. Ava soaks herself till her skin is like a prune and Joseph comes looking for her. Their lovemaking is quiet, reassuring.

The wind is howling and fierce. Joseph suggests they nap until it dies down.

Ava wonders about introducing Joseph to her family. It's easy to picture her back-slapping brother and her gregarious aunt as they welcome the newest member of the family with hugging and teasing, no matter how they really feel. Her father would be more transparent. Ava can visualize his stern you-could-have-done-better look. And then the yelling would start.

When she knows Joseph is asleep, Ava creeps down the stairs and asks to use the house phone. She hands the proprietor a dollar bill and goes to sit in a quiet parlor.

For the last two years, Giorgos Paputsakis has rarely answered a ringing phone, believing it can only bring more bad luck. He stopped answering his home phone when he'd been called by a Dr. Karacostas to come to the deathbed of his wife. Today, he surprises Ava by picking up on the third ring and jumping right in.

"I hear I didn't raise you right, that you eloped with a wild Indian."

"I think you'll like him."

"We'll see what we can do to have it annulled. I can't have you married to some savage."

"I assure you he knows how to use a knife and fork."

"A knife, that's what I'm afraid of. Don't want any scalping going on. Especially with your head of hair."

"Dad. . ."

"Couldn't find some Greek boy from Chicago? There's thousands of them would love to marry you, you know."

"You didn't marry a Greek and it turned out okay."

"Or a Polack, right. Some Polish boy from the old neighborhood. Like Eugene. Gene, you used to call him. Nice kid."

"Gene's a priest now, Daddy."

"I thought I could talk about this, but I can't. My little girl hitched to some…"

Ava hangs up this time. She can't bear to hear what he has to say.

A few minutes later, she calls back.

"So, what does Tonto do for a living?"

"He's been working at a museum." She says nothing about a ranch in Kansas.

"A what?"

"An archeological museum."

"You send your kids to school and then you can't even understand what they're saying."

"His name is Joseph. And he's not all Indian." She is not proud of herself for making sure her father knows this. "He's part British."

"Well, la-dee-dah. I have no use for the English. Snobs and savages, what kind of ancestors are those?"

"And Ukrainian. You're going have to get used to this, Daddy, because it's a done deal."

Pause. "Ukrainian? They do the fancy Easter eggs, right?"

"Right."

"Your mother mighta liked that. She always liked a good Easter."

"I miss her." Ava knows her voice is cracking up.

"I can't do this. Your Aunt Dena's giving you a party. Don't expect me to be there."

When they start down the highway, Ava is as tense as a high wire. They are headed to her beloved home city, Chicago. Her people, her family. People as different from Jesse as day and night. Maybe she herself is just too different for him and that is the real worry. She imagines Jesse walking out of the party, leaving without so much as a goodbye, getting into his turquoise truck and driving off without her. Her creeping mental catastrophe is cut short by the sound of singing. A made-up song about flying trains, changing lanes, and palomino manes.

"You're just trying to be one of those Basque guys, improvising on the spot."

Joseph sings on.

Goodbye and thank you, Dr. Baines
Sure could use some clean underwear Hanes
Ever heard of a flying train?
If this were spring, we'd see sandhill cranes...

"Sam Hill who?"

"Cranes. Migratory birds. Fifteen-foot wingspans. Sometimes you can see them here on the Nebraska sandhills." He brakes and gets out of the car. She watches as he studies the ground.

"See! A crane feather." He studies the feather, the interlocking pattern of its barbs, the places where it stayed together and where it came irreparably apart. He knows from endless tries in childhood that once the feather is split, it can't be put back the way it was.

Ava looks up. "I wish I had a fifteen-foot wingspan. How great it would be to fly with giant wings."

"You kinda look like a sandhill crane. Long neck, stately, elegant."

She loves these compliments, files them away for a rainy day. She doesn't have long to wait. Lightning zags across the huge gray and purple sky. Clouds open up and pour thick rain. Just running to the truck soaks their clothes, which stick to them like second skins. When they are hidden behind a veil of rain and fog, Ava puts her hand on Joseph's lap. They are honeymooners and the sight of each other's curves and mounds still excite them in an instant. The very idea of wetness propels them toward each other.

Iowa

The sky clears. Ava loves the rolling hills in Iowa, the patchwork-quilt farms, the silos and cornfields. Since they both remember Amana refrigerators from their childhoods, they stop at the Amana colonies. Besides, Ava would like to get her laundry done and what better place than where they make washers and dryers? Sidetracked by an old brick building with a sign announcing lunch, Ava drives over gravel into a parking lot. They walk in and smell the lovely scent of real food. Sauerbraten and dilled potatoes, wiener schnitzel and sauerkraut are passed around the oilcloth-covered communal tables. Bowls of beans and salad. Pies and ice cream. Even better than hot-turkey sandwiches.

"You like this stuff?"

She answers, "Schurrrr" with a mouthful of food.

On the table is a flyer about the utopian community that was here long before there were refrigerator plants. He muses, "Weren't they some kinda Anabaptists?"

They start out in pursuit of an Anabaptist laundromat, but Joseph is entranced by the remains of the community. Grapes on trellises grow up the sides of the brick dormitory-style buildings. They find a graveyard with row upon row of uniform, unadorned markers. Except for a few infants, most of the dates indicate that these utopians lived well into their 80s and 90s. Ava thinks about how healthy this life must have been. She wonders if this is what Kansas will be like. She gets down on her knees to photograph the headstones from different angles.

No laundromat, but on the road back to the highway Ava spots a tag sale at a community center. She is desperate for clean, dry clothes and finds herself in luck, with a table of jeans and shirts her size, priced at ten and fifteen cents each. A white dress with embroidered ribbons down the front hangs from a nearby tree. Ava admires it, holds it up to herself. A woman just her size, but with blond hair and freckles, says, "Go on inside, try it on."

Inside, Ava uses the pay phone to call her father who waits through at least nineteen rings to answer and starts right in. "Speaking of celebrations, how come you went and did this on the sly? Why you take that away from me, walking you down the aisle? Ever since you were a little girl, you always wanted me to walk you down the aisle. You were gonna wear a fancy wedding dress."

"With ribbons down the front."

"Yeah, with ribbons." She can't bring herself to tell him she's trying it on this very minute.

"He's the best, Daddy. He tucks rosemary behind his ear, just like you."

"I don't understand a bit of this. Nothing. Not a bit."

"But I'm a grown up."

"I can't say anything to change your mind, Baby Girl?"

"Done deal. And I'm so very happy."

There's a silence, then the sound of her father's hand covering the receiver, covering his fuming thoughts: Not the way I wanted it. Kids these days. When he speaks, his voice is cracking. "So, get yourself that fancy dress. With the ribbons. I'll pay you back. It's my job. And we'll have a party. A helluva party. I'm Greek and you're not gonna take that away from me."

"Sure, Daddy, we'll have a helluva party."

Chicago

Ava insists on driving across the Mississippi River. The landscape changes and flattens, towns become more frequent, cars more numerous, the air noisier. They are close to Chicago, a place she still calls "home," and there is no way she can convey the joyful anticipation and abject terror that occupy her thoughts in alternate spasms. In the City with Big Shoulders, they maneuver through traffic in this bright vehicle that seems as out of place as a spaceship.

He drives; she navigates. She has timed their arrival well, after lunch but before the prep cooks start their evening work. Aunt Dena is off getting her hair done and her nails shimmered; her dad taking his daily walk to the cemetery. Ava gives instructions: "Park in a spot marked 'reserved,' otherwise, the cops might tow the truck. But they'd never touch a vehicle in Auntie Dena's space, she pays them too well." Joseph does a doubletake and then says, "Oh, yeah, your Al Capone connection."

Ava turns the key, opens the door, and hums her way up the stairs loudly, not wanting to find anybody naked. She calls out loud "Hellos" around the familiar rooms with their dark ornate furniture and family photos. She opens and shuts the refrigerator as if expecting someone to be hiding inside. She reopens it to behold sprigs of rosemary woven into a traditional Polish bridal wreath. Rosemary for remembrance. With a cube of sugar to sweeten life's sorrows and one of bread so one is never hungry. Undoubtedly, the work of her cousin Julie.

"No one's home. We can catch a nap before they come back."

They carry in everything except the red cedar tree, which has become too heavy for anyone to steal. Ava heads for her old childhood room, with its reassuring familiar bed and Frankie Avalon posters. Her father's best suit, reserved for weddings and funerals, hangs in its dry-cleaner plastic on the door of her closet. Her nightstand now displays an ashtray filled with cigar butts. Her father moved into her room after her mother had fallen ill. Ava turns and heads for what she regards as her parents' room. When she sees the large carved headboard, she turns away. Joseph picks up a note from the bed. It says, "*Kalos Orisate*." Welcome. Joseph gives her a hug, then throws himself on the flowery bedspread and falls instantly to sleep. Ava drops her shoes, pulls up her feet, puts her head on Joseph's chest. Road weariness hits her hard and she falls into a dream.

When they walk into Café Athena, they are greeted by an explosion of celebratory flame as a platter of saganaki cheese is ignited, accompanied by cries of "*Opa!*" Glasses of ice-cold ouzo are put into their hands and squares of warm toasty cheese are placed in their mouths. The hugs begin, enclosing the young marrieds in soft bosoms and generous upper arms, hugs that seem to end and then start again with yet a tighter squeeze. One can't help but feel welcomed wrapped in so many enclosing arms.

Just when they think they might get to sit down, Auntie Dena takes one of each of their hands and leads them to the small dance floor with its wobbly microphone. As if she needs amplification. "Ladies and gentlemen: Ava and Joseph!!!" Applause, applause. Then, into Ava's ear, "I like him!" and to him, "You need to eat! Look at you, so skinny!" She ushers them to their place at the head of the table, between the Catholic and Orthodox priests.

The men take off their suit jackets and neckties. Ava doesn't know if they are trying to make Joseph more comfortable in his simple white shirt and black pants or if they are just trying to cool off. Her own father keeps his formal dignity and his jacket on. Giorgos Papatsakis is wearing what Ava thinks of as his serious smile.

Joseph surveys the facing wall with its mural of the goddess Pallas Athena, grape vines, olive trees, and the Parthenon set against a blue sky. Following his gaze, Ava finds the blue-and-white wall suddenly overly bright and brash, the colors trying too hard to make a statement, the mural embarrassing. The image of Athena seems to bear too much of a resemblance to her Auntie Dena. At the edge of the room sits the potted red cedar. Tucked into its branches are envelopes containing checks and hundred-dollar bills. Ava's critical thoughts dissolve as she thinks of her father and aunt hauling the heavy pot into the café, making something nuptial of the thin tree.

The Orthodox priest is asking Joseph if he's ever seen the movie *Zorba the Greek*, then blesses the food: the spanakopita, the stuffed grape leaves, the feta, the olives. Ava wonders if the olives are too salty. They eat the tender bites, the tangy bites, the juicy bits.

New aromas waft into the banquet room. Her Uncle Hank walks in, followed by his wife and six daughters, all carrying platters of kielbasa, kapusta, horseradish, and braided bread. Ava's brother calls out, "The Polacks have arrived."

Ava doesn't know if they were given a different arrival time—it's happened before—or if they are simply late—it's happened before—but she's delighted to see them. Her Uncle Hank and Aunt Dottie are the reigning polka-dancing champs of the world, and their blond daughters are as close to Ava as sisters.

Her cousin Julie runs to her, embraces her mightily, then sits in the chair where the Orthodox priest had been sitting before he started blessing everything. Ava and Julie chat conspiratorially, their noses almost touching. Julie is so excited to hear that Ava has returned to the Midwest. And she shares her own news that she has been accepted into grad school at the University of Kansas.

"We'll be right around the corner from each other!"

"You're kidding me!"

The priest returns. Auntie Dena nods Julie to her seat. On her way back to her gang of sisters, Julie takes an appraising look at Joseph and gives Ava a thumbs-up.

Everyone in their place, lamb and sausage eaten, it's time for toasts. Ava looks over at her father, who uses a rosemary twig to get a bit of food dislodged from between his teeth. Giorgos Papatsakis rises from his seat and clicks his fork to his glass. Others follow suit until the noisy conversation quiets. His face is showing a little five-o'clock shadow. He puts on a broad smile and speaks.

"Where does the time go? When Ava was four, her mother found her in our room, pennies scotch-taped to her fingers. She was dancing in front of the mirror, wearing her mother's silk scarves. We asked her what she thought she was doing. She confessed that she had sneaked downstairs from our apartment to watch a belly dancer we had hired. She was clicking the pennies together, like finger cymbals." Giorgos demonstrates with his own fingers. The family laughs, already familiar with the story and the antics of little Ava. Ava is grateful he has not told the more detailed version of the story, with its miniature dance of the seven veils.

"Kids. They grow up. Our Ava has grown into a young woman her mother would be proud of." Giorgos chokes down tears. Ava notices an empty place has been set next to him at the table. For her mom.

"And now, she has brought to us a young man with the name of a saint, the name of the carpenter Joseph. I am here, we are all here, to welcome Joseph to the family. May they have a long and happy life together! *Ya sas!* And *Sto lat!*"

"*Ya sas!*" shout the Greeks.

"*Sto lat!*" shout the Poles, even louder, not to be outdone.

They raise their ouzo, their retsina, their vodka, their beer. Giorgos stands with formal dignity after the toast. Hushed, everyone watches and waits. He takes his half-full glass and places it carefully on his balding head. He does a little shimmy to demonstrate his balance and agility. He escalates into a bit of a dance. Not a drop spills. Cries of *"Bravo!"* egg him on. Ava blushes. Joseph breaks into a full, appreciative smile. He is enjoying this rambunctious, expressive family. Several of the men try to imitate the balancing act with varying degrees of success.

The Polish priest leaves, saying, "I hope one day we will bless your marriage." The Orthodox priest leaves, saying, "I hope one day we will bless your marriage."

Ava's brother sits down next to Joseph. A man with a mission, he speaks in an uninterruptable stream. "Hey, Buddy, thanks for taking my kid sister off my hands. And uh, here you go. I didn't want to put a thousand bucks in the Charlie Brown Christmas tree there, so here's a little somethin' toward a down payment. Polacks like to give cash. I guess we're too lazy to shop. Now, I gotta tell ya, I'm a little relieved to see you. I kinda expected some Chief Tonto with a braid down to his butt, a headband and feather on his head."

"Y'mean like this?" Joseph pulls a red kerchief out of his pocket and quickly knots it on his head. He inserts a tall feather into the headband. From its comical enormity, she realizes that it's a sandhill crane feather. She wonders where he's been hiding it. The room has quieted to a murmur. All eyes watch. Joseph starts laughing. They like a man who can laugh like that. Joseph pulls the feather off his headband and touches Ava's nose with it.

Like the Chicago gangster he seems to be emulating, Mickey says in a low tone, "You hurt her and I'll kill you."

Joseph says to Ava, without irony, "I like him."

He then puts the ridiculous feather and kerchief down next to his water glass, where he notices a pink WHILE YOU WERE OUT note with his name on it. Auntie Dena is on her feet, smiling a stage smile. As she makes her way to the microphone, she signals Nikos, her favorite bouzouki player, to begin.

Nikos works his fingers over the stringed instrument as if it were a woman he loved. Dena begins to sing in her deep, throaty, Melina Mercouri voice. She looks like a goddess. She has gone from Auntie Dena to Athena. Her voice lilts and seduces. She is at once sultry and celebratory. Strong and wise. At the instrumental section, Dena grabs Joseph's hand and drags him to the dance floor. Several of the younger men leap to their feet—some pushed by their mothers—to join hands and form an impromptu line. Dena pulls the red kerchief off the table and waves it in the air as if she were tempting a charging bull. The musicians quiet down and slow the beat. Dena hands the kerchief to Kostas, one of the young cousins who erases the smile from his face and pulls himself up to all the dignity his five-foot, six-inch frame will allow. The others link arms and follow suit. They look adolescent, earnest, and clumsy. They watch Kostas closely. He moves his feet in a complex pattern on the floor. The others follow. A dancer himself, Joseph picks up the pattern quickly. Kostas twists and leaps, waves the kerchief. Ava swells inside with a pride akin to patriotism.

The kerchief is passed down the line and each man in turn solos with his own moves. Some are accomplished and confident; some demonstrate a desire to get off the stage as quickly as possible. At last, it comes to Joseph, who improvises with a mixture of Greek and Indian steps. Dena nods appreciatively.

Ava looks down at the pink phone message and reads what it says: "For: Jesse. From: Kaya. Call. ASAP."

The dancers wipe the sweat from their brows and take their seats again. Dena summons Giorgos up to the microphone as Nikos starts playing a familiar love song. Dena starts in her husky voice and Giorgos joins in. The siblings' voices blend and separate in complex patterns. When the chorus starts again with the familiar phrase *agapi mou,* Joseph takes his cue and pulls Ava to her feet. They dance together to a slow song in an ancient language they only partly understand.

❦

Ava's Polish cousins, her near-sisters, pull a chair for her to the middle of the dance floor. Julie whispers in her ear, "He is one sexy guy!" Then, she joins the others in their ancient tasks. They remove the bridal wreath from Ava's head and tie an apron around her waist. Tiny plastic babies are tied to ribbons sewn on the apron. Ava's mind is filled with *Ms. Magazine* objections, but her memories of attending hundreds of Polish weddings win out. Even without a church or court wedding, she has become a wife.

Ava knows what comes next. Uncles and male cousins crowd around, waiting for the chance to dance with her. Some come willingly, others are urged by elders. The musicians play a medley of old American standards, like "Let Me Call You Sweetheart" and "Always." Each man spins her around the floor then pins "cradle money" to the apron. Behind them, baklava and kolaczki are eaten with ice cream.

The older people leave with a squeeze to say goodbye. Little children dance around Ava in a circle. Joseph is on the restaurant reservation phone, nodding, serious. He hangs up and comes to her with the WHILE YOU WERE OUT note. He stands across from her, unmoving, waiting. She stops her dance. She bends her head toward him to hear the news.

"My father. He's fallen."

The next hour is a rushed clutch of hurried goodbyes, quick changes, packing and loading.

❦

Ava gives directions on how to exit the city. Joseph beeps impatiently.

"What did he think he was doing up on the roof, a man of his age! When did he get so stupid?"

Ava is biting her tongue. She knows he doesn't mean it. Joseph's jaw is set. She doesn't know what to do with his anxious anger. She wants to be back with her family, opening wedding presents, reminiscing with cousins.

"Is he all right?"

"If he was all right, do you think I'd be driving like a maniac?"

"Did he just slip and fall or. . . ?"

"He's in the hospital. It could be something else."

"You mean like a stroke?" She feels her voice rise.

"Don't even say it."

"What, ya think the Great Spirit is gonna hear me and punish you?" She sounds like her brother. But the words are a release. Turning to anger helps her stay awake.

When they turn onto smaller roads, Ava knows they must be getting close. But instead of driving into a hospital parking lot, Joseph is driving up a gravel driveway. In the morning light, she sees a field of flowers, an old farmhouse. Joseph says, "You get some rest. I'm going to the hospital."

There is no discussion. Only Joseph showing her where to sleep and which bathroom to use, where the phone is for calling her father to say she's arrived safely.

Ava is too wired from coffee and anxiety to rest. She walks through the house with its creaky stairs and pocket doors, its wooden floors and thousands of books. She did not expect this. Books. Everywhere. In every room, horizontal and vertical, in orderly and disorderly arrangements.

She finds what must be a study. A wooden desk much like the one in Carlo's San Francisco office. More books. Classical archeology. American archeology. Joseph's father is an archeologist? Of course. Another reason why Joseph was involved in the Ozette dig. Ava is curious about her father-in-law, this man Joseph never talks about, but even more curious about Kaya. She wanders the house looking for traces of her. She opens doors, becomes an invader.

Fifteen rooms. Some of them have been closed off for years. Maybe decades. One room is furnished with nothing but a dusty highchair and a pair of children's socks on the floor. Another bears a calendar from 1952. Still other rooms are piled high with boxes, tools, old furniture, as if someone went to too many tag sales and never looked at the purchases.

Ava circles back to the room where she and Joseph will stay. A note on the bed offers "Welcome." Her eyes are heavy, but she roams further. She finds what must be the father's room: bed unmade, a pile of books next to it, papers piled on the window seat. She leaves quickly. It would be bad luck to go in.

Next door is a tidy, plain room with a hand-crocheted bedspread and a powwow poster on the wall. Kaya. He married me, she reminds herself. She fingers the ring on her finger, carved not of gold but of cedar root. Kaya's bed is close and inviting. The pillow smells of lavender. With that scent for comfort, she lies down and falls asleep.

Voices. She tries to shut them out but they continue. "Episodes before." "Why didn't you tell me!" "Didn't want to interrupt." "What are we gonna do about. . . ?" "You had your life, your white-man dreams."

Dreams. Like a child pushing away the sounds of parents arguing, Ava tries to shut out their words and stay in her dream. She likes the idea of dreams, of herself sleeping inside a comforter called "dream." The sound of voices, of doors closing, of stairs creaking is part of a deep, delicious dream in which a fuzzy white dog is nestled behind the crook of her knee snoring peacefully, rhythmically, and everything is simple and right with the world.

Ava senses that she is being lifted. She is a small child who fell asleep in the car being carried by her father to her own bed. She enjoys the comforting strength of his shoulders, his arms. She nestles in and resists the putting down. And then, with her face clinging to the strong, safe body, she realizes this is not Aqua Velva aftershave but sweat and earth she smells.

Ava opens her eyes for a blink and closes them again. She is in a large bed. She is resting on pillows. But she doesn't care about whether her bed is hard or soft. She wants to see the face of the father, brother, or lover who carried her here. She opens her eyes and sees strong hands adjusting covers. Joseph's hands, calloused, with dirt behind the fingernails. In a state both drowsy and anxious, hoping for a reply that will allow a return to dreams, she asks, "How is he?"

"We'll talk about it in the morning. Sleep."

"Just tell me. The *Reader's Digest* version. I won't sleep until I know." Her fumbling language wakens her further. She opens her eyes in full alarm now. Joseph's sleepless dark-circled eyes, worried tight lips. She is flooded with a liquid feeling like sympathy mixed with urgency. "Tell me."

"They think he'll live."

"Good." She tries to quiet herself, to achieve some sense of decorum.

"He will probably be impaired on one side. He'll need some care. And then there's this place." Joseph gestures impotently at vastness. "He has horses, crops, gardens, pet bison. . ."

"Pet bison?"

"Did I mention my father is a tad eccentric? I've got my work cut out for me." Joseph almost smiles. "When he tried to speak, it came out in Ukrainian. He must have learned it when he was a kid. I had no idea. The doctor said it's like the stroke closed some doors in his brain. But they may open again."

Ava thinks of the closed-off rooms in the house, this mysterious, bookish house surrounded by acres of land, pet bison, and flower fields. A puppy jumps up on the bed and nestles against her leg. Or maybe she's drifted back into dreamland. Half-asleep, she kisses Joseph's hand, too sleepy to reach for his face.

"I planted the tree. The red cedar. It's in the ground."

"That's why I smell dirt."

"What were we thinking hauling that damn twig across the country?"

"What were we thinking?"

His full weight falls onto the bed. They sleep in their clothes, their teeth unbrushed. A young dog sleeps between them, running in its dreams.

PART THREE

Big Springs
Seven Years Later — 1978

You spread oil over your shoulders and arms, your thighs, your calves, the calloused and rough heels of your feet. Platty Puss licks up the small puddles you've dripped off the edge of the tub, onto the bathroom floor. You wonder why you let your children name the animals. From the laundry basket, you excavate a bra held together with safety pins. You do up the hooks and search for more underwear. You put on his jockey shorts, your long underwear, his turtleneck, your jeans, his flannel shirt, your socks. It's been way too long since you've done the laundry.

You reach for the phone before feeding yourself breakfast, even before having a sip of water. You dial Dena's number.

"What does it mean when a fly sticks to the wall when you're taking a shower?"

"You okay? You sound like an old Jewish comedian."

"Getting over a cold." You feel like you've just risen from the dead, like you're seeing things for the first time after weeks of only looking at clouds of Kleenex spilling out of trash cans, your haggard red face in the unkind mirror, your impatient children's faces. You unsuccessfully try to stifle a cough.

"A fly on the wall. While you were showering. In December. In Kansas."

You just "Mmmmm-hmmmm," swallowing phlegm. You wait for the augury, the secret to living your life. You love divination. Every morning you study your horoscope in the Topeka daily paper, devour fortune cookies to get to the message and lucky numbers, study your own palm for signs of happy endings.

"Maybe a visitor will arrive. Could be good news."

"Or. . . ?" While you wait, you try not to think of the phrase "pregnant pause." You study the frost on the windowpane. You love the white shapes, the feathery crystal continents with rounded edges in relief against the plain glass. You want to find your camera, capture the image before it melts away.

"You know what, Auntie Dena, that's okay. It flew away." Sweat is already developing on the windowpane, white frost continents losing ground to the sun.

"It flew away?"

"It's no big deal. I'll call you later."

"Or it could mean there's somebody keeping an eye on you. She's moved to a safer distance from which to observe."

"I'll whack it. They're dirty. They lay their eggs in buffalo poop."

"Check the mail. If there's nothing in the mailbox, kill it with my blessings."

You snap the photo before the last bit of frost disappears, make your way through the house, navigating through Lego architecture and doll furniture. In the kitchen, you see the results of a morning's getting-ready-for-school tornado: swollen Cheerios float in sour milk, half-eaten slices of toast lie abandoned on plates, a coffee cup sits in its own puddle of dark stain. You try not to get mad at your husband who is, after all, taking the ill-fed and undoubtedly rag-taggedly-dressed, mother-forgotten girls to nursery school and your father-in-law to somewhere, maybe the library. In a sudden burst of hunger, you bite into the burnt leftovers of toast; you swallow a few of the abandoned Cheerios; you follow it all with a sip of the rank milk and then you spit it all out into the sink. Not having eaten for days does not give you an appetite for bad moo juice. Or, uh-oh, you're pregnant again.

You see Homer making his way over, needing to go outside. Your constant companion for the last two weeks, you are grateful for his shaggy warmth. You open the back door. Even a blind dog needs to pee. You are greeted with a blast of Arctic air. You yelp and Homer backs his way into the house. You slam the door and icicles fall off the gutter pipe, stabbing the snow beneath. Homer wags his tail and makes for the door a second time.

Success. Homer yellows the snow.

A flash of feverishness pulses through your body. You plop down on the couch and luxuriate in the fur of the buffalo throw. Exhausted. You want servants, a staff, a nurse. You want somebody to deliver you to normalcy. On the TV, Gene Kelly is singin' in the rain. You love Gene Kelly. So much more desirable than the delicate Fred Astaire. Gene has working-class shoulders, substantial thighs, dark glossy hair. Suddenly, you love him more, want to be embraced by him. You think about him kissing your hurting feet, your throbbing head.

Your hand moves along your thigh but detours to a Kleenex box so you can swipe the snot off your face. No Kleenex. Not one thin tissue. Its emptiness makes you cry. This is what you're like when you're sick. You cry over the slightest loss. You spy a roll of toilet paper next to an empty water glass. You pull off an overly long stretch of paper and wipe the slime off your upper lip. Two weeks of flu and it's not over yet. When you blow your nose, your ears suddenly pop and you feel a tiny hope of wellness. You look up at Gene of the Nice Shoulders. Your hand moves under the waistband of your husband's underwear in rhythm to the music. You bring yourself to a climax, wipe your hand on the buffalo throw.

You think how you're a terrible mother to be doing such a thing while your kids are innocently singing the alphabet song at preschool. You should be baking gingerbread cookies, frosting cupcakes. But Gene Kelly is more delicious. And can't make you pregnant.

When you return to the kitchen, you spot the fly, floating in pinkish milk, asphyxiated by Fruit Loop juice. You spill the bowl out but the fly sticks to the sink. You congratulate it on its resurrection. You let it live.

Ten minutes later, after emptying ashtrays and restoring boxes to cupboards, you spot the insect again, another of its kind atop it, humping the hell out of it. You yell "BLEH!" and run water on the copulating couple, sending them down the drain.

You drink lemonade straight out of the bottle. When you come up for air, you can sense a few brain cells rallying. You have a few minutes of clarity to check the calendar.

And there it is, on today's date in big red caps: CARLO!!! Crap. In a panic, you run down to the family-sized chest freezer and bend over into it. You could fall into this freezer and never be heard of again. You survey the contents: bison burger, buffalo ribs, bison pot roast, buffalo short ribs, bison stew, buffalo steaks. You yank out a couple hard-as-granite packages of ground bison and vow to make bison/black-bean chili before Carlo Spinelli arrives in his rental truck for his annual visit. You gather up every bit of trip-on-me detritus, every pull-on-my-cord-and-make-me-squeal toy, every fragment of the flotsam and jetsam of family life.

You take a breath—omigod, you can breathe—that's one advantage of panic, it opens the bronchial tubes. And then you enter what was once the sewing room. You traverse the empty, naked, forbidden, near-sacred room, once the province of Jesse's mother, to get to the closet. Once you open the door, time slows. Inside, the filmy, plastic dry cleaner bags with their contents: moose-hide dress and powwow regalia. You shake the ankle bells and feel your blood flow. A flash of memory from when you still called him "Joseph." Before family and Kansas and a dependent old man. You force yourself to avert your eyes which land on your children's powwow dresses, all beads and shells on black velvet, sent by Jesse's Makah grandmother. And never worn. A feather falls.

Flying on nerves, guilt, and hunger, you declare yourself well.

⁂

Every December, Carlo Spinelli drives a U-Haul truck from San Francisco to Big Springs. He calls it his "Kiss-my-ass, Uncle Sam" tax-deductible trip in which he lowers his inventory and his taxes while getting a short, refreshing snort of winter. He gets to see old friends and smoke dope in the sauna. Carlo loads his truck full of unsold Asian-imported merchandise from his San Francisco warehouse, heads south and then west, drinking date shakes in the desert, buying santos in New Mexico, making his way up to Kansas, to his friend Jesse's ranch. Okay, Jesse calls it "farm." Carlo calls it "ranch." There he sells off his geegaws to old customers and small shops, gets a dose of family life and winter, loads his truck with Jesse's hand-crafted furniture to haul back to sell in California. After a few days in Kansas, Carlo always leaves before dawn on an undesignated morning to everyone's surprise and relief.

⁂

The long white truck crunches over snow-covered gravel and comes to a stop. Xenia and Sequoia, hyper-excited about Christmas vacation and the sight of "Uncle" Carlo, squeal out to meet him, followed by Homer the Samoyed, and then, more sedately, their parents. Carlo steps out of the truck's cab wearing a sheepskin jacket, jeans, and cowboy boots with a comically small tiara on his head and another in his hands. Jesse says, "What are you doin' with the girly crown on your head, man?!" Jesse grabs it, runs, and throws it like a Frisbee; Carlo catches it on the fly. He tosses it again in the air and then throws another.

"'Tiaras,' you inlander-know-nothing." They play like this for a few tosses. Trying to reach the sparkly crowns, the girls jump between them and find themselves in the center of "Monkey in the Middle" until the soft-hearted Carlo pretends to drop one, then the other, tiara. He reaches into the truck cab and produces a third, larger, rhinestoned crest. Foolishly, Ava thrusts herself into the middle between the guys. Children squeal, "Mommy, Mommy," and try to tackle the grown men quintuple their size. Carlo ends the game by crowning Ava with her own fake diamond tiara. He hugs and sloppy-kisses everyone. On the way into the house, Carlo pauses to look up. "I missed this sky. This wide-open big sky. And the sound of the wind, don't you love it?"

Ava hates the sound of the wind. Pioneer women had to be lashed to prairie schooners, gone mad from its constancy. It blares like a vacuum cleaner. It whistles around the edges of windows and doors. The howl equals loneliness. The Chicago winds, the "Windy City" gusts, never sounded so desolate and haunting. Ava realizes she has gotten lost in her own thoughts when Carlo nods back toward the driveway, "There's a box out there." Ava remembers how, in her pre-guest frenzy, she neglected to get the mail. She tears down the just-melted road, happy for an excuse to run. Mail is the highlight of her day.

In addition to Christmas cards and catalogues, there is a box. Ava knows from the return address that it contains Dr. Baines's books, the Christmas gifts she will give to everyone this year. What Ava enjoys most about the season is the feeling that she's gone a little too far, spent a wee bit too much, which she equates with the Christmas spirit. This year she has something special to give. It's taken seven years from that summer in Seattle to this moment. Seven years in which Dr. Baines conducted research, analyzed data, wrote, and found a university press to publish The Book.

Ava ducks into her dark room and uses a pair of scissors to split the tape. Ten books and she smiles to see them. On the cover, half-hidden by title and author, is her photograph of an Indian dancer at Pioneer Square in high contrast and bright color. Ava's name is printed in the credits as photographer. PHOTOGRAPHER!

☙

Jesse is giving Carlo the annual tour of his building projects. The huge old barn converted into his carving shed. The treehouse where Carlo observes that the little red cedar tree brought here in the terra cotta pot is now gigantic.

The girls are prancing in their tiaras and hugging their new Barbie dolls. Ava follows the men as they walk through the breezeway joining the old house to the new addition. When they reach Ava's darkroom, Jesse follows her eyes to the corner, where she had hastily covered the box of books with old mail. He grins. Damn him.

In the big living room, the senior Joseph waits, enjoying the warmth of the wood-burning stove, wearing more turquoise than any white man should be allowed. He is adorned with belts, buckles, bracelets, wristwatches, and a bolo tie. He is topped off with a hat too large for his old-man head, but also turquoise-laden, so it's part of the outfit. He loves company and after dinner joins the guys in a game of cards. He may have only one useful hand, but he is sly as a fox.

When Jesse comes to bed in the early hours of morning, he tells a half-asleep Ava that Carlo wants to stay through Christmas. He and Paulette are having marriage trouble.

☙

Ava loves Christmas. Ava hates Christmas. She loves the excuse to glitz up the house and listen to schmaltzy music; she hates the long weeks of the children's antsy anticipation, the tiresome jingling bells, the impossibility of any Norman Rockwell dreams actually coming true. She is already disappointed. She wanted a cozy family holiday, everyone oohing and aahing over her book cover. Now the scene will be altered by boy banter, card games, and break-up stories. Carlo will want Kaya here.

Bleh. She should be over this by now. She should be grateful for all Kaya has done over the years. How she helped with Joseph I until some of the doors in his mind opened again. And how she stayed when the girls were born, how she cleaned, bathed, fed, and rocked Ava's babies.

Ava is grinding her teeth. She tries to stop her jaws, but let's face it, you can't make yourself like what you don't like. Even though she knows it's a good thing to have a grown Indian woman in the girls' lives. Even though she knows it's a good thing to have someone who knows about babies when there's a baby in the house. Even though she admits that Kaya knows her way around the kitchen better than she does. But these are the very things she's resented over the years: Kaya's insider-ness, her ease with babies and guests, her knowing-better-than.

Ava's not sleeping. When it's late at night and she can't sleep, Ava is not kind in her thoughts. She sits up in bed to give full weight to mentally dishing Kaya. At least the woman doesn't live here anymore. When Sequoia was born, Kaya's room was needed. Jesse had refused to put his daughter in the sewing room, keeping it as a shrine to his departed mother. He had also refused to put his daughter in the same room where his baby brother had died decades ago, "the forbidden room." Jesse does not believe in the efficacy of wafting sage, but he does believe in the Makah deity who steals babies. The room remains unused to this day except for storing out-of-season clothes.

Trying to be grateful for Carlo's arrival, Ava thinks of the full house they will have at Christmas. She recalls a day a few weeks ago, when she had grown tired of photographing the sickly empty sky—sky the color of skeletons and dirty snow—and the leafless trees reaching up into it, like gnarled fingers. Opening her worn, black address book, she started calling former classmates. Most of them weren't home at two in the afternoon. They were working or lingering over a late lunch or headed off to a museum. Those who did answer sounded delighted to hear her voice but were on their way out the door or had a paper to write. Ava's mood sank. The telephone had become her lifeline, bringing news, continuing old friendships. Jesse hated the phone. A device, according to him, only for setting up appointments or announcing tragedy. Just like her father.

On that day, Ava cradled the phone in her hand, its dial tone waiting for the next attempt at connection, and she started to shudder with a realization. She had married a farmer. True, he carved splendid handmade furniture. But she had become a farmer's wife, living a life centered around planting and harvesting, the agricultural calendar of births and deaths. She had come here thinking Kansas would be exotic and, for a while, it was. But on that particular day, the wind didn't so much whistle as wail with a deep sound of mourning. The Uhhhhhhhhhhhhhhh of the earth moaning its losses when the land was scoured of leaf and flower and covered with a prickly stubble.

Thinking she should face the wind head-on, she went to the closet to get her coat and instead walked inside. She fought the hanging clothes as if the jackets and shirts were rude passengers on a Chicago El train. Exhausted, she slumped to the floor and sat on the collection of shoes and boots. Shoes she had worn when going out with friends to argue about movies or practice new languages, shoes too fragile for this soil. She missed her old life. She loved her husband and her children, but here she was, sitting on the bottom of a closet, weeping over shoes.

Looking up at her moose-hide dress, she shouted, accusing the guilty frock of dragging her into this life. Spent, Ava raised herself into a squat and then pushed up with her legs as hard as she could, toward the incandescence of the bare lightbulb above.

She braided and wrapped her hair, put on the dress, and went out into the cold in search of Penny, the oldest female of the bison herd. Penny, too old to bear calves and too ancient to run, was standing, as usual, on the leeward side of the barn, sheltering herself near the water tank. Ava situated her camera high on the windowsill of the barn, set to take a photo. She climbed up the old stone steps that led nowhere and hoisted herself onto Penny's back. The camera clicked too early. On the third try, Ava got the timing right, but Penny had grown impatient and started to snort at the barn wall and its clicking camera. Ava pitched forward and fell to the ground, grazing her chin on the old stone steps. Fortunately, Penny had no interest in trampling and Ava was able to grab her camera and sprint away before the other buffalo came running. She bandaged her chin, changed her clothes, and thanked the dirty white heavens that she was still alive. When she developed the prints, she loved the sense of action and adventure in the photo of Penny charging and Ava tipping forward. She sent it to all her old friends.

Ava dons a coat over her nightgown and grabs her camera. Going out into the night with the intention of shooting the outline of the barn against the sky, she spots Carlo, a cigarette poised in his hand, looking like an old-timey detective in silhouette, right down to the 1940s hat. Ava quickly takes a few shots and nearly escapes back into the house unnoticed, but he hails her.

"Hey."

"Hey." The moon shadow is kind to his face. She takes another photo.

"Looks like you're gonna have to put up with me for a bit. Jesse insisted I stay for Christmas."

"That's great," she lies. "We'll shoot a turkey."

"Not one with a name, I hope."

"They all have names. The girls have named more animals than Adam and Eve."

He points to her camera, "Hoping to catch someone dancing under the stars?" He does a quick, impromptu tarantella and she indulges him by snapping a few more photos. "I've always liked you, Ava. Y'know, if it weren't for damn Jesse getting there first, I'd have gone after you myself."

"Never mind that you wouldn't have known me if it weren't for Jesse." Ava is complimented by the comment and hates that she is so easily flattered. She quickly adds, "I'm thinking of inviting Kaya. Maybe my cousin Julie and her husband Trent. Y'know, make it a party." Ava hopes Julie will save her ass, keep her from actually punching people.

"Kaya. She's a looker. You must be a very confident lady to have put up with her all these years."

Ava thinks: Confident? How far from the truth appearances can be! She says, "What's Christmas without Kaya?"

Her hand curls into a fist. She imagines punching Carlo.

And here it is: Christmas morning. Ava surveys the living room. Xenia, five, is painting Uncle Carlo's fingernails a glittery hot pink. Xenia, this child given the more Greeky name, turned out to have her father's straight black Native American hair and features. She is painting ever so carefully, but, any second now, a wave of Homer the Dog's wagging tail could topple the bottle of glammy polish, resulting in tears. Uncle Carlo may or may not be enjoying his manicure. He seems to be attempting a nap. Sequoia, three, with her mother's curly Greek hair and her father's miraculous green eyes, is sticking Christmas bows onto her daddy's head. Jesse's eyes are closed in forbearance.

Grandfather Joseph, 68, dozes on the couch before the warmth of the wood-burning stove, still wearing the now-crumpled Santa suit he put on last night to distribute presents. His fake beard has been pulled below his chin onto his chest and makes a bed for the cat. Any pretense at Santa-ness has been extinguished. The girls don't seem to notice. They have decorated him with tinsel.

Ava experiences a sudden paroxysm of Hallmarkian emotion, looking at her people in the tableau of crushed tissue paper, forgotten presents, and tilted tree. When she notices the time, her affection turns to panic. She still has to chop apples and celery, stuff the turkey. His name is Poochy. She wishes the children didn't name the animals. She opens a window despite the cold, to shoo out the last wafts of pot smoke before the guests arrive. Did they really stay up and smoke dope after Midnight Mass?

Kaya comes in the backdoor unannounced and starts setting the table. She knows where everything is because every Tuesday she is here to help. She says it is for the senior Joseph, the old family ties, but Ava knows that Jesse pays her on the sly. Despite the cleaner house, the calmer children, the eased grandfather, Ava has been uncomfortable with this arrangement for seven years. It is an untouchable subject.

Ava runs around refolding already-tented napkins, reprimanding children, mashing potatoes, dropping potato-laden mashers on the floor. She has a tendency to forget asparagus in the fridge or bread in the oven. She sometimes burns the gravy. Will she ruin Christmas again?

She catches a quick glance of Kaya and Jesse chopping comfortably side by side, teasing and laughing. She thinks about how she is and always will be the white girl in the room. Never again will she wear her moosehide dress or braid her hair in public. No amount of turquoise jewelry or suntan will make her Indian.

Carlo walks in, freshly showered, hair wet, and smelling of musky cologne. He pours from the bottle of Mendocino he brought with him. He is clearly happy to see Kaya.

"Look at you, foxy lady."

"Go to hell, city slicker."

When Julie and Trent arrive at the door, Ava practically jumps up and down. She hugs her cousin so tightly she nearly crushes Julie's compact body. Julie is her only tie to her childhood, her own blood, her earliest memories.

Julie lifts a glass to toast. She is holding up the book with the bright photo on the cover. Ava's eyes are tearing up. It's probably the lack of sleep. And the slight pot hangover. She'd break into tears if she heard so much as a Pepsi commercial. She hides her face by snapping a picture of everyone assembled at the table.

"To my artistic genius of a cousin. To Avie!"

Everyone raises their glasses and calls out. The little girls are delighted with the ritual and the attention their mother is getting, at hearing their mother called "Avie." Kaya picks up the book from Julie's hand and studies it.

Ava realizes she did not order a copy for Kaya, didn't include her when counting heads. She runs to retrieve her own personal copy, hurriedly scribbles an inscription to Kaya. Love, Ava.

Dinner is served at last. Platters are passed. The food is tender, fragrant: Ava's roast turkey, Jesse's gravy, Julie's roasted vegetables, and Kaya's home-baked rolls. The feasters drink up the Mendocino. They consume the tender bites, the tangy bits.

After the gobblers attack the gobbler, Ava surveys the table. Smears of cranberry sauce puddle with brown gravy. Half-eaten rolls sit in piles of crumbs. Bones adorn plates like after a medieval feast. Everyone is sated and woozy. The drowsy little girls are still fancied up in their Christmas dresses and the tiaras from Carlo. Xenia fusses with the lace trim on her sleeve. She likes dressing up and insists on wearing party dresses even when riding her pet goat. Led by Joseph I, they all join in a clumsy version of "The Twelve Days of Christmas." Then, over pumpkin pie and whipped cream, Kaya, unaware of Carlo's marriage breakup, asks after his wife.

After an overly long pause, Carlo mumbles, "Dunno. I don't know how Paulette is taking it." Then, without thinking of the presence of children or the naiveté of his audience, he blurts out, "But I just couldn't do it anymore. I realized I wanted less cock, more quim. It finally dawned on me, at this late age, that I wanted a real woman."

Ava blurts out, "What are you talking about? Paulette is a real woman!" Then, she realizes that the one and only time she met Paulette was on the stop in San Francisco seven long years ago. She mentally reviews Paulette's clothes, shoes, makeup, her eagerness to go to Finocchio's to see the drag show. She asks herself how she could be so naïve. Paulette was a cross-dresser? Does that make Carlo gay? Or formerly gay?

There is a hush. Sequoia turns to her big sister and asks loudly, "What are they talking about?"

Xenia, the sophisticate, responds, "Men's and ladies' parts." Ava thinks how she needs to instruct her daughters on language. Men and Women. Lords and Ladies. Before she can utter a word, Xenia adds, "Y'know, penises and vulvas." Both girls giggle, then start chanting: "Pee-niss. Pee-niss. Pee-niss! Pee-niss! Pee-niss!!!" Stifled laughter all around the table.

When Ava gives them the That's enough, girls! look, they quiet for a moment. Sequoia then smiles with delight and chimes in, even more loudly, "My mommy has a GREAT BIG VULVA!" Ava turns red, Julie coughs up a sip of coffee, Trent shifts in his seat, Kaya looks like she is biting her tongue really, really hard, and Jesse smiles his wry smile. But Carlo laughs. He laughs louder and longer than he has in years. Sequoia thinks this is the most fun ever and starts howling.

But Xenia looks mortified. Grandpa Joe quickly comes to the rescue. "Well done, children. If you just keep in mind the Latin derivation." He pauses. "Jesse, the O.E.D?" Jesse lugs over the gigantic two-volume *Oxford English Dictionary*, a Bible to Joseph I. He reaches in its little drawer and takes out the magnifying glass. He flips through pages with his one good hand. The girls love looking through the magnifying glass at the impossibly small print. They adore it when Joseph I reads aloud about swords and sheaths and wrappings, decodes the mysteries of Latin and Medieval French. But enough about men's and women's parts. They want to look up other words, like "dog" and "Christmas." They want to use the spyglass to see a cat hair up close, a piece of turkey stuffing under glass. Joseph I indulges every whim. There are oohs and aahs. Ava snaps pictures.

⁂

The phone rings. Ava runs to get it, knowing before she picks it up that it will be her brother's annual Christmas phone call.

"How ya doin', Babe?"

"Didn't burn anything."

"Good job."

"I only forgot to serve one of the appetizers."

"Mom's herring with the sour cream and onions?"

"That's the one."

"Good. That stuff gives me gas."

"The girls ended dinner by chanting 'penis, penis, penis.'"

"HA! Give them my love. Big hugs and kisses."

"Hope you're having a Merry Christmas, Mickey!"

"That'd be nice."

"What's goin' on?"

"Y'know how it is, Avie. Business. Up and down."

She doesn't know how it is. She and Jesse try to live off the land, raise their own food, make their own beer, barter for clothes. Joseph I pays for the kids' Montessori School.

"On the down, I take it?"

"Might just declare a little bankruptcy."

"Whoa!"

The conversation continues about downsizing, selling the business, maybe moving to another state. Ava wonders about the legality of what her brother has been doing. She suspects that he's been involved with some unsavory characters. She remembers a particular incident from her childhood involving an uncle who collected "rent" on juke boxes for the Mafia. "Remember that time Father Pete asked Uncle Hank to donate bingo prizes?"

"Bingo prizes that just happened to 'fall off the truck.' Those old ladies played for prizes so hot they'd burn your fingers. And you, kiddo, you were pretty damned shocked."

"I was twelve. When I overheard that conversation, I felt like I'd lost my virginity."

"There's no target on my head, if that's what you're worried about. We're not all crooked in Chicago."

"Not crooked, just a little bent."

"Bent? Y'know, that's code for homo. I ain't no fag neither."

Since she's heard Mickey use words like "chink" and "wop" her whole life, she is not surprised by his language. He speaks the sexist, racist, insensitive working-class Chicago-ese they grew up with.

And he continues. "Hey, how's that Redskin of yours treatin' you?"

She looks over to Jesse, winks, and speaks extra loudly. "Ain't scalped me yet."

"Glad to hear it. So, Avie, when you comin' to Chicago?"

"Mickey, when you comin' to Kansas?"

"Yeah, right."

"Love ya."

She is consumed with questions for Jesse: Did you know about Paulette? Did you really spend years of your life sharing a house with a gay guy? Did I marry a gay man? Instead, she pulls off her nightgown and climbs onto him, licks his neck, his shoulder, his chest. She concentrates on the little divot near his hipbone. She wants to find the answers in their bodies. Jesse pulls her up and turns her on her back. She cries out loudly when he rocks on her. She wants to be heard, again and again.

Afterward, she hums.

He says, "You've been watching Gene Kelly movies again."

"What?"

"You're humming 'Singin' in the Rain.'"

She playfully punches his shoulder.

Carlo is gone in the morning.

Winter arrives full force. The bison and horses stand motionless in their heavy coats close to the house. When Ava walks out on the road, she finds herself in a stark landscape of bare branches and dirty snow. She watches the skyline for movement, but she only sees a broad expanse of sameness. She listens for the sound of a truck on the road but hears only the persistence of wind.

Darkness comes early. Joseph I retreats into his books. Joseph II retreats into his carving shed. Sequoia and Xenia retreat into sibling fights over toy ownership. After the children go to bed at night, the house is silent. At first there is relief that the high-pitched squabbling has ended, but then there is an overpowering stillness. Ava recalls her noisy growing up, the evening lights of the city, her family's restaurant with its warm aromas of lamb and roasting garlic, the way her father would joke with customers, even the loud patrons themselves. She knows in her heart of hearts that she loves her husband and that her children are everything to her, but she is missing a life lived at higher volume.

Cold, Ava nestles into the bison throw and pretends to read. When she works up enough energy, she tears a page out of the book she is reading. She crumbles it up and throws it into the wood stove, as if punishing the book could possibly help. She spits on the stove and her saliva evaporates into a split second of steam. She does it again and again.

Winter makes you pale. Winter makes you glum. Winter makes you eat every bit of chocolate within a square mile even it means stealing from your own children. Winter makes you turn on all the lights and leave them on all night. Winter makes you impatient. Winter makes you want something, anything, new to begin.

Ava tries to waken Jesse from a deep slumber. Their New Year's Eve plans were cancelled when the blizzard hit. They decided that they badly needed a good night's sleep so headed off to bed early. But Ava isn't sleeping, and she has the sudden urge to celebrate, so she shakes him gently, then less gently.

"C'mon, sleepyhead, we have a new year to greet."

"Grmmph."

"Time to count down with me! 10, 9. . ."

"No. I mean okay, as long as I don't have to leave the room and there's no loud noises involved."

"The whole world is making loud noises and painting their front doors red and eating grapes."

"So, we don't have to, right?"

"They are setting off fireworks."

"And singing 'Auld Lang Syne.' I know."

"Stand up." She's feeling a surge of enthusiasm that might not last more than 10 seconds and doesn't want to lose it.

"What?"

"Get up here with me!"

"Stand on the bed?"

"And jump."

"You mean do the very thing we tell our kids not to do."

"5, 4, 3, 2, 2, 2. . ."

He smiles, knowing that midnight probably happened hours ago but what the hell. "One."

And they start jumping. Hesitant, at first. And then, with laughter. And falling. And thinking how they might just want to do this every year.

⁂

Ava stumbles out of the house in old clothes. She doesn't have the energy to do more than add another layer of long underwear. The women's group is meeting at the Topeka home of Linda, a small woman who enunciates clearly and precisely. Her house is tidy, her furniture covered in afghans. Ava seems to remember liking these women, but tonight she finds their chatter irritating. Everyone is drinking warm apple cider and laughing in the kitchen. The others have known each other since teenage-hood, and they lapse into reminiscence, talking about teachers they used to have, boyfriends they used to date, houses they used to live in. "It was back when we lived on Jewell." "Y'know, when Carole wore those pigtails?" "Jeremy Schoenvelter!" Laughter. They may as well be speaking a foreign language. Ava stays a few steps out of the group, feeling unknown and unwelcome.

Ava is so inside herself she barely hears the transition to a conversation about the Equal Rights Amendment. Something about how Kansas has ratified, but several states have not. Something about how some states are even rescinding their approval. How female ERA opponents are baking pies and bringing them to state legislators. The necessity to secure an extension. But opponents claim that if the ERA passes, women will serve in combat, start marrying each other. Ava thinks maybe that wouldn't be such a bad idea. She sometimes thinks of men as alien beings she cannot understand.

Linda proposes a campaign in which members of their group will write letters to the legislators of the recalcitrant states explaining that this is not the intention of the ERA. "We have to assure them this will not happen." Women in the room nod in agreement. Linda has taken the liberty to draft a letter and passes around copies. Ava reads the polite, apologetic language, the entreaties, the summations. She speaks out of turn in a volume that steadily rises.

"Do we really want to sit quietly and write letters? Don't we want to make a point? An impact? A change in society? Don't you sometimes just want to yell? Shout! Don't you just want to go to these men in their suits and ties and fat bellies and tell them we want our rights! We are citizens, for Chrissake! Listen to us!" By the end of her impassioned speech, Ava is sobbing. Her cousin Julie reaches over and squeezes her arm.

Linda waits a moment to respond. "That's what we have to avoid. No matter how strong our feelings, we have to present ourselves as rational. Women are often accused of being overemotional, shrill, and lacking reason. We can't feed that gristmill."

"Bull-fucking-shit! If there are women who want to fight to defend their country, we shouldn't deny them that right! Think of the Amazons of the ancient world. And what about same-sex marriage? Are you against it?"

"No, I'm not against lesbian love, I just think it isn't a necessary consequence of the Equal Rights Amendment. I think we want to be reassuring."

"Reassuring? Why don't we just bake our own damn apple pies? Why don't we just become Phyllis Schlafly and ask permission of our husbands to speak?"

"We don't all have husbands like yours, Ava."

"Yeah, a super stud AND does the dishes." Nervous laughter follows.

Another voice joins in. "Right. I can't go off to some other state and start chanting at their statehouse. I can barely get my guy to put the kids to bed when I come to these meetings."

And the conversation shifts to "the sock wars": talk about how to manage sharing household chores, getting their men to pick up their clothes, wash kids' faces, do some of the cooking. Julie adds an example of her own life with Trent, how hard it is for her to speak up to him since he was once her teacher. Linda reminds everyone to please send copies of the letter to the addresses she has provided.

Once they get in the car, Julie smiles. "Well, that was fun."

"If what you mean by fun is having your tongue cut out and roasted on hot coals."

"I see you've lost your gift for hyperbole." Julie reaches into her big tote bag and pulls out a small flask of brandy and passes it over.

"Seriously. Don't you ever feel, here in Kansas, like you've got to sit on your hands?"

"True, you and I did not grow up with our ankles crossed and our hands folded in our laps."

Ava takes a hit off the flask. "Maybe if I had known Jeremy Schoenvelter in junior high, I wouldn't have turned into such a screaming banshee."

"Jeremy Schoenfucker can kiss my big city ass. You and me, we grew up with people who, let's say, lived at a higher volume."

"Y'mean ate grotesquely gigantic meals and danced like lunatics?"

Julie agrees, "And gestured wildly."

"And screamed really loud! Ready? At the count of three: One. Two."

They both wave their arms around and scream at the top of their lungs. "THREEEEEEEEEE!!!!!!!"

Ava knows she's not about to go to sleep when she gets home, but that's what everyone else in the house is doing. Joe I is making guttural sounds on his exhales but seems to be smiling in his slumber, so she moves on. Sequoia has kicked off her covers and Xenia is sleeping flat against her headboard, her knees tucked under her chin. Ava replaces covers, kisses foreheads. Without waking, the girls stretch out again. She tries to imagine their dreams and can only come up with pink teddy bears and unicorns. Then she remembers the girls who shouted "Penis!" at the tops of their lungs at Christmas. Get real.

Jesse doesn't budge when she comes in. She turns on her bedside lamp and writes about the evening in her journal. She loves the fine pen she is writing with, its delicate deep black line, the permanent ink. She turns to survey her husband, frames him in her mind's eye in various photographs she will never take. She sketches him in her notebook. His hair is still the same blue-black comic-book-hero color it was seven years ago. His shoulders, smooth and beautifully sculpted. She takes her pen and, on the flattest plain she can find on the middle of his back, she draws a pair of wings.

Lawrence

Julie and Ava slide their way over the snow-struck campus paths. The class is a Christmas gift to each other. An excuse to get out of their houses and maybe get back into the groove of learning. In nervous anticipation, Ava hypothesizes about their teacher-to-be.

"Professor Christopher Raleigh Grenville. Is that really his name? I mean, I'm seeing a pince-nez, tea-stained tweeds, rumpled vest."

"Eighty-seven years old. A small, wrinkled man."

"Withered. Miniscule. Eats only what his mother puts out for him. She's one hundred and three. Wears wellies."

"The natives where he did his doctoral research never boiled him up in a pot because there wasn't enough meat on him."

"I'm thinkin' a stammer."

"Definitely a stammer. Maybe two."

Ava mimics a haughty British accent in an ancient trembly voice, "G-g-good afternoon, colonists. I am Professor Christopher Raleigh Grenville,

Newcoalingshire-Up-Up-Upon-Whitsun-Avon. . ."

They've made their way into the classroom. They bite their tongues as they take seats behind eight earnest-looking male students. Ava opens her notebook and writes the date on the first page. Three times. Then, "Fieldwork. Again." They dare not look at each other. Finally, Julie clears her throat. "Actually, Trent says he has substantial credentials. FAT resume."

Ava shifts her image to a short, pink, fifty-year-old scholar wearing a pith helmet and oversized jodhpurs with lace-trimmed cuffs.

"Ruddy, round, squat, and bald."

"Henry the VIII meets Teddy Roosevelt."

"Sleeps under mosquito netting."

"Pudgy but carries a big stick?" They both splutter as the clock hits the hour mark.

A tall, slim figure strides in, wearing an Edwardian suit with a Poor People's March button on the lapel. If one could walk eloquently, he is walking eloquently. He carries neither textbook nor notes. He reaches the lectern but ignores it, turns around and beams a slow, infectious smile. He looks each student in the eye, one by one, lingering on Ava's face as if he's trying to recognize someone he's seen before. He can't be more than thirty. His skin is poreless and he has wavy maple-syrup-colored hair and mustachios curled up and waxed. When he finally speaks, his voice is softened by a honeyed Southern drawl. He announces that everyone in the class is getting an A.

"Let's not bother with all that grading nonsense but rather get on to the more important matters." He says "Rah-thah" for "rather" and manages to make it sound warm instead of uppity. Ava studies his hands, which look as if he's accustomed to holding a plumed pen. Everything about him looks like he might carry a quill pen and speak in seventeenth-century language mellowed by warmer climes. He speaketh further: "After today's class, we will be meeting in what I hope you will find to be the relative comfort of my home." Then, he writeth his address on the board in an elegant calligraphic hand.

Ava and Julie look at each other. Professor Grenville manages to quote Franz Boas, Samuel Beckett, and Bob Dylan in a single sentence. He even makes a reference to neo-Futurists without laughing. He bows graciously and then he is gone.

Ava and Julie leave the classroom, dumbstruck. What tornado dropped him in Kansas?

The next morning, after Ava drops off the pre-school carpool, she heads to campus to see if the library has copies of the books assigned for class. Money is scarce as usual. The sun has melted most of the ice into rivulets. Typical Kansas weather, she thinks, shifting from arctic to mild in a few hours' time. Ava hurries her pace, checks her pocket to make sure she still has the class syllabus.

She thinks about the various classes she has taken over the years. Anthro. Women's Studies. Photography. If she manages to finish this one, she might actually finally graduate. Ava Paputsakis with a degree. Ava Paputsakis. . .

"Miz Paputsakis? Miz Paputsakis?"

A voice calls her from behind. But who would call her "Miz Paputsakis?" She finds Professor Grenville striding beside her.

"Just the shortest interruption, Miz Paputsakis. I just wanted to let you know how much I admire your work."

"My work?"

"I have been looking forward to meeting you. I recognized you yesterday. From the display at the faculty show. There's a bio of you on the entrance-hall wall."

"Oh, that. No, I'm not really faculty. I teach a few pre-school children to snap a few pictures, that's all."

"Even better. Teaching our children is the most important work of all, don't you think?" He doesn't stop for an answer. "I'm also an admirer of your work in the gallery downtown." He says "Bett-ah" and "Ad-my-rah."

"You mean the Co-op?" She and Jesse recently joined a few other craftspeople in town who rent an inexpensive space in Lawrence. Maybe twelve people have walked in since it opened two months ago.

"And on the cover of Baines' book, how did you ever manage to capture such a rare moment? And what you did with color!"

Ava is blushing. She does not know how to accept such a string of compliments, how to be both light and appreciative at the same time.

"Again, I do apologize for interruptin' you. Where might you be headed?"

"The library. To read my assignment."

He stops short. Stops striding as if she had announced she was heading to death row. "The 'lie-berry?' No, no, no. You are not goin' to no lie-berry." She does a double take when she hears the purposeful bad grammar and mispronunciation of "library." Her professor just demoted the temple of academia with an offhand shrug and childish word. She catches the boyish smile on his face. "You are coming with me, Ms. Paputsakis. We have a party to go to."

No use protesting. Besides, it is his class she will be short-shrifting if she doesn't get to the library. And, she is curious. Damn curious.

They arrive at a stately house near campus. He smiles and shakes hands at the door with a gray-haired couple who are clearly expecting to meet Mrs. Emma Jane Grenville, but he introduces her instead, "I just knew you would want the opportunity to meet the photographer, Ms. Ava Paputsakis. I'm sure you're going to want to grace the walls of this fine home with her incredible work." Wine. Hot appetizers. An array of blue-veined cheeses. French breads in various shapes. Senior faculty members. Community dignitaries. An hour of polite conversation about campus politics. And then, with a gentle hand on her elbow, he ushers her out.

When they are out of earshot, he says, "Lovely people with consummate social graces." Ava understands that this itself is an indication of a consummate social grace: a polite put-down which, if quoted, could not be construed as negative. He's saying they aren't much fun. He does not wait for a reply or comment, but streams on, "I hope you and your husband will join Emma Jane and myself on Saturday night. Eight-thirty." He smiles a Colgate smile. "Be sure to wear your dancin' shoes."

"Life is just one party after another."

He shakes her hand, does an endearing bow, and walks away. After a few steps, he turns around, pauses, and lets another slow smile emerge on his face.

Ava has trouble finding her car. She has forgotten the "lie-berry" completely.

Big Springs

"What are you laughing so big about, Grandpa Joe?" Sequoia hopes to solicit a joke or story.

"Did I ever tell you about Old Hiram, my father's hired hand?"

"You don't have to tell us again," Xenia adds, wishing for the opposite.

"Well, Old Hiram loved to eat frog legs."

"Yuck." Sequoia scrunches up her small face. Ava moves quickly and catches the expression with her camera.

"Sauteed in butter, you'd like 'em. They taste like chicken."

"Then why not just eat chicken?" Xenia clearly repeating something she's heard an adult say.

"Well, Old Hiram was a bit lazy but clever." Despite a useless hand and a crooked smile, Joseph I has recovered his ability to tell stories. When he's not drinking, cussing, or gambling, he tries to live up to being their resident village elder. Ava snaps a few more pictures of the old man and his adoring granddaughters.

"Besides, that Old Hiram, he had a sixth sense about the weather. He could predict the exact second the pond out there would freeze, and he was always right." Both girls turn to look out the window to see if the pond is frozen. "Old Hiram would go out when it was just about to freeze." At this point, Joseph I claps his hands and both girls jump. "Then, he would clap his hands and all the frogs would jump into the pond, just as the water turned to ice. They got frozen with their heads in the water and their delicious frog legs sticking out on top of the ice. Then, Old Hiram, he just went out with an old-fashioned lawn mower and harvested the frog legs. Mmmmm-mmmm. My Daddy and me and Old Hiram, we had ourselves a tasty supper of frog's legs cooked up in butter." The girls' faces are screwed up in horror. Snap.

"Yuck."

Then, just as quickly, "I wanna clap my hands and see the frogs jump in the pond."

"Me, too. I wanna see the frogs jump in the pond!" Snap. Snap.

"It's gonna freeze any minute now, so we might just catch 'em." And with that, Joseph I puts his Santa hat back on, even though it's weeks after

Christmas. Jesse gets the girls' coats. Father and grandfather take the girls out to the pond, hoping to see the frogs leap at their command.

〰

Kaya walks in the door just as Ava is emerging from the shower. There are not many people she trusts with the girls, so Ava has swallowed her pride and called Kaya to babysit. Ava closes her bedroom door and tries on five outfits, that is, everything in her closet. She can't appear in overalls. She can't dance in her work boots. She settles on a turtleneck, skirt, tights, and a pair of flats. She wishes she had some interesting ethnic jewelry. The kind female anthropology professors wear. Ava walks into the kitchen to gather up the wristwatch and wedding ring she left on the counter above the sink when she was doing the dishes.

Kaya watches her put on her red cedar wedding band and comments, "You should tell him to give you a gold ring and marry you for real."

Outside, the clapping of several sets of hands as the girls try to get frogs to jump in the pond.

"There's milk in the fridge. They can each have one graham cracker before bed. And yes, they are allowed to brush each other's teeth."

Half an hour later, Ava slams the pickup door hard.

Lawrence

They are surprised to find the Grenville house in a low-income neighborhood, by the railroad track. The houses around it are low, squat, ramshackle, with washing machines on porches, weeds and dogs comingling in scrappy yards. The grand Grenville house stands tall, with two large chimneys sending up smoke, a two-story brick abode painted in handsome sedate colors. It is dignified and perhaps the oldest house Ava has seen in Kansas.

The street is lined with cars parked on the grass, so they have to leave the turquoise truck two blocks away. Ava and Jesse can hear people singing:

And only say that you'll be mine,

And in no other arms entwine.
There beside where the water flows,
Down by the banks of the Ohio.

Through the tall, narrow windows, they can see someone playing mandolin, someone else with a banjo. Dozens of people with beers in their hands are singing along. The door is unlocked, the living room crowded. Ava nods to students from her class. She notices children sleeping under tables.

Standing apart from the clusters of laughing, drinking, singing guests stands Professor Grenville, smoking a blue-and-white porcelain pipe, surveying the room. He catches Ava's eye and smiles. She would not have predicted it in a million years, but Jesse and the professor are both wearing cowboy shirts, black pants, and belts with big buckles. Their host speaks directly to Jesse.

"Why, we're a match made in heaven," he jokes. "You must be Joseph Lightfoot."

"You can call me Jesse."

"And I will, if you'll call me Raleigh." He shakes Jesse's hand. "I am honored to meet you. I have seen a desk with your mark at the Dean of Faculty's house. So I immediately purchased one of your hand-crafted boxes from the Co-op when I saw it. Being a follower of William Morris, I admire a true craftsman. I have been looking for someone like you to help me with a project. Please, let me show you." Jesse follows him with an enthused look on his face. Professor Grenville is capable of charming men as well as women.

The living room is furnished with antiques and heavy satins, warmed by a fireplace with two gaudily painted andirons, both shaped like George Washington. Above the doorway to the kitchen is something written in Grenville's now familiar calligraphic hand. Something in Italian or maybe Latin. Ava wanders from room to room, overhearing conversations about who's playing in town and underground movies she's never heard of. She leans in when she hears Grenville's name, hoping to catch some gossip about their hosts. She is rewarded with a tidbit about how Mrs. is several years older than Mr., how she was married before and has a child somewhere back in North Carolina, but left her first husband and child for the moustachioed professor. Ava suspects the story is untrue but finds the legend compelling nonetheless. It reminds her of stories written in the supermarket tabloids about the rich and famous. She pictures the Grenville name in bold headlines. Grenville makes her think of the French word for frog, *grenouille*.

Enticed by the smell of baked ham and biscuits, Ava makes her way into the kitchen. Over the doorway, more calligraphy reads: "Give me love and work—these two only." William Morris is clearly a Grenville favorite.

The kitchen is furnished with a soapstone sink and an ancient stove, but there's no sign of a refrigerator. Women are congregated here. Ava thinks she may have found Emma Jane Grenville in a small woman with a dark brown braid down her back. Mrs. Grenville stands at a big scarred table, slicing ham and putting it on biscuit halves without removing the cigarette from her mouth. When she finally does open her mouth, it's to announce to the women assembled that there is going to be a race. All the women are to call for their husbands. Right now.

"And we'll see whose man comes runnin' first."

A couple of the women sing out their husband's names as if they were calling hogs. Others go to the living room to collar their men. Emma Jane doesn't move. Neither does Ava.

"Raleigh wouldn't run if I was one of Homer's sirens callin' him. Hi, I'm Emma Jane Grenville." She slathers mustard and jam on a biscuit with ham on it, hands it to Ava and takes one herself. "It might look like sin, but it tastes like an angel shat it out." Ava can't decide whether this is a recommendation. She has to work up her courage to take a bite but ends up delighted at the mixture of salt, sweet, tang, and fat.

"'Kissin' don't last but cookin' do,' Raleigh is wont to say."

"And this is mighty good cookin'." Ava finds herself imitating the lilt in the Southerner's voice.

In the background, the protestations of husbands who will not follow their wives into the kitchen, husbands who want to stay where they are, dammit, drink a beer, and play a little banjo, dontcha know. Emma Jane smiles, fixes Ava another ham-biscuit with jam and mustard and turns to meet her eyes. "And you are. . ."

"Sorry. Ava Paputsakis."

"You do kinda look like you could pose for a 'Come to Greece' travel poster."

"Only half of me. The other half is Polish. Ava Odesza Paputsakis."

"Mongrels are strong."

Trying to find a starting place for further conversation, Ava looks up and finds a carefully painted quotation above the door. Before the request for a translation is out of her mouth, Raleigh Grenville is behind her, offering: "My course is set for an uncharted sea."

"Don't know why he couldn't have put it up there in English," says Emma Jane. "I get mighty tired of translatin' these here walls."

"Guess I'm just a pedantic show-off." Raleigh emits his captivating smile.

To a freckled woman with long, pale straight hair who pulls her husband into the kitchen by his hand, Emma Jane offers only this dismissal, "Too late, Louise, we got two come in ahead of your Tim." Clearly, she means that she herself and Ava have won the husband-calling contest. She smiles to Ava with a self-satisfied and conspiratorial glance. Their men were summoned by the power of thought alone. Tim and Louise leave with a shrug.

Jesse eyes the calligraphy on the wall. "It's Dante, from the *Paradiso*." Ava realizes Jesse is talking about the quote. She thinks about how her husband often surprises her with his knowledge. Then he adds, "I thought of this very line the first time I met Ava."

The party is followed by weeks of gatherings at the Grenville house. There seem to be parties for any excuse. A visiting banjo player or a fiddler's contest. Elizabeth Cotten visits, a Lomax or two, Alan Dundes. After the official reception, there's always a party at the Grenvilles', with studious-looking men singing unaccompanied Child Ballads or raucous guys in rumpled work shirts playing blues guitars.

Big Springs

At Jesse's request, Ava invites Raleigh and Emma Jane to dinner. They arrive in the early evening with four ragamuffin children in tow. Xenia and Sequoia, excited for the company, jump up and down when the old Mercedes unloads. Emma Jane carries a cake fragrant with orange and ginger. Raleigh exits the car, then stands gazing first at the barn, then up at the treehouse. He walks slowly and gazes appreciatively at the yard, the buildings. He walks into the barn and Jesse hurries to catch up with him.

The cake is delivered to the kitchen, and Emma Jane gives Ava a warm hug. "The kids seem happy enough out there, let's see what those menfolk of ours are up to."

When they move into the woodcarving shed, they hear Raleigh praising Jesse's workmanship: the mortise-and-tenon joinery, the dovetailed drawer boxes. "This is what we're missing these days. Craftsmanship. Pride in workmanship. Everything now is made of plastic or glued-together cardboard. This is what my man William Morris talked about." Ava sees it, too, the care Jesse has put into his work. The satiny finish on the wood, the result of hours of sanding and waxing. Ava looks from man to man, seeing how different they are. The one tall and lanky, almost delicate and feminine in his gestures; the other, not much taller than Ava herself, sturdy, broad-shouldered, and brown.

"Joseph, I hope you will honor me by building the cabinetry for my library. Emma Jane is mighty tired of having boxes on the floor. Name your price. It'll be worth it." Jesse blushes. Ava half expects him to crack a joke, but he stands silent and proud. She experiences a surge of admiration for this man she's been with for seven years. She feels a pang of guilt over how invisible he has been to her lately. Just someone to negotiate with about who's going to pick up the kids, return the library books, feed the livestock. But once again she sees the beauty in his face, remembers his craftsmanship, enjoys the way he turns his hands up in a what-can-I-say? gesture. Ava takes Jesse's hand, feels its warmth. A wahooing begins inside her as she realizes that this deal means buying clothes, food, film. Stuff.

The children have found their way into the warmth of the main house, where Joseph I is narrating how Odysseus was lashed to the mast with his ears stuffed with wax so he wouldn't hear the tempting call of the sirens. Sequoia holds her hands over her ears. One of the Grenville children is holding a candle, clearly considering the option of stuffing his ears with melting wax. The other children listen with mouths open, anticipating the call of the siren. Ava complies in her totally pedestrian mama-yell voice, "Come and get it."

They delve into bison pot roast and homemade bread, followed by

Emma Jane's gingerbread cake with orange sauce. Emma Jane takes a walk around the house, nonchalantly commenting on how Ava managed to capture movement, then asks if Ava could please do portrait photos of her children. Ava says, "I don't usually," but then agrees.

The Grenvilles don't seem to care about bedtimes or tooth-brushing, but Jesse and Ava do, so they compromise and tuck the children two and three to a bed for a rest until the grownups are ready to call it a night.

When the house quiets and Joseph I retires to his room, the two couples find themselves comfy places to sit, with their glasses of Mendocino left from Carlo's visit. Ava puts out chocolates from Christmas. She is eager for an adult conversation.

Raleigh runs his hand over the smooth surface of the coffee table. He continues his examination until he finds the small abstract winged boat carved into a corner edge. "So, when I recommend you to others for your fine work, do I say Joseph or Jesse?"

Ava answers, "I thought his name was 'Chief Joseph' when I first met him."

Jesse notes, "'Chief' is one of those names white men are always calling Indians. Like 'Tonto.'"

"But your name is Joseph Lightfoot?"

"People think Lightfoot is an Indian name but actually I'm named after a white ancestor who came from Liverpool."

"A Liverpudlian? Like the Beatles?" Emma Jane asks.

Ava says, "Don't you just love to say 'Liverpudlian?' Sounds like they're a people descended from Lilliputians who dwell in puddles.'"

Jesse clarifies, "My friends call me Jesse, but Joseph Lightfoot is my official voter registration name."

Ava's curiosity takes over, "Kinda like you're called Christopher Grenville in the university catalogue but Raleigh in person."

"Raleigh's given name was Christopher-Robin," Emma Jane enlightens them.

"Like in Winnie-the-Pooh?" asks Ava.

"Yes, my Mom was a Pooh fan. But when I was twelve, we took a trip to Roanoke Island."

"Sir Walter Raleigh's outpost? The Lost Colony?" asks Jesse.

"Mmmmm-hmmmm. The British dumped off settlers, got distracted by a war with Spain, and forgot to come back for a few years."

"So you changed your name from Christopher-Robin to Christopher Raleigh?" Ava asks. "From a sweet boy who hangs out with a honey bear to a pirate?"

"It's a lot sexier, right?" says Emma Jane. "What is it about a pirate?"

Ava visualizes Raleigh twirling his grand mustachios as he plunders and pillages.

The present-day Raleigh once again runs his fingers over the signature boat carved into the coffee table. He turns to Jesse. "Wherever did you learn to do this, this beautiful work?"

"Thank you. I learned some basics at Haskell, though I resented it at the time."

"Haskell was a manual-labor school, am I right?"

"That was before my day. When I was there, we took classes in Native American religion and philosophy, Indian crafts and music. We had to work forty hours a week besides going to classes, but y'know, I learned a lot."

"You worked forty hours a week when you were at Haskell?" Ava never knew this.

"Isn't that where our neighbor Kaya went to school, Emma Jane?"

Emma Jane nods, "She tells some horror stories about the bad old days of the school. Forced assimilation, cruelty, abuse."

"Kaya is your neighbor?" Ava's voice is tense and high-pitched. She realizes that she has never been to Kaya's house. Never was invited, never tried to find out where it was. She wonders why she has been so negligent in her detective work.

"She lives right behind us, little blue house."

Raleigh shifts the conversation back to Jesse. "But you went on to university."

"KU, eventually."

"I'm glad someone had the good sense to teach you what you were born to do. You craft gorgeous pieces of furniture that people will admire for hundreds of years."

"A Mr. David Morris taught me cabinetry at Haskell. And I spent a few summers out on the reservation."

"What tribe are you?" Raleigh asks and Ava marvels that he knows the right way to ask.

"Makah."

"Ah. Those Northwest Coast Indians do know their way around a piece of wood." He wraps his long, slim fingers around the stem of a fragile wine glass and looks up. "But then you are a chief. Woodcarvers, whalers were from the chiefly class, am I right?"

A blush colors Jesse's cheeks. "Times have changed. As the Makah say, 'Honor the past but adapt to survive.'"

Ava feels this evening is teaching her things about her husband that she never suspected.

Jesse agrees to let Raleigh's fieldwork class visit his carving shed to interview him as a traditional craftsperson. Emma Jane insists that Ava visit with the children on Wednesday.

Raleigh raises his glass, "You two are what we hoped for, coming to Kansas."

Lawrence

Tuesday morning, while the kids are in daycare, Julie and Ava drive to the Grenvilles' neighborhood. They are in Julie's highly identifiable yellow Volvo station wagon, so they park two blocks away. They pretend to be walking to the Grenvilles' and have a trumped-up excuse, returning Emma Jane's cake platter. True, she did indeed leave it at the farm, but they could have easily returned it in class the next day. They are walking toward Kaya's little blue house. They are here to snoop, and they are hoping that no one is home so they will be free to peer in the windows.

Ava and Julie try to keep themselves looking purposeful, but then Julie starts chattering on about how thrillingly handsome Professor Raleigh is. "I wouldn't mind finding his boots under my bed." Ava howls. They've been co-conspirators since they were eight years old.

When they cross the street to take a peek at the little blue house, they see a too-familiar turquoise truck and run for the car. Ava drops the glass cake platter, which shatters. In haste, they pick up the shards and drop them into Julie's handbag. Ava's finger is bleeding and her face is pale. Julie is muttering a nonsensical stream of reassurances.

"He's just probably dropping off something she left at your house when she was babysitting. Like we're doing with the cake plate."

"The cake plate was a lie."

"Maybe that wasn't even Jesse's truck."

Ava takes a quick glance over her shoulder. "Yeah right, there's such a profusion of turquoise pickup trucks in Lawrence with moon-shaped dents in the left rear fender."

"Ava, don't let your imagination run away. Jesse and Kaya have been friends for years."

When she takes her seat in the truck, Ava wraps some Kleenex around her cut finger.

"Make sure there are no splinters in that cut."

"Are you going to try to solve ALL my problems? Do you really think I'm not an adult?" Then, her voice rises to a fever pitch, "Did you see that house? It's the same damn color as Jesse's truck. She painted the house to match. That's not friendship. It's obsession. You know I'm right."

Julie makes several false starts getting the old Volvo going. "It could be anything. Coincidence. A paint sale."

"Obsession."

"Maybe he's there to tell her off, to say she should go live her own life, marry some nice Kickapoo from the reservation and move on."

"Right. After all these years he's gonna do that."

"Ava, you would have known if there was something going on."

"I'm married to the best poker player in the county. He does not show his hand. Ever."

"You think he could hide for seven years, from you, his wife. Besides. . . "

"There's a besides?"

"Besides, I've never seen a couple so much in love as you and Jesse. He loves you bad."

"Lately, I've been a cold, heartless bitch, always longing for something else, someplace else. I haven't been there for him."

"This will all look better after a good night's sleep."

Ava starts keening. Pent-up tension from years of wondering and worrying come flooding out. Julie stops the car.

"Now get over here."

Ava sidles her way closer to Julie who holds her until the sobs stop. When Julie thinks Ava is ready for a joke, she says, "Besides, I thought Jesse had a thing for Carlo. You did think he was gay, like a week ago."

This shouldn't work but it does. Ava finds a laugh down deep in the place where her sobs came from. She manages to speak, "Turns out, the REAL story is that Carlo didn't want to go Paulette's parents' place for Christmas, so he staged a big fight with her and came here."

Julie smirks. "Now, there's a reasonable husband. And I take it Paulette has been a girl-girl all along?"

"What girl-girl wears stilettos, glitter lipstick, and looks to drag queens for fashion tips?"

"Stilettos. America's answer to Chinese foot-binding."

"I'm told she is a girl-girl. Not that I've seen the goods."

Ava heads out to find a replacement cake platter for the Grenvilles. It takes her three stores to locate one in a dusty second-hand place piled high with old washboards, roller skates, and dishes. She washes the plate five times, bakes some brownies, and writes an apology note. When she picks up the girls, she takes them to the Grenville house, as promised. She explains to Emma Jane how terrible she feels about having dropped the platter.

Emma Jane fake-flutters her eyelids, "Frankly, darlin', it had belonged to my great-great-grandmother back in Charleston. I hope her dear departed soul forgives me for leaving it behind."

"Oh, no. I feel just awful."

"Aw, c'mon, Ava. Raleigh picked it up for 25 cents at some yard sale in Topeka."

"Really?"

"Anyway, I meant to leave it behind. It was yours to keep, break, or give away."

"Really?"

"Can you stop with the 'reallys?' The only thing that puts me out about all this is that you were right here in the neighborhood and didn't stop by yesterday. I saw you and Julie runnin' like the dickens, like two school girls who'd been peekin' over the fence at some nekkid person and near got caught."

"I am so embarrassed."

"If you're curious about Kaya's house, well, let's you and I just walk on over there and bring her some brownies." Emma Jane gives that conspiratorial look she wore after the husband-calling race. She adds, "Any woman who'd paint her house the same color as my husband's truck would need lookin' into, and I'd hope, as my only friend in town, that you'd join in on the research expedition."

Ava looks in on her girls, who are upstairs trying on giant picture hats under the supervision of the Grenville's live-in eighteen-year-old niece, so she gives them a quick kiss and says she'll be back in a few. They are too entranced with this room full of period costumes and mirrors to care. She makes a mental note to come back with her camera and get pictures of her girls in bliss.

Emma Jane lights a cigarette, sticks it between her lips, and holds it there tightly. Her eyes are squinting against the smoke as she leads the charge across the backyard and over to Kaya's. Instantly, Ava feels culpable, excited, and incapable of speech. Emma Jane exudes nothing but confidence when they knock on Kaya's door.

"Emma Jane! Ava! Please come in." Kaya never looked so pale.

"My, this is a pretty house. We just wanted to bring you over some brownies."

Ava's heart throbs wildly. She tries to keep her eyes on Kaya while taking in as much as she can of the small living room. Her guilt quotient is rising even higher as she notes how poor the place is. The powwow poster that used to hang in her room on the farm, worse for wear, is mounted on the wall with different colored push pins. The walls are paneled in cheap imitation wood-paneling and it looks like someone punched a hole in one place. The couch is shabby, with collapsed cushions, but it is covered with a hand-crocheted afghan Ava has seen before. There are at least three cats and a scrawny dog. Other than the poster, there are no pictures on the walls. There's a gap in the kitchen where a stove should be. A hot plate sits on the counter with a calendar above it. It's a tidy place, but it's a poor house where everything needs to be painted or fixed.

Kaya puts the platter of brownies down and asks the women to please help themselves while she gets some tea. Ava notices that the coffee table is one that Jesse has crafted. So is the kitchen table, and the end tables. Incongruous items in this poor house. Some wooden boards act as bookshelves with bricks holding open the space for books, like in a student's home. Among the books and carved eagles, Ava recognizes a carved turtle Jesse had given Ava when they were first married. Or its duplicate. Ava tries to remember when she'd last seen the little turtle.

Emma Jane searches for an ashtray, flicks her cigarette butt, makes polite conversation about weather and the neighborhood. Ava smiles and nods. Kaya takes a bite of her treat, brightens and says, "Good brownie. It's nice to know you use my recipe!"

"Guilty as charged." Kaya has been helpful and generous. Ava, snoopy and suspicions.

When Emma Jane and Ava are walking back toward the Grenville house, Emma Jane says, "I'd keep an eye on that one. Those were your husband's tables in there."

"They've been friends for years."

"She comes out to the farm, helps with the kids, right?"

"Yeah."

"We had someone like that when I was growing up. She'd cook all day in our house. It would smell so good and then she'd take all the food home with her."

Big Springs

Ava can feel the steam of the shower trailing her husband. She can smell his aftershave. He is facing his dresser, away from her. He's only got as far as putting his T-shirt on.

"I can see your butt," she says.

He doesn't turn around. "If you took off your jeans, I could see yours, too."

It doesn't take long for her to step out of her jeans and panties. She turns and lies face down on the bed. She loves this room that Jesse built high off the ground, a treehouse bedroom with windows all around. How much she admires this bed he's made with his own hands. She enjoys the weight of him on her. He kisses the back of her neck, licks her earlobe. Her body responds convulsively. She jolts and in that second, he slips his hand around to the front of her.

"Mommy! Daddy! Where are you?"

They jump. Jesse pulls on the rest of his clothes and hurries out to the children. Ava showers and dresses slowly before joining the rest of the family.

On the dining room table is a copy of the Topeka paper with a want ad circled for a staff photographer. Ava reads the ad, then looks around the room to see who might have left it for her. Jesse is tossing Sequoia in the air and catching her, much to her delight. Xenia is holding up a drawing of a mermaid she wants her mother to see, "Look, Mommy, look!"

Ava says, "That is the best mermaid ever!"

Joseph I catches Ava's eye and smiles. With his one workable hand, he beckons her to where he is sitting, near the wood-burning stove. He is reaching into his pocket for his wallet. He fumbles for several one hundred-dollar bills.

"Christmas went by and I never gave you a present, Ava."

"No, no, no," she says, but he is adamant.

"I'm sorry I don't know what kind of camera you'd like to have, but I want you to go down to the camera shop in Topeka and get yourself the best you can. Then, head down to the newspaper office and tell them you are the best person for the job, because you are. You can do this. I've seen your work. You can do this." His shaky hand holds out the large bills for her.

Jesse says, "He's stubborn, so you better take it. Besides, he's right."

Joseph I nods. Xenia says, "Can I see one?" Ava bites her lip to stop any tears and holds out one of the bills for Xenia to see. Joseph I talks about Benjamin Franklin on the face of the bill, his accomplishments, his worthiness. Ava wonders if she'll ever see a woman's face on a bill. What would a woman have to do to be depicted? If her girls could be presidents someday. But then, more practically, she wonders if she herself could ever get a job as a newspaper photographer. Sequoia runs over and tries to grab the money from her hand, but Ava pulls it away with more force than she would have expected. Her body has spoken. She wants this.

Topeka

Ava drives past the *Capital-Journal* office three times before parking. She plunges her boots into the slush, walks up to the door, turns right and passes it. She has a portfolio under her arm, cameras slung from her shoulder. She tries to assemble herself. She thinks of her father's dignity even while balancing a glass on his head. She straightens up and walks in the door. Blown-up photos are displayed. Ava recognizes some by Brian Lanker, who won a Pulitzer prize for his work at this very paper, and others by Jim Richardson, who became a *National Geographic* photographer. She is officially intimidated.

"Can I help you?" Her heart is beating in an unnatural rhythm. She might faint. She pretends she just remembered something, snaps her fingers, and walks back to the truck. Her boots are too old and her camera too new. She heads home where she can page through Dr. Baines' book, re-reading her name in the acknowledgments, staring at the cover she helped create.

Big Springs

She knows better. She shouldn't bring stuff up late at night. She shouldn't confront her husband because she's disappointed in herself.

"I know." At first, that's all she says to him.

"You know. . . ?"

"I know what you did." She'd read an article somewhere saying anyone will feel guilty if they are told this. Everyone has done something they wish they hadn't done. She thinks this will elicit a confession. Knowledge, guilt, and repentance. Maybe they'll move to Chicago.

"Why don't you tell me what I did." This is not what Ava expected.

"I know what you did. You know what you did."

"I know I made the kids bacon for breakfast. What are you talking about?"

"I know what you did. You know what you did."

"You said that. Wanna give me a hint? When? What?"

"Wednesday." Ava thinks she notices a flicker of a blush on Jesse's face. He turns away. Ava is trying to feel the rage in her bones again, the suspicion, the eating away.

"I don't like guessing games, Ava. I don't like distrust. Out with it. Speak up."

Her eyes narrow, she bites her lip.

"Okay, then," he says. "I'm going back out to do some work." He nods his head toward his carving shed.

"I saw your truck outside Kaya's house."

"Since when do you follow me?" Was he really going to make this about her?

"Julie and I went to return a cake plate to the Grenvilles'."

"Why have you waited days to ask me this?"

"Why don't you answer? Why were you there?"

"I don't have to account to you for every second of my time."

"Her house is the same color as the truck."

"Lots of people like turquoise. My dad is crazy about it."

"Can't you just answer me?"

"Why do you get flushed every time Raleigh Grenville sneezes? Why do you and Julie trail him and talk about him for hours as if you didn't have anything else to do?"

"Really? You're going to make this about me?"

"I know what you did, Ava."

This feels like a knife between her ribs. "I didn't do anything."

"You hang around his house. Kaya told me you two skittered around like schoolgirls, breaking things and snooping. Is it a girlish crush? Or more? I know what you did, Ava."

She looks at him and sees seriousness and pain, but she also sees something of what she's always been attracted to. The strong face, the gentle eyes. She does not want to hurt this man whose children's faces echo his. "I didn't do anything except be silly. I couldn't bear to lose you."

He pulls her toward him. With her head on his chest, she hears his voice, sounding deeper than usual, as if in a cavern. "Some of the Haskell kids have experienced trouble in downtown Lawrence. They aren't getting served in one of the restaurants. They're being called nasty names. I've gotten myself involved. Maybe I should have told you. I've gone to a couple of meetings. I've been talking to Kaya."

Ava pushes away from him. She needs to see his eyes.

"Ava, this is the world our children are growing up in and I don't like it. Kaya said that somebody made fun of Xenia at school, called her a Redskin."

"She didn't say anything to me."

"She told Kaya. Weeks ago. I wanted to check it out before making a big deal of it."

Ava wonders how she managed to miss this hurt in her own child. Anger rises. Everyone in her family is going to Kaya with their troubles? "I'll talk to Xenia's teacher."

"I already have."

"Why didn't you tell me?"

"It's an Indian thing."

"I'm her mother."

"I didn't want you to worry.

"I want to worry."

"No, you don't."

"I want to know the truth. Always."

"The truth is that Kaya lives in a rental. She has no say on what color the outside of the house is painted. The truth is that I was trying to be a good dad. You've been distracted lately. I took care of it. Just like I take care of earning money and putting food on the table."

Topeka

Ava dresses in her best clothes. She studies the kids' faces when she gets to the preschool, looks for signs that they feel anxiety about going in. They seem like their usual squabbling, giggling selves. Or maybe she doesn't know what to look for. She kisses their foreheads when she walks them in.

She drives straight to the *Topeka Capital-Journal* offices. A kind-looking older woman asks her if she's here to place an ad or renew her subscription. The woman is wearing red patent leather boots and reminds Ava of her Aunt Dena, which is a comfort. Ava blurts out that she wishes to apply for a job as a staff photographer. Time slows down and voices get louder. The woman asks if she's made an appointment. Ava mentally kicks herself.

"No, I'm sorry. No appointment. Just passing by so I thought, since I read the ad. . ."

"Just a sec." The bright boots make clunking noises. Talking, pointing, someone looking at her. Ava's heart is thumping too loudly. She's signaled to a chair. The man has better things to do, "Let's see what you've got." He gestures for her to hand him her resume. An academic book cover. One show at a cooperative gallery.

"No J School?"

"What's J School?"

"No working under deadline?"

"I have two children and a ranch. I'm always working under deadline."

He makes the harrumphing sound some men do when they hear you have kids and there might be sick days and dance recitals and husbands with priorities. He taps his finger on his desk and looks away. She's been dismissed. Ava stays glued to her seat. She pulls out her portfolio. He deigns to look at the photos.

"Sorry, little girl, I can't use you right now."

"That's all right, I'm going up to Chicago for Easter anyway. Just wanted to get acquainted." Ava looks him right in the eye. "I'd be good at this."

"Let me tell it to you straight. You've got a good eye, and you know how to frame a picture, but this is not *National Geographic.* This is a daily paper. I need news photography." This last is emphasized by thumping on a marked-up page on his desk.

"Yessir."

He turns his full attention back to his cluttered desk.

When she comes back after the Easter trip, her camera won't be so brand-spanking new. She'll have more photos then. She'll take pictures in Chicago. News photos. She'll do a bang-up job. She'll impress the hell out of him. She'll knock him dead.

On the Road

It's almost 80 degrees on April 11 when they pack up Julie's car to head to Chicago. The weather has gone from slush to summer. This would be a pleasant day in July but now it feels odd. No one knows how to dress, what to pack. The girls are squinting accusingly at the sun, as if it has done something wrong. Sequoia says, "I'm sweaty."

The grown women are as excited as schoolgirls. Ava gives a lingering kiss to Jesse, grins widely, and hops in the car as quickly as she can. Julie peels out. And then the car breaks sharply, spitting gravel. Ava hops out again, gives Joseph I a peck on the cheek, and runs back to the car. She's sixteen again, out with a girlfriend who just got her driver's license. Once out of male earshot, the two of them yell out the windows. "One, two, THREE!!!!"

They sing along with the radio and remind each other of childhood trips. Especially trips to Florida when they were taken out of school and spent a month with their two moms in a beachy cottage. Everything was magical about those trips, even the long rides getting there.

"Remember how our moms used to say we 'walked to Florida,' you and me."

"Ye-ah, we just stood in the back, walking around behind our mothers' heads."

"Mommy, can we do that?" asks Sequoia.

"Nope. Times are different now."

"Different how?" Xenia wants to know.

"There weren't even seat belts or car seats back then."

"You and Auntie Julie lived in the Olden Days," says Sequoia.

"Yeah, we wore bonnets and carded wool."

"You wore bonnets walking to Florida because it was so sunny and sweaty out, right?" asks Sequoia.

"You got it, Muffin."

Ava and Julie reminisce about their younger vacationing selves. How they brought along their schoolwork and finished it in an amazingly short time. How they went shopping with their moms for tropical-looking clothes, feeling somehow a little sinful getting bathing suits and sandals in the middle of winter. How they lounged on the beach under palm trees and went to Parrot Jungle, where colorful birds pulled out their hairpins.

Soon, the little girls are bored with the sunny, sandy stories and fall asleep in their car seats. The landscape changes. Julie is clearly itching to talk.

"When we went on those Florida trips, y'know. . . "

"Ye-ah?"

"Do you think our moms were just a little bit happy to get away from their husbands?"

"Not happy. Eager! I think my mom and dad liked each other, but running a business together sometimes made things a bit tense."

"Once, when my mom was leaving for Florida, my dad said, 'Don't let the door hit you in the ass on the way out.'"

"But he welcomed her back with flowers, right?" Ava notices Julie looking out the window with more concentration than the Missouri landscape deserves. "So, Julie, feeling a bit relieved to get away from the routine?"

"Just a little bit. Just a bit. Just a real lot, actually."

"Uh huh?"

"Y'know, I gotta admit since we started taking that class from Professor Grenville. . . "

"Raleigh."

"Um, yeah. It's sorta kinda made me think twice about my marriage. I mean, if I'm that attracted to another man, maybe there's something wrong at home. And right now, I'm not missing my beloved husband at all."

"She said after being away from home for an entire three hours."

"And you?"

"I am dee-lighted to have a break from Big Springs, bison burgers, and boys."

"Woo-hoo!"

Xenia wakes up long enough to say, "Would you two please behave yourselves?"

Chicago

After spending the night in St. Louis, treating themselves to what Julie calls "dy-no-mite I-talian food" on The Hill, they drive the rest of the way to Chicago, or rather Arlington Heights, where Ava's recently-divorced brother Michael lives.

"Did you know the front door was going to be purple?" Sequoia inquires. They are standing at the curb outside Michael's suburban house. The neighborhood is tidy and prosperous; the houses, repetitive brick structures with unimaginative landscaping. Ava takes a deep breath before gathering children and bags to cross the carefully-edged lawn.

On the inside, the house feels hollow without the noise of the recently-vacated wife and boys. Even the mirrored wallpaper reflects emptiness. A few sticks of gold-spattered carved furniture stand starkly in the deserted living room. The white shag carpeting has been vacuumed into a herringbone pattern, evidence that the divorced and unemployed ex-husband doesn't have enough to do. Fortunately, this is also clear from the cooking smells emanating from the kitchen. A Greek Lenten fish so besotted with garlic and peppers it will hardly be a privation to eat it.

"I learned to cook, can you believe it?"

"Smells great, big brother, but didn't Greek Easter come early this year, like a week ago?"

"I know, I know. Christ is already risen in Greektown but we gotta balance out the time you're gonna spend with Aunt Dottie in Polkaland." Mickey says, wearing an apron not unlike their Aunt Dottie's, a flowery print with an abundance of pockets.

No one says a word about the apron or the bankruptcy or the subsequent marital break-up until the dishes are put away and the little girls are tucked into twin beds in a blue room wallpapered with the Cubs logo.

"So, Mickey. . . " Ava begins.

Mickey is pouring everyone a tumbler of vodka. "I don't wanna talk about it."

"O-kay."

"So, you guys are here to do some class project together?"

Julie answers, "We're studying our roots. Easter customs, stuff like that. I'm gonna write and Avie is taking pictures."

"I'm gonna take the pictures, but I'm not sure I'm sticking with the class."

"Why the hell not?"

"I'm thinking about getting a job. Besides, the teacher has become a friend and it feels weird being in a class where the instructor's gotten sloshed on Irish whiskey in my living room."

Without so much as a polite transition, Mickey says, "She left me for the dentist. She fell for someone who caused her pain while watching her slobber." It took Mickey all of nine seconds to get to his divorce. "Someone who drilled in her mouth."

"Sounds tough," says Ava.

"I never liked the bitch," adds Julie.

Mickey returns to the theme, "I mean would either of you guys leave your husbands for a dentist?"

Nopes. Unh-unhs. Don't think sos. "So, what happens now?"

"Dad and Dena say they want me to take over the restaurant. Got nothin' else to do, so I'm working there three nights a week. Been doing it for two months and I still can't balance a fucking glass on my head."

"Ya don't need no glass on yer head." They are all lapsing into the street language of their youth.

"Downtown, I used to have a building named after me. Now I'm trying to balance a fuckin' glass of ouzo on my head. Besides, I don't look like no Greek. I'm six foot five and have blond hair, for chrissake."

Ava tries to reassure, "You'll do great. Everybody knows you since you were knee high."

"Everybody moved to the 'burbs. There's Greek restaurants in all the strip malls now. Things have changed, kiddo. We're gettin' tourists who don't know me from their own assholes. It ain't the same. Ya better come down to Athena's tomorrow night. On me."

"To hell with the 'on me' shit. You're puttin' a roof over our heads here."

Ava lies awake in the unfamiliar bed, wired and tipsy and afraid to turn over because it might awaken her cousin. But it's Julie who starts the whispering.

"You awake?"

"Yup."

"About Raleigh? What I said?"

"Yup."

"Just a crush."

"Every woman on campus has a crush on Christopher Raleigh Grenville."

"And every man." Ava tries to suppress laughter.

"I think I married Trent because I looked up to him. He was my teacher. I don't look up to him so much anymore."

"Hard to do when you've seen his poop in the potty." Does she have to sound like a mommy every minute?

"Avie! I've never ever seen his poop in the potty. He's fastidious."

"Fastidious is good. Somebody in the family's gotta alphabetize the spices."

"Shhhhhhh!" This from Mickey in the next room. Ava is embarrassed into more stifled giggles. She turns away from her co-conspirator but continues to lie awake, wondering if marriage is even possible, worrying if she is a bad wife and mother, asking herself if she should be visiting some Native American Cultural Center for the sake of her husband and kids instead of tromping through her old Polish neighborhood and Greek town. She wonders if her marriage, going through a rough spell of jealousies and unkind words, is as fragile as her brother's. Ava gets up and tiptoes into the room where her children are supposed to be sleeping.

Sequoia has climbed into bed with Xenia and is placidly sucking her thumb. She opens her eyes. "Where are we?"

"Chicago. It's an Indian word that means 'wild onions.'"

"Does everything have to do with food?"

Ava answers confidently. "Yes."

The next day is Holy Thursday. In Ava and Julie's childhood, a big part of the day was devoted to visiting Polish churches around the city with their grandmother. Walking on their knees up the aisles of Baroque-styled churches, feeling the hardness of the marble floor. Weeping over the impending death of Jesus as if lying to their mothers about eating candy before dinner could actually cause god incarnate to be beaten with a hooked whip, crowned with thorns, and crucified.

They decide to go to one church for old time's sake: St. Stanislaus, Bishop and Martyr, the church where they were baptized. Among the ethnic wars her parents fought, Ava's father won the battle of the Greek restaurant—"We gotta eat!"—and her mother prevailed in the conflict over church and school—"A mother knows about these things."

Before going inside St. Stan's, they shepherd Xenia and Sequoia to the Garden of Graces, an outdoor site dominated by a twelve-foot statue of the Blessed Virgin. Ava recalls the honor of being the child chosen to crown the statue with a flowered wreath one May Day. How her five-year-old self teetered on the ladder. Julie bursts into song, "Oh, Mary, we crown thee with blossoms today! Queen of the Angels, Queen of the May." This is met with grimaces from the little girls, who say, "Who's Mary?" and "What's a virgin?" Ava's children's lives have been completely devoid of any religious training. She and Jesse have avoided the topic. Although Ava remembers with fondness her early years in the cocoon of this churchyard, with its school, garden, convent, rectory, today the buildings look smaller, older, dingier.

They herd the girls over to the stone steps of the church. Sequoia says, "Carry me!" and Ava does. Once inside, she thinks: Now, this is more like it. The church, with its seven altars, gilt trimmings, choir loft for a hundred, and huge pipe organ, has retained its grandeur. Julie points at the ceiling. The girls look up and then spend the rest of their time in the church studying the multitude of angels painted three stories above them, lit grandly by chandeliers and stained-glass windows. Ava thinks the angels, in their familiar celestial poses holding harps, lyres, and trumpets, look paler and less impressive now, repainted in pastel pinks and baby blues. Or perhaps memory is more intense than reality. Isn't that why she photographs? She positions her camera to catch the awe on her daughters' faces and then shifts to the celestial beings above.

Ava is glad the statuary is draped in purple, so she doesn't have to explain how baby Jesus grew up to be tortured, bloodied, and killed. She snaps more pictures of the angel-adorned ceiling, the gilded altars.

Thankfully, no one is walking on their knees.

They hurry out, happy for the spring air. "Remember that place?" Julie indicates a Mexican bodega that used to be a Polish-owned candy store. Boys with slicked-back ducktail haircuts used to idle out front, pitching pennies on the sidewalk. The dangerous boys; "hoody" boys they used to call them. Some of them Italians from the next parish. How appealing they were, with their up-turned collars and Frankie Avalon looks.

"Hey, look at the time! My mom's gonna kill us!"

Sequoia gets a worried look on her face, "Your mommy's gonna kill us?"

As they speed their way, they hear a siren. Traffic accident. "Since we're already stopped," Ava leaps out with her camera to see if she can do some "news photography." She tries to distance herself, put the camera between herself and the mangled cars and crushed bodies. When a news truck pulls to the curb around the corner, she runs to it, yanks the roll of film out of her camera, and hands it to them. Phone numbers are exchanged. When she returns to Julie's car, she throws up into the gutter.

"I coulda told ya, you don't have the stomach for that kinda thing."

Julie parks behind her widowed mother's house. Ava surveys the two- and three-story brick apartment buildings, all with wooden back staircases zigzagging their way up. She photographs this domestic sight, so familiar from her childhood. The backyards in rows of rectangles. The gray-painted porches with their metal gliders and flowerpots. She continues shooting as they climb the stairs.

The door is slightly ajar. Ava, Julie, and the little girls can waltz right into the Chicago apartment as casually as if they'd run to the corner store to buy a quart of milk. But instead, having driven 500 miles from Big Springs, Kansas, they yawn, stretch their necks, and look around the place, waiting for their elder relative to greet them. Aunt Dottie sits on her doily-enhanced burgundy couch, raptly watching *The Young and the Restless*, making a Wait! Wait! sign with her upturned index finger. Her living room is graced by the same Duncan Fyfe furniture it sported some twenty, thirty years ago, except for the significantly larger TV. A faded picture of Jesus showing off his sacred heart hangs above the screen where, finally, the credits roll. Released from the daily daytime drama, Aunt Dottie turns her wide smile to the new arrivals. After sloppy kisses and tight embraces, after children have been whirled in the air and twenty-dollar bills tucked into their little fists, Aunt Dottie leads her visitors into the kitchen. On the counter are three jars of Manischevitz horseradish: two beet, one plain.

"Easy breezy these days, huh, girls? Not like the old days, remember? Grating the ends of your fingertips into the horseradish, your eyes watering, the coughing, the running out to the porch to get away from the sting in your lungs. All the crying, remember? Now, look, thanks to the Jews, we got it made. It's even kosher, whatever that means."

In Ava's revered memories of this old Polish neighborhood, Holy Thursday was indeed the day for grating horseradish. Sure, they'd visit the obligatory seven—or maybe it was nine—Polish churches, put their knees to marble and walk their way toward the suffering Christ, but the real business of the day had been the peeling and shredding of white and red winter roots in her mother's kitchen. The very reason they are returning to Chicago is to record the fondly remembered anticipation of Easter: the making of sausages, the grating of beets, the baking of breads, the carving of butter lambs. When Ava and Julie were children, Polish Easter was the biggest holiday of the year.

Ava's camera hangs heavily from her shoulder. Her shutter finger is itchy. She tries to word her response carefully. "If we were to run over to the Serafin's around the corner, do you think maybe they'd still have a horseradish root and a coupla beets?"

"You remember that dusty old place? You had to ask for everything. You wanted a can of beans on the top shelf? They used to grab it with a claw on a stick. Long gone, girls, long gone. A big Kroger opened up and now we get everything in one store. You don't have to go to bakery here, butcher there. You don't have to talk to nobody. They got everything. They even sell pineapples in winter, can you imagine? We are so lucky we live when we do." Aunt Dottie lets Ava and Julie squirm with discomfort, recalculate, and hem and haw for a few minutes before she slowly and dramatically opens what she still calls "the icebox." A pungent Easter fragrance blasts out like a cloud of smoke from a locomotive. The scents of garlicky sausage and boiled eggs, horseradish root and beets fill their nostrils. Dottie pulls out a long, yellowish, waxy-looking root and a couple of hefty, earthy beets. "I don't know why you wanna do it the old way when they done all the work for you. You call it tradition, I call it hard work." With mild distaste, she hands around aprons. "You're gonna wanna wear these. Those beets bleed like a goat with its throat slit."

Everything Dottie says is true: the crying and nipped fingertips and overwhelming nostril-antagonizing pungency. The little girls, in aprons tied under their armpits, first turn up their noses, then each try a bite of boiled beet. Xenia dutifully chews and swallows. Sequoia spits out the first taste but then grabs another, bigger piece. Dottie wears an apron that covers her from shoulders to mid-thigh in pockets and flowers. She jangles keys in one of the pockets as she instructs Julie how to add the vinegar and salt. When she's given a sample, Dottie screws up her face, "Strong! Bitter! Salty!" she exclaims. Dottie herself stirs in the deep purple grated beets, "Helps take the edge off, like a good joke in hard times." A pause and then Dottie, with a bit of a flourish, raises a full tablespoon of the mixture to her nose, then her mouth. Like a wine connoisseur she furrows her forehead, concentrates on the bouquet and the complexity of tastes. She nods her approval, "It's like life, right? You got the bitter and you got the sweet."

Next, they tackle the carving of the butter lambs. Ava shows the girls how to attach what will be the head and neck to the body with a broken-off piece of toothpick. Then she uses a small knife to carve the likeness of a lamb in a lying-down pose, calm, sacrificial. She wields a spoon to mark the stylized fleece. A tiny clove for each eye. Four-year-old Sequoia wants to touch one of the lambs. When she has it within reach, she grabs for it and squeezes it between her fingers. Grown-ups cry "No" but laugh despite themselves. Sequoia licks the delicious damage off her fingers. Xenia manages to make a lamb of her own, though Ava thinks it bears more of a resemblance to Dottie's spaniel Trixie. Even though it's technically still Lent, Dottie delivers secret treats under the table to Sequoia, Xenia, and Trixie. Plump red jellybeans, her favorite.

When there is a moment to breathe, Ava looks up to survey the room, to take more photographs trying to capture the setting, the context, for the sake of their class. Dried fronds from Palm Sunday, woven into crosses and fans, are tucked behind the crucifixes and pictures that adorn Dottie's walls. Family photos. Ava stops short at a picture of Helen, Dottie's sister, and her own recently deceased mother. If she were alive, she'd be the one teaching her granddaughters the old ways. How beets sweeten the horseradish. How cooking from scratch means more work but, for better or worse, more time together. How to use an eggshell to pour the right amount of brandy into the batter to flavor the lamb-shaped cakes. "More fun than using some aluminium measuring spoon." To put a toothpick in the head part of the lamb-shaped cake form so the ears won't break off. How working for a holiday is exhausting and frustrating but somehow makes you feel like you belong somewhere, to somebody, to several somebodies at once. How families are flawed and irritate the hell out of you, so forgiveness is repeatedly necessary.

Xenia, Ava's sensitive six-year-old, says, "Mommy? Why are you crying?"

"Horseradish finally got to me."

They go to Athena's Café as promised. Greek Easter came early this year, so here they can feast and dance. When they walk in, there's a "While You Were Out" slip waiting for Ava. Jesse called. She reaches for the hall-reservation phone, but her father sweeps her into a hug. He is glowing. On his arm is a woman. Clearly his date. More than a date, since his arm is around her in a gesture of belonging. Ava looks for and sees a fat diamond on her hand. So soon after her mother died. Is this how he honors her memory? And then she recalls that it has been nearly a decade, that she herself never so much as went to her mother's grave. When she missed her mother, she married as quickly as she could. While her brain is calculating her lack of filial piety, her father is making introductions. The name of her father's fiancée goes in one ear and out the other. Is it Angela? The children are screaming to see the balancing act, and their grandfather indulges. Then, the pretty middle-aged woman joins in and manages to balance a glass on her head as well. Ava's mother would never have done that, stolen the spotlight from her father, but he is pointing at her with appreciation and fondness. Everyone is clapping and shouting, "*Opa!*" Flaming cheese arrives to the little girls' delight.

No sooner are they seated than Dena arrives, with a date on her arm as well. Ava leaves town and look what happens, and so quickly. But it has not happened quickly, not really. Change always feels quick when you are the child, no matter what your age. Besides, Dena has a new boyfriend every five minutes, that's who she is. She is making introductions to Johnny, who she married on Valentine's Day. She eloped, didn't even tell Ava. With his hair puffed up and slicked back, Johnny tells of plans to open a new Athena's Café out in Itasca, where they'll live and work.

Itasca? Way the hell out of the city. What about Auntie Dena's trailer with its tiny Italian lights? Ava's hearing the answers faster than she can think of the questions. Johnny's a builder. Yeah, right, thinks Ava, construction tied in her mind to the Mafia, not to speak of the sharkskin suit, the pinky ring on his fat little finger. She is being told her father is retiring, and Mickey is taking over. The old days are done and it's time for a fresh start. Everyone else has been out in the suburbs for years. Decades. Ava herself went all the way to Kansas.

Ava studies the two couples as they tell how the two men bowl together every Tuesday and how they double-date and are planning a trip to Jamaica together. How dare her father and her aunt move on with their lives. But she can't help but see a refreshed glow on their faces. Their smile lines are deeper, their hair thinner, but they are laughing. Loudly. They have found mates who clearly adore them. Ava looks at Julie, who shrugs and smiles, then at her two daughters, who are being hoisted on the shoulders of these older men and given rides around the room as they squeal.

Mickey looks frayed and out of place as he greets customers, slapping backs and winking as he removes "Reserved" signs off tables and seats special customers. Platters of food arrive with their aromas of oregano, olives, and feta. Ava tosses down a glass of ouzo faster than she should. She eats a few dolmades and savors the piquancy, despite herself. Heaps of stuffed peppers, roasted lamb, and lemony potatoes are put before her. Yes, everything IS about the food.

Dena comes and sits next to her. She looks around as if she is about to commit a crime. When the coast is clear, she hands a fat envelope to Ava.

"I love Johnny, but his kids are greedy and spoiled like you wouldn't believe. I don't want my money getting into their hands. God willing, you'll get more when I die. You are the daughter I never had. I want you someday to do what I never could. I want you to go to the Old Country, go to Greece. Find out where you came from. Find the village on Crete where there are people named Paputsakis. Eat, listen to the music at the taverna, watch the men dance. See the real thing. Can you promise me you will do this for me, carry out my dream?"

"You go, Auntie Dena. You still can!" Dena presses the gift into Ava's hand. The envelope is filled with singles, fives, and tens. Tip money saved for years. Ava changes tactics. "I'll hold it for you. Maybe next year, we'll go together."

Dena shakes her head in a firm "No," squeezes Ava's hand, and rises to sing a love song to her dear Johnny. He glows.

To honor Good Friday, a hungover Ava and Julie take the girls to a matinee performance of *Jesus Christ Superstar*. Ava starts crying five minutes into the show and is shaking convulsively by the end. The little girls cry, too, so they don't notice their mother's tears. They are shedding tears for the sad story, but Ava is weeping for her mother. She misses her mommy. She wants her mommy next to her daddy. She wants things the way they never were but how she will always remember them.

On Saturday, they perform the ritual Ava loves best. They line baskets with cloth napkins and fill them with samples of all the foods that will be eaten on Easter Sunday. A piece of each sausage, both smoked and fresh; a few neon-colored hard-boiled eggs; jars of horseradish, both plain and beet; a small cellar of salt and one of pepper, slices of rye and braided cardamom bread with raisins. A lamb carved from butter. The children carry the food baskets into the church basement where they will be blessed and where a dozen or so women and children already wait. Father Gene, who grew up across the street and is now the pastor, enters with a silver wand full of holy water. The women fold back the carefully pressed white napkins as if the blessing couldn't get past these flimsy barriers. Holy water is splashed on the food, along with holy words. Ava is happy the holy words are still in Latin, though she suspects it isn't very Vatican II. She may no longer believe in religion, but Ava does believe in this. In ancient words over shared food.

Before they leave, Ava catches the eye of Father Gene, who responds with a wink. Out of that glance, Ava excavates memories of their playing kick-the-can and hopscotch. Cops and robbers. Cowboys and Indians. Crack the whip. She remembers when they skinned their knees together and yelled rhyming epithets at each other. When they witnessed each other's first broken bones and erections and kisses. And now she is a mother and he is a priest blessing her children's food. Ava relishes the common history and wonders if her own children will enjoy such a sense of camaraderie and shared memory. She winks back.

Back at Dottie's place, the smell of soup welcomes them, a Polish *barszcz* made of sausage, broth, and beets. They add the blessed items to the table. Ava knows that the Easter-blessed food, with its smell of baptism, will taste better than any other. Maybe because it used to follow forty days of fasting, a meatless Lent. Perhaps even the memory of a certain hunger can make the food especially flavorful.

She puts out the butter lamb she carved, with its eyes of small cloves and its red-and-white flag of resurrection hoisted on a toothpick. From the backyard, she herself picked the violets that surround it, a field of surreally oversized flowers celebrating spring. She hesitates for only a second before she slices her knife through the lamb's butt and slathers her bread with it.

"Mommy! How could you! You killed the lamb!" Xenia squeals.

"It's what we do at Easter. We kill the lamb," says Julie.

Ava adds, "Don't worry, I'll make another one tomorrow."

She consoles herself with the taste of butter-lubricated caraway seed and yeasty grain smashed into flavor explosions by her teeth. Ava grunts with pleasure, sure that Poles did this kind of feasting in spring long before the advent of Christianity. The horseradish on homemade sausage. The eggs with beets. The sharp soup that opens the sinuses and the heart. No one talks. They chew and swallow like they haven't seen food for weeks.

After lunch, she leaves a message for Jesse, back on the ranch in Kansas. Here with her relatives, where she is right now, she has such strong feelings of attachment. Here where she has known people her whole life long. This is memory, but where is home?

That night, after they've tucked the girls in, Ava excuses herself and closes herself in the kitchen. Her home phone rings eight times followed by the mid-ring click of the receiver being picked up. She doesn't wait for a hello.

"Jess?"

"Oh, good, it's you!" Kaya answers the phone, then calls out loudly, "Jesse, it's Ava!" And then to Ava, "I'm so glad you called. I wanted to ask you if I can sign the girls up to dance at the spring powwow at Haskell. There's some kind of silly form that needs to be signed by Monday and Jesse didn't want to do it without your permission."

"Sure, fine. They've never danced traditional dances before. The dresses have hung in the closet gathering dust for so long."

"They've been using them for dress-up, so I know they still fit."

Ava did not know this.

There is a shuffling and Ava can hear Kaya say, "She says it's okay," then the clumsy moment of a hand muffling the receiver and then Jesse's voice on the phone. Ava is both relieved and anxious. At least he's alive.

"Sorry! We were getting Dad situated when the phone rang."

Okay, she thinks, Kaya is lending a hand, some necessary assistance. "I've been trying to call you!"

"We were at the Grenvilles'. They've had us over to dinner every night. Something about collecting the Easter orphans. Tomorrow, too, for the big feast. I'm there every day anyway, putting in the bookshelves. How's it going up there?"

"My brother's divorced, depressed, and dating an aging Playboy bunny. My dad is engaged. Dena got married to a slick guy named Johnny who's in the Mob. Everyone in my family is re-mating." Ava searches quickly in her handbag for the large envelope of cash. It's still there.

"Wild."

"But the project is going well."

"Hey, a guy called from the Topeka paper. Wants you to call him back on Monday. Sounds like they need somebody to shoot a few things. Like that rally for the ERA."

"Really?" Ava was planning to attend that rally. WHAT DO WE WANT? EQUAL RIGHTS! WHEN DO WE WANT THEM? NOW!!! She's not sure it's kosher to cover something she has a stake in. But it's not like she'd be writing, she'll only be taking pictures. Besides, reporters and photographers cover elections and then vote in them, right?

"How are my girls?" Jesse brings her back to earth.

"They miss their daddy. I miss their daddy."

"Tell them I miss them, too."

When Ava hangs up, she exhales a huge sigh. She has always thought of Chicago as home. Kansas couldn't possibly have become home.

⚜

Easter Sunday is a blur of relatives, loud voices, pungent smells, fleshy hugs. There are two dozen places set for the afternoon's feast. The dining room furniture has been augmented with a card table from the garage and the kitchen table. Sequoia is impatient and whiny. Xenia says, over and over, "Who are all these people?" No recognition of blood relation until their Grampa Paputsakis arrives, then their Uncle Mickey. The two burly men carry pastel baskets of candy for the girls, hide sugary eggs for them behind knickknacks and chair legs.

⚜

Even though Easter is officially past for half the family, the day turns into a culinary battle, Polish vs. Greek. There is a cacophony of pots banging in the kitchen. Lambs and hams being roasted. Eggs painted unreal colors. The older women are in their Easter finery topped with aprons, the younger in silk blouses and jeans, the little girls in frothy princess dresses from San Francisco. Ava feels a little guilty that she holds a camera in her hand instead of a mixing spoon. She was taught by both her Polish-American mother and her Greek-restaurant-owning father: Cooking is an honor. Eating, a pleasure. Hospitality is the first rule. Julie is tape recording the cooks of the two tribes as they vie for space and admire one another's creations.

The dining room is steamy, the fragrances heady, the table groaning. Finally, everyone sits and beholds. Fidgety children calm down to admire the lambs carved in butter, molded into sugar, and baked into cakes. Platters of carved lamb and ham are passed around the cloth-draped tables, along with bowls of green beans, spanakopita, lemon potatoes, and braided bread. Salads. Pitchers of red wine. Everyone eats ravenously, drinks gratefully.

Older relatives ask politely but pointedly about the absent husbands, Jesse and Trent. One, the Indian, tending to bison and his ailing father. Julie's, the Brit, at a conference in Buenos Aires. The others nod as if they understand, but Ava suspects that they do not. To be here today, the elders have crossed ethnic lines wider than miles. Greeks and Poles have learned to sit at the table together, what's the matter with these young people? After an uncomfortable silence, Aunt Dottie mentions how she used to have to work on Easter at the hospital sometimes. Giving them an out, indicating a precedent.

With frosting on her chin and chewing on a raisin, Sequoia moans, "Can I eat another lamb, please?"

It's hard to extract themselves. Everyone must be hugged and kissed. Tupperware must be filled with slices of ham and peeled eggs "for the road." Ava's father tears up when he says goodbye. Mickey barks, "Don't do anything I wouldn't do," and looks away. Dottie gives the little girls one last squeeze and jellybeans for the road. Trixie licks their faces.

Ava and Julie drive straight through without an overnight. They take turns at the wheel, handfeeding each other and the girls from the Tupperware. They stop only for fuel and potty breaks. The girls are sticky with marshmallow candy, hyper, and spent. They fall asleep collapsed over each other, entwined in unfamiliar affection, too tired to even ask "Are we there yet?"

At dawn's first light, they are fifty miles out. Ava and Julie smell like rotted fruit. Their hair is tangled, their armpits rank. They have given up any semblance of politeness. They can't possibly finish this stupid project together. They might not even speak to each other again. Ava is driving fast, fueled by spite.

Big Springs

It's early morning and Jesse has just showered and dressed. He is helping his dad with a glass of water when he hears car wheels crunch over gravel. He spills the greater portion of the water on his father's lap, utters a quick "Sorry," and rushes outside. When he sees the dusty car come around the bend, he stops short. His body is poised in concentration, leaning forward. Waiting.

When Ava sees him, she brakes hard. She gets out of the car and starts running. Deaf to the sounds of her children crying out, impervious to the sharpness of the gravel cutting into the bottoms of her bare feet, she is running.

She stops short. He leans toward her. Her chest is throbbing loudly. She tries to quiet herself, to assemble herself into some kind of dignity.

Julie lets the children out of the car and they scream, "Daddy, Daddy!" They climb his legs as if they were tree limbs. Homer the Dog circles the bunch of them, barking. When Ava steps back to let the children hug and pummel their father, she takes things in. The horses Little Joe and Red China have wandered close to the fence. The flower fields are in bloom. She can see where Jesse has been ploughing the hill. The red cedar has grown so tall. She turns back to him, takes in his questioning smile. His hair is braided like Willie Nelson's and bound with rawhide and cowry shells. He wears a beaded cuff on his wrist. His legs are bare and brown.

He is beautiful.

She says quietly, "I brought you horseradish."

PART FOUR

Topeka
Seven Years Later — October, 1985

7:21. Finally. After all the auditions and rehearsals. The pre-teen tears, screams, and hand-holding. The endless metronome of the practice tape. The pleading with Jesse to please do this for his girls. The putting up with Carlo smoking around the house for weeks. At last, it's tonight. But Ava feels frozen, pale, spent.

7:24. Ava zips and unzips her parka, wishing she would have worn something with a little more class, for god's sake.

7:27. People wave at her, wearing their composed, practiced grins. Friends, family, editor, boss, neighbors. If people keep coming at this rate, there won't be enough food at the reception on the lower level. Let's call it what it is: basement. Uh-oh. Omigod. Ava plunges her hand into her over-stuffed backpack, searching for one of her multitudinous lists. Clumped Kleenexes fall to the ground. Wallet, sunglasses, Tampax. Oh, great. Finally, the checklist emerges on the back of Xenia's math homework. Cupcakes, cut-up fruit, check. Fall-themed napkins and plates, check. She got a good post-Halloween deal on those. Apple cider, check. Cups. People will share plates but they won't share cups. Uh-oh. Ava decides to tell everyone she knows to come quickly over to the house where there'll be a whole 'nother party, with baklava and spanakopita and kolachki. And booze, plenty of booze. A much better party, the second party, the unofficial party at the house. With cups. She'll force herself to cheer up by then.

7:28. She tries to center herself, to remind herself this is a kid's recital, a one-night event most people will forget by tomorrow. To calm herself, she recalls the sequence of events. The auditions. The casting announcement. Let's face it, maybe both were cast because of the family resemblance. Sisters who could play sisters. Sequoia even had her hair straightened so it would match Xenia's. Her spirally springy hair now flat as Twiggy's. Omigod! My girls are in a ballet! They will dance tonight not at a powwow, not at a Greek restaurant, not at a polka competition, but in pink satin slippers with straightened hair. They have chosen this pale elite strand of culture that speaks to neither of their parents, none of their grandparents.

Ava reminds herself that, at their age, she was gyrating to "Rock Around the Clock," rolling her eyes with disdain at her father balancing a glass on his head. Her father. Her father. She bites her lip so she doesn't cry out. It's been a month since he died, but it feels like a day. She's managed to push all mourning, all grieving aside to concentrate on this night. For her girls, she tells herself to buck up.

7:29. A chill of anxiety. The auditorium is only half full. Maybe the audience will be too small and the applause too meager. Maybe the audience will be huge but the performance will be embarrassing. Carlo will drop Xenia. Sequoia will storm off the stage in anger. Jesse will stay backstage and not even enter. Afterward, people will be overly polite. Because that's what nice people do when someone's child has failed. When someone's father has died.

7:30. Ava looks down at the program her hand is sweatily clutching. She tries to concentrate on the words, to read the words as written. Miss Gloria's "Fall! Dance!! Spectacular!!!" Ava lets out a singular "Ha!" then jerks her blushing face around to see if anyone noticed. She reminds herself to be dignified, to sit tall. She reminds herself that her husband and his best friend Carlo are behind that red curtain along with her daughters. She concentrates on reading Carlo's name, listed on the program as "Guest Lead Male Dancer from San Francisco," and again she emits a "Ha!" prompting Mickey to reach over and squeeze her hand hard, silencing her with brotherly pain.

7:31. She looks up at the exit sign. Her father told her to always know where the exit is. She absorbs the red letters onto her retina and then gives a long stare to the red velvet curtain. She whispers, "Abracadabra" and commands it to open.

❧

7:19. He is hiding behind a red velvet curtain, surrounded by a bunch of squealing pre-teen girls with glitter on their eyelids, adjusting each other's tiaras. Somebody's mom is smearing clown white on his face. He's already wearing a way-too-pink latex forehead with a few clumps of white hair around the edges. He is playing an old white man, the mad scientist Coppelius. Were they thinking Copernicus or what? He has a hunchback stuffed into his jacket and will chase people around the stage with a cane. What we won't do for our kids.

7:21. Carlo is pacing around in his tights, saying, "I'm so nervous! I'm so nervous." Jesse has no sympathy. Carlo's the one who decided he wanted to take classes. Worse, he encouraged Xenia and Sequoia to do the same. He even paid for their lessons, as if they needed encouragement. Their friends were already wearing leg warmers. Then, one of the Grenville girls starred in *The Nutcracker* and that was it. The girls wanted tutus. Sometimes he thinks his kids dropped to earth from another planet. And now, because, let's face it, there aren't an abundance of guys in Miss Gloria's classes, here's Jesse, now a "volunteer," being powdered and wigged. And Carlo, the "Guest Lead Male Dancer from San Francisco," worried about living up to his billing.

7:23. Carlo is still saying, "I'm so nervous. I'm so nervous."

Xenia snaps, "Get a grip! I'm the one doing all the work!" Playing Swanhilde at age twelve, she turns with a pleading look in her eyes. "It's true, Daddy. I leap and he gets all the credit. Why the hell do they even call it 'lifting?'"

"Xenia, language!" Jesse feels a parental obligation to be offended.

Carlo stops pacing. "She's absolutely right. Besides, she weighs less than a bag of potato chips."

7:26. Pissed off that her sister has the lead role, Sequoia stands stiffly. She is practically spitting, "At least Swanhilde gets to be lifted. I have to play a stupid doll, just sitting there."

"C'mon, you have the title role, the most important part," Jesse lies. "You play Coppelia! And hey, you get to dance with me!" He tries for a sheepish grin.

She cheers up. "Yeah, who would want to be called Swanhilde anyway?"

Xenia a.k.a. Swanhilde rolls her eyes. "Da-ad!!!"

Sequoia can't help herself, "From now on I'm calling you Swinehilda."

"Da-ad! Make her stop! I must get centered! My public is waiting!" Instantly realizing how haughty and ridiculous she sounds, Xenia lets out a loud snort. Sequoia starts laughing and Jesse has his girls back. Tears come to his eyes and, when he wipes his face on his sleeve, he smears his mascara, much to Carlo's amusement.

7:27. Carlo strikes a pose and says, "Are my seams straight?" They're all on the verge of hysteria and happy for any excuse to laugh. Let's face it, Carlo has no seams to straighten. He's playing Franz, the young swain. The hot straight guy.

7:29. It's nearly time for *Coppelia.* Or, at least excerpts from the junior amateur Miss Gloria Dance Academy version of *Coppelia.* This is the story of a mad inventor and his wish to make his creation, his doll, his Coppelia, come alive. This is the story of a young suitor who, despite being extremely happy with the soulmate love of his life, falls in love with A DOLL named Coppelia. This is the story of a young woman whose suitor has fallen in love with a doll and therefore wants to become the doll, marry her handsome suitor, and live happily ever after.

7:31. "Places!" someone's mom yells. They find their marks. They assume their positions, their characters, their roles. Carlo holds his head high. He looks strong, handsome, princely. For the sake of his girls, Jesse tries to get into character by thinking of himself as one of the masked dancers at a potlatch, here to tell the story of how Raven stole the Moon. It's not about him. It's about the story. He steps into Coppelius, the Old Man with the pale face and bent body. He will totter. He will try to make people laugh, make her laugh, and maybe that's not such a bad thing. He'd like to make her laugh.

7:32. Jesse glances over at his girls. They are beautiful.

7:33. The music begins.

The music is a mazurka, a Polish dance song, a melody painfully familiar to Ava and Mickey because their mother played it on the piano almost daily. It's as if there's a conspiracy to make them grieve not just one parent, but two. Mickey squeezes her hand so tightly she thinks he's going to break a bone. For the sake of her girls, she tells herself, she must push aside the flood of childhood memories running across the screen of her brain. For her girls, she must heighten her attention, watch with her whole body, lose herself in the spectacle of movement.

Carlo looks not forty but twenty in his regal jacket and with his noble profile. He escorts Xenia around the stage, moving with dignity. Then, in his princely character, he notices the doll sitting woodenly on a balcony, with exaggerated eyelashes and red circles painted on her cheeks. Sequoia, as Coppelia, sits unblinking, porcelain. She's never been this still in her life! Jesse moves stiffly, chasing Carlo away with his cane, wearing an unfortunate wig, his makeup smeared so one can see his darker skin under the white paint. Julie snorts briefly, then covers her face.

Then something happens, bewitchery or artistry take over. Xenia extends her arms and legs with grace. Ava is enchanted. Damn if her daughter doesn't look like some latter-day Audrey Hepburn. Xenia conveys longing, joy, cunning, with her limbs and eyes. Ava has no need to make up kind things to say to her. She's a ballerina. Her daughter is a ballerina!

Trying to win back the affection of the man she loves, Swanhilde pretends to be the doll now. Jesse as Coppelius tries to breathe life into her. She moves haltingly at first, an abstraction of life, then she takes off. The audience exhales as one with relief. But then, she falters, almost falls. Stricken, Xenia freezes. She doesn't run off the stage, at least there's that. And her father rises to the occasion. He guides her, lifts first one arm, then another. Xenia responds, holding her hand in each position. He moves her head, her limbs, in turn until she starts moving on her own. The audience applauds. Because she has recovered? Or because there was never a mistake in the first place?

Ava wonders when she herself will come to life again, find her steps. The music, the dancing, everything in the room reminds her of him, her daddy. How did this happen? A real human being is irrevocably gone. Where to? Where did he go? She experiences grief as a trembling, as someone taking over her body. She understands why people talk about spirits, ghosts, possession. Someone is shaking her. Her daddy. He is shaking her.

The burst of applause returns Ava to herself. Mickey and Julie have each taken one of her elbows and are lifting her to a standing position. The dancers are bowing and receiving flowers. Miss Gloria is placing bouquets into the hands of her daughters. Her own lovely daughters.

Ava starts to clap. Long after everyone else has stopped, long after they've left the room, she continues her applause.

Big Springs

After a quick visit to the official reception in the basement, where there are cups aplenty, Ava breaks away to re-assemble at home with friends and family. Who are we if not our friends, family, community? When she arrives, the room is already abuzz. Guests have helped themselves to wine and are chatting.

"Wasn't that lovely!"

"Sequoia! Why, I wouldn't have recognized her in a million years with those big eyelashes painted on her face!"

"Is Xenia okay?"

"One of our kids stopped dead silent in the middle of her piano recital. I walked up on stage, I mean it was a small church basement, not like tonight at all, and sat down next to Emily on the piano bench. I played a few notes and then put my arms around her. She had tears in her eyes, but she continued."

"Aren't the leaves gorgeous this year?

"I thought Jesse handled it so well!"

When Jesse enters with his two daughters hanging on his arms, trailed by Carlo, applause breaks out. He nods, skirts around the food-laden table, and guides the girls to their room. Away from company and inquiry, he tells them how proud he is of them, how proud they should be of themselves. Xenia's eyes are lowered. Sequoia is looking straight at him with her big doll-eyes. She's refused to remove her stage make-up and looks falsely cheerful and unbearably bright. Smiling broadly, she follows Jesse into the living room, which is crowded with family, friends, and strangers from her parents' lives. Someone she doesn't even know hugs her.

Xenia remains in her room. She takes a pair of scissors from a drawer and cuts her costume to bits. She forces the mass of tulle and satiny shoes into a trash can.

The table is crowded with food: spanakopita, smoked salmon, dips and crackers, cheeses, raw veggies that some people are calling "crudités. " Ava vexes over what she might have forgotten. She opens the fridge to retrieve any orphaned dishes but instead pulls a bottle of vodka from the freezer and pours herself a glass, not bothering with ice or tonic or orange juice. Straight from the freezer, sharp and cold on her tongue, it leaves a trail of heat in her throat. She pours another glass and carries it to the living room.

Ava notices white creases on Jesse's face where he didn't quite get all the make-up off. Despite his gracious demeanor, she detects a familiar worry in his eyes. Though he listens modestly to reviews of his performance, he looks back frequently toward his eldest daughter's door.

When Xenia emerges, she is wearing her mother's old moose-hide dress. Her hair is braided and adorned with cowry shells. She is barefoot. The dress is too big and falls off one shoulder. She puts an old cassette tape on. What plays is the powwow music that Ava recorded maybe fourteen, fifteen years ago. The sound of drums beating, voices calling and responding in a high wail. Xenia bursts out, "I'm not really a stupid-ass ballerina, anyway. I'm an Indian. Do you hear me? I'm an Indian!"

Ava makes her way to Xenia's side, tries to pull her into an embrace, but Xenia tugs away, closes her eyes and starts to dance. People step aside to make room for her as she slowly moves around the room in a step-step-together pattern. At the end of her dance, which she performs with closed eyes, there is silence. Her father applauds. Others join in. Xenia looks at no one but walks, with as much dignity as she can muster, out onto the deck where Carlo is smoking. Kaya turns off the tape player and follows.

Joseph I drags a drum to the center of the living room. With his one good hand, he thumps a rhythm. Sequoia improvises a few dance steps and Jesse joins her. A conga line weaves through the house, people moving awkwardly, colliding with one another but too drunk to care, everyone trying to lift the spirits of the room. When the music ends, people try to resume some semblance of conversation.

"That Xenia is an accomplished young lady, I'll say that much! Ballerina and Indian dancer, all in one night!"

"So, you work at the paper? Must be fun being a news photographer!"

"The girls are one-quarter Indian so I'm wondering if that gives them some kind of tribal rights."

Ava nods amicably but makes her way to the person she's known the longest. When she gets to his side, Mickey looks her straight in the eye and speaks as if the rest of the evening hadn't just happened, "I'm goin' back home tomorrow, so I gotta know. You're gonna do this Greek trip, right, Sisso?"

"Mickey, not now."

"You're a photographer, for Chrissake, and this is the perfect job for you!" She tries to concentrate on what Mickey is saying. She tries to tell herself that Xenia is okay, she's with her Uncle Carlo and Auntie Kaya and that if she has a chance to work through this, she will learn from it. Sometimes less is more in parenting. She dares to think: Maybe she's better off without me.

"You do know what I'm talking about, right?" Ava struggles to focus. Something about being a photographer on a summer heritage trip to Greece, taking photos of people visiting the villages of their yia-yias and pappous, maybe showing them how to shoot better pictures? Odyssea Tours. "Dad's friend from the old neighborhood, Spiros, runs the company." Mickey's been talking about this non-stop since he arrived a few days ago, but she's closed her ears, made it background noise.

He reassures her that it wouldn't be all of Greece, just Crete. Crete of the Minotaur. Crete of their ancestors. Crete, where she could release her father's ashes into the Aegean, as he wanted. Ava thinks back to the difficult discussions about her father's remains. The American Greek Orthodox church doesn't allow cremation, nor does the Catholic Church, which insists on "dust to dust." But his wife Angela insisted that, even though it's not what anybody else may have wanted, their father wanted his ashes to be set free in the sea. He dreamed his whole life of making this trip to Greece, his homeland, but never managed. Until now.

"C'mon, you're perfect for this, Avie."

"I can't imagine a better person for the job." A different voice joins in the conversation, the familiar drawl of Raleigh Grenville. "You are such an amazing photographer, those travelers have so much to learn from you." He puts his blue-and-white porcelain pipe back in his mouth, inhales, then exudes smoke mixed with words, "The girls will be fine. They do have a father, y'know." Ava can't help but smile at his use of a saying she's only heard women use before. "Besides, you'll have Emma Jane, Julie, Kaya, all them good females watchin' out for your girls." He adds, "It sounds like a fabulous trip. Hell, I'd be tempted to sign up myself."

Mickey adds, "Once you get to Greece, one tour group leaves, the next group comes. Somewhere in there, you'll have a couple of weeks to go to Daddy's village."

Ava takes another hefty swallow of vodka.

⁂

The drumming and dancing have stopped. Carlo and Xenia have chosen this gap in the soundscape to re-enter. All eyes go to them. Carlo still looks like Franz from *Coppelia,* holding himself straight and tall. He is guiding Xenia, his hand on her back, giving her support. These men have become downright chivalrous. Xenia sidles up to Ava and enunciates carefully, "Mother, you should go to Greece, like Uncle Mickey said. You really should, Mother. You've always wanted to go." Mother? Since when did her kids call her "Mother?" Only in anger and impatience. She's Mommy. She wants to be Mommy.

Sequoia adds a clearly rehearsed line, "It's a lifetime opportunity."

Ava can't help but laugh. Others join in, breaking the tension. And then her eyes go immediately to her boss, as if she's asking permission. He responds, "We'll talk about it." As if on cue, Joseph I pulls out books on Greece, both archeological monographs and some handsome coffee-table editions. He puts them around the dining table, now depleted of food. He opens them to stunning shots of boats drifting on the sea, cliffs, statuary and ancient artifacts. He puts ashtrays on top of the tomes to keep them open. Ava's eyes graze over the pages to dwell on turquoise water and marble bodies. She longs to enter the photographs, to escape into the endless blue.

A thought occurs to her: I've been ambushed. This has all been choreographed. Jesse wraps his arms around her. She enjoys the feeling of warmth but doesn't know if he's asking her to stay or go. Ava looks around the room. Julie is clearing dishes from the table. Kaya is holding Xenia gently by the shoulders. Aunt Dena is opening her mouth to sing a Theodorakis favorite. Mickey successfully balances a glass on his head. People are laughing, having a party. She downs another glass of vodka.

173

Big Springs

"Okay, so I'm thinking I had this dream. But maybe it wasn't a dream." Ava has a splitting headache, but she needs to talk.

"So, tell me already!" Ava and Julie have the geldings by their reins, leading the horses Little Joe and Red China to the stream after a good run.

"After the party, I wasn't sleeping so great. Jesse, either. I felt him shifting around and he's usually such a sound sleeper. I gave up, grabbed my camera and went to sit in the comfy chair. I took a few pictures of Jesse sleeping. . ."

"That's so sweet!"

"And then, I must have dozed off. When I woke up. . ."

"Or did you?" Julie interrupts.

"Through the window there was this gorgeous light from the moon."

"Some of us call it 'moonlight.'"

"Jesse's eyes were closed, but he was moving his head from side to side and moaning a little. He had tossed off the covers."

Julie has a wondering look on her face. "Ooooh, you managed to take a few sleeping nudies?"

"Carlo was there. With him. On the bed. Had to be a dream, right?"

"Go on," says a now very curious Julie.

"Slow shutter speed, moonlight, two men with very different bodies. One blond, one dark. The two of them kinda wrestling. Jesse kept pushing Carlo away but not very convincingly, like it was part of the dance. I watched but I didn't feel the slightest bit of jealousy. I was just super curious, and, truth be told, a little bit excited, watching. Things progressed and Jesse's face, I don't usually get to see his face like that, his face was in ecstasy. I felt close to him. Weird, huh? I'm weird."

"No. I mean, two very good-looking men. . . "

"I got in close with my camera. Jesse saw me and reached for my hand. I put down the camera and let him pull me down to the bed. He pushed Carlo away and started kissing me. Lips, neck, um, lower. . . " Ava takes a deep breath.

"Yeah, well, he is Jesse, that part might be real."

"Not done yet. That's when I felt something. A sensation. Not unpleasant." She pauses, reluctant to go on, but hey, this is Julie. She tells

Julie everything. "On my thigh and moving higher."

"Something nice?"

"Orgasmic. Carlo."

"Omigod! You dreamt you were having a threesome with Carlo and Jesse?"

"It was a dream, right? Do you think it really could have happened?" Ava steps carefully on the rocks that cross the stream. "I was pretty much three sheets to the wind."

"More like six. But in the morning? How did you face them in the morning? How did everyone act?"

"Carlo was gone. Completely packed up and gone."

"He always does that, though, leaves unannounced at dawn, right? The camera?"

"Empty. No film in it."

"C'mon, Avie, you always have film in your camera. You threw away the evidence."

"Or it was a dream."

"Can I have that dream? I mean you dreamt about doing Carlo. I'd like to jump his bones."

"Really?"

"Oh, yeah, like this minute. You only live once." Julie looks over to Ava, whose face is showing a new curiosity over Julie's taste in men. "Oh, c'mon, Ava, you've been having these kinds of orgasmic dreams since you were twelve. Look, you got the great guy AND the good dreams? Why don't I get some?"

"But why now? Why this?"

"Uhhhh, because you need some adventure. You're the girl who rode with wild horses in Chile and lately you've been cooking bison burgers and taking pictures of poodles. You've been such a good stay-at-home mommy."

"Adventure? You think the dream's a message I should have an adventure? Maybe go to Greece, like Mickey says?"

"Wow. Hadn't thought of that. I like that. Or—alternatively—there's been a lot of tension and sadness since your dad died, maybe you needed the release."

"The release. God knows I can't seem to get that when I'm awake. Jesse treats me like I'm a broken piece of china, and if I do feel at all sexual, have any naughty urges, I think I'm a bad daughter disrespecting my father." And then, immediately after saying the word "father," a quake rises in her, starting in her belly, then her chest, then rising into her throat. "Daddy." She tries to swallow down the grief, but she fails. Instead, she falls on Julie's shoulder and starts to sob. And remember.

How she knew it instantly when her Aunt Dena called. How she'd cried out, "No, no!" before Dena could even tell her what happened.

"He's gone," Dena said. "Thank the gods, he had no tubes in him, he died at home, in his own bed. May he rest in peace."

Ava should have been there. She wasn't there, at her father's deathbed. In the months that he warred with the cancer that took his life, she had gone up only three times. Brought him a huge pot of soup once, carried it frozen in the car, letting it melt as she drove at high speed to Chicago, as if chicken soup really could cure something so invasive, so evil, that spread to his liver and pancreas, thinned him, made a ghost of the man who had so loved life. Life, in all its shades and music. And, all at once, the quakes in her body stop as suddenly as they began.

When she looks up from the safety of Julie's sweater, half-relieved, half-embarrassed, she sees that the leaves have turned. There are layers upon layers of translucent reds and golds, and that particular light that only comes in autumn, filtering through the leaves, trying to give hope despite the coming of winter. Bright leaves, skeletal tree trunks. Life and death together in some glorious last light.

Ava watches the leaves already fallen into the stream, damming up in places, already turning brown around the edges. When she speaks, it's in a blurt.

"I'm bloody pissed at him."

"Who?"

"My dad."

"For why?"

"I missed fall because of him. I love fall and I missed it."

"Yeah, right, that's it. You're mad at him because his death distracted you. It has nothing to do with him marrying that D.A.R. WASP and then dying in her arms before you got there. Or just dying. You're not mad that he died and left you an orphan?"

"Am I an orphan? At 35, can I still be an orphan?"

"Or maybe because he took what should have been your inheritance and gave half of it to the wicked stepchildren."

"I got some rugs. I always liked Daddy's rugs. Besides, the step kids are younger and need the money."

"What bullshit. Your stepmom has your mom's rings. Her gold locket. The ungrateful rude stepkids got all the money. And you are pissed. Go ahead, say it."

"I am soooooooo bloody pissed!!!!"

Ava thinks about where the money could have gone. The orthodontist's bill, a new furnace, a better truck, a vacation. She is embarrassed again, this time that she can think such ordinary, mercenary thoughts two breaths after such a jolt of grief. Then, she wonders if she could she even find her father's village. She imagines treating everyone there to a feast. She pictures whole legs of lamb on the table, bottles of ouzo, platters of artichoke hearts cooked with cream and rice, the raising of glasses and villagers who all look like her father shouting, *Ya mas!!!* To us. *Ya mas!!!*

"Ava! Still there?"

"Yeah. Sorry."

"I was just saying, at least you still have erotic dreams about Jesse." The subject has reverted to the earlier topic. Ava needs to get more sleep. Stop being so scattered, so mind-wanderingly scattered. Julie continues, "Do you think you married a boyfriend or a husband? I think I wanted a boyfriend but married a husband. Anyway, I never have sexy dreams about Trent."

"I barely knew Jesse when we settled down. But then, we never really got married, not legally." Then she realizes that she missed a beat. Her cousin, her best friend, must have been talking about Trent, her husband, and she missed something important. "But hey, about Trent, how are things with you two? I've been going on and on. . . ."

"Same old, same old. I married my teacher and he still thinks he's my teacher. It's his way or the highway. He's a man with a big temper who wants me to stay home, y'know, belong to him. If I don't, I'm a whore. Oh, Ava, I'm not sure I can hang in much longer. If it weren't for you and Jesse and the kids, I think I'd be outta here. Maybe move back to Chicago." Ava wonders how much her mind wandered while Julie talked about her own woes. She hadn't listened to poor Julie.

The horses are restless, eyeing home. End of conversation. Once mounted, Ava looks again at the leaves, looking so fragile yet glowing. Julie's voice comes through her reverie. "So, jerkoff, enjoy the memory. Of the, uh—dream."

Ava pulls up her reins. "Julie, you asshole!"

"Ava, you bitch-girl."

When she gets home, Ava digs into the trash basket and pulls out Xenia's discarded toe shoes. She cleans them with a damp cloth and sews new pink ribbons on them. She tries to squeeze her own feet into them, but like Cinderella's stepsister, she can't wriggle them on. She puts the shoes in the closet, next to Xenia's old Barbies, just in case. When Ava licks her lips, she tastes salt. Ava doesn't know yet that one day, when her daughter is attending the University of Washington in Seattle, Xenia and her friends will start a modern dance company called BarbieNot.

Ava walks into the yard and sees Jesse supervising the girls practicing archery, as if the last few days never happened. When they first showed an interest in this sport, Ava thought it was a joke. In her own childhood, she sang, "One little, two little, three little Indians," and images of cartoon Native boys with toy bows and arrows danced in her head. But now, she realizes that her girls have spent their whole lives watching their father, a serious bowman, hunt, following in the footsteps not only of his Makah mother but of his white father. This same white father, Joseph I, has been preaching that the deer herds were getting too large, causing some animals to die of starvation. Ava wanted to put food out for them, to feed them. Josephs I and II sighed. Now, there's Bambi stew and Bambi stir-fry in their freezer along with the bison burgers. The girls hadn't killed anything yet except a squirrel, and that by accident. "It'll make them strong," pleads their grandfather.

She watches them for a while, a dad and his daughters, with their bullseyes and quivers. But she doesn't want them to see her, the weak, crazed woman she's become after losing her own father. She doesn't want to have to speak. She escapes down the meandering country road.

Sometimes you can't finish sentences, your thoughts remain incomplete. You've wandered, forgotten to change your clothes. You've spent too much money or too little. You've stopped answering the calls of friends. You've forgotten how to comb your hair, you've left your cameras in restrooms. When you least expect it, you remember him, your father. Gone.

You recall what a good daddy he was when you were little, how patient and funny, sneaking you bits of honeyed baklava and shrugging his shoulders as if he had no idea where it came from.

You spend a lot of time wandering country roads, hoping that no one will notice you. If they could see how broken into pieces you really are, how crazily you wander, how compassless, surely someone would take you away, put you somewhere for your own good, saying: She was always odd, different. It's for the best. . . Or worse, they'd take your children away. Your children who you love more than anyone else in the universe. You know what people would say: She was no good for them. The kids will be better off without her.

Topeka

Thank the goddess for work. Ava can push herself into this other sphere, distract herself, get absorbed into the world of angles and perspectives, depth and focus, the lives of other humans. A cosmos where she is rewarded for tangible accomplishments. She relishes her own images on the pages of the newspaper, the respect of her editor. Most of all, she loves the world of the camera, of living through her eyes.

Her weekend is Monday and Tuesday. She works Saturdays and Sundays, so she can cover school sports, concerts, plays, art openings, and civic debates. When she doesn't have a specific assignment, she walks or drives around, hunting the news down. It's what they're supposed to do, the photographers on the paper, look for the visual stories. A chihuahua that can skateboard, a kindergarten play. She watches for the last leaf falling, the first crocus blooming. She shoots.

Usually, there is an assignment. Today, her boss sends her to

Lawrence to cover the Haskell powwow with a reporter named Helen. Ava doesn't think she's the right person for the job since she has a connection, a possible conflict of interest. Her own children will be dancing. But Mr. Taylor shrugs and sends her anyway, reminding her that she's not the one writing the story, she's illustrating. "And yeah, take some of your family. Your kids are so damn photogenic, we might not be able to help ourselves. And that little one of yours, I mean she's got the name, right? Sequoia Lightfoot! C'mon."

Lawrence

Jesse, Xenia, Sequoia, and Kaya. They appear as a family, the four of them, dressed in Native costume for dancing. They are sitting at a picnic table, eating fry bread tacos and joking together. They face toward each other and Ava is on the outside with her camera. She takes photos of them from this distance, before they are aware of her, before she is seen.

Jesse senses her first and he opens his face with a smile to her. The same old wry grin.

It doesn't take more than a second for Sequoia to notice and run up to her. "Mommy, Mommy!" She hugs her with all her 10-year-old might and then, not able to contain herself, she spills out, "Auntie Kaya is gonna take us on the powwow circuit this summer!" The more sophisticated Xenia is watching the transaction and biting her lower lip. "We'll travel to Indian reservations all over the country. And then go visit Daddy's tribe, the Makah."

"Wow! That's your tribe, too, y'know!" Ava introduces Helen, who quickly excuses herself with a wink to talk to one of the other dancers. Ava wants to die on the spot.

"So, you can go to Greece now and not worry about us. Auntie Kaya says you can find out who you really are, and we can find out who we really are."

A lump the size of Idaho rises in Ava's throat. She wants to scream that they are also Greek and Polish and American, but she bites her tongue. Jesse seems untroubled by the idea of his children wandering the country like nomads, sleeping in tents, eating enormous amounts of fried food, and not being with their parents. The stream of catch-up continues. Sequoia adds, "Did you know that there is a building on this campus with my name on it that used to be the library? Daddy wants to turn this place into an accredited university."

Using her most grown-up sophisticated voice, Xenia adds, "'Get Haskell out of a high-school mentality and into a university environment,' is what people are saying now."

Ava assembles herself. "You can be very proud of your dad, because he's been working hard for Haskell. Someday his dream will happen." She thinks of the long nights when he's gone to meetings, working to make what had been an Indian boarding school, and then a trade school, and then a junior college, into an accredited four-year college. The politicians he's courted, the nasty letters he's received in the mail, the threats. He and Kaya, too, worked hard at it. Ava should be proud. She is proud. But she is also something else, something like jealous, even resentful of the time he's spent away.

She thinks of how Academy Award winners often thank their families for doing without them while they worked on the movie. Or how, in the acknowledgements of novels, a male author might thank his understanding wife, whom he abandoned while holing up in his study for three years. Ava wonders if those families, those wives, felt fulfilled and challenged or were they jealous like she is. She wonders how her own children feel when she is gone on the weekends. Perhaps we are all both abandoners and the abandoned, feeling this tug between home and away, adventure and safety. Ava's children could be gone this summer while she wanders islands with a bunch of strangers. Right this minute, she vows to talk to Mr. Taylor about a leave of absence so she can take the Greek job. She just might do it. She breathes deeply and notices how good the fry-bread tacos smell. She samples some tidbits.

"Mmmmm."

"Mo-om!"

She picks up Xenia's forbidden coke and washes it down.

"Mo-om!"

And then the sound begins. The loud, wonderful beating. Voices call and respond. The drumbeats resound. The sound is strong. It makes her forget hunger, fatigue, her fears. She gets absorbed into the sound.

Ava snaps photos of boys the age Jesse was when she first saw him. Young and eager. Their regalia is brighter these days, feathers in neon colors, beading more elaborate. Now, most of the boys modestly wear leggings and shirts under their bustles. Ava is a bit disappointed, wanting things the way they were at her first encounter, longing for the first time.

The girls' event comes up and they hold their heads high, move with dignity and grace. Ava looks over to Jesse, to smile at him and gush over their children, but she sees that he is exchanging whispers with Kaya, both glowing with pride over the girls' performances. And they should. They were the ones who taught them. Bleh on that. Ava can't help it. Right this minute, she wants to slap Kaya silly, ban her from her home. But the feeling passes when the girls run up to Ava after their dance, one on each side, jumping up and down and clinging to their Mommy. Their own true Mommy.

***

Later that night, after the girls have listened, for the five millionth time, to the story Joseph I tells about how Odysseus managed to trick the Cyclops, after the children and Joseph I are asleep and lightly snoring, Ava turns on Jesse.

"You're letting the girls tromp around the country like homeless waifs, eating junk food and sleeping in tents."

"You think summer camp is better?"

"I think you're trying to punish me."

"I think I'm trying to give my daughters a sense of their own culture."

"You're trying to get back at me. For even considering the trip to Greece, for even thinking of taking my father's ashes there, for honoring my father."

"I'll honor your father. I'll carve him a totem pole. I'll build him a mound."

"So now you're an Indian again. Make up your mind."

"You make up yours."

"I've made up my mind. I'm going. To Greece."

"On a plane."

"How else would I get there? I'm not going to live and die by your fears."

"And I'm not going to live and die by yours."

There's a slamming of doors and he is gone. She throws one of Joseph I's gorgeous Greek books at the door after him and it falls to the floor, broken at the spine.

Now look at what I've done. Ava tries to put it into words, to compose in her brain the true words she never says aloud: I want my family back. I want my husband back. I want to be held and made love to. But I also want to go, to leave, to explore, to wander, to see the world. I want to be on a boat with wind in my hair like in a damn perfume commercial. I want my children to admire me and build altars in my name. I want everyone I know and love to live forever. I want my father back. I want my mother back. I want to dance with pennies Scotch-taped to my fingertips with everyone around me smiling and clapping.

And I want to beg my husband, Embrace me, take me, make love to me. Love me.

─✦─

She waits until midnight. Then, she dials. Kaya puts him on.

Ava says two words, "Come home."

When he stands in the door wearing his brown leather jacket, he has tears welling up in his god-help-us-fucking-mortals green eyes. He takes her into his arms and leads her to the bedroom. She lies, cold as a fish, stiff as a doll, like Coppelia, not a warm, breathing woman. When he enters her, she cries out in pain.

Lawrence

The next day Ava returns to the Haskell campus without an assignment but with both her cameras. She goes directly to the cemetery. She's heard about it for years. Maybe if she had been a good wife, she would have come here earlier, shown more of an interest. Ava knows the Haskell story, how Indian children were forcibly taken from their homes and culture, brought here to a boarding school where they learned domestic skills and trades, where they learned to serve white people. She knows they weren't allowed to speak their Native languages, that their hair was chopped off, their clothing and sacred objects burned, their names taken from them. That they were marched in military-style drills, to train the Indian out of them. That was back in the late nineteenth century. Things have changed since then, even since Jesse went to school here. She knows Jesse is part of the change, working toward making Haskell an accredited college, a true Indian Nations University.

In front of her is the cemetery. The headstones, a hundred identical slabs, gray, uniform, sit in even rows. It resembles a military graveyard with its measured evenness, but instead of a mown lawn, it is overgrown with tall grasses. She takes the first photos from a distance. Then, she does a walk-around to get an overview before she hones in on the small headstones. Some of them have offerings next to them: real and plastic flowers, stuffed animals, tokens. She photographs.

CHARLES PANTHER
OSAGE
1865-1885

AGNES McCARTY
MODOC
1870-1886

NORMAM BROCKEY
PAWNEE
1861-1885

BIRD McGUIRE
OSAGE
1869-1887

Ava pauses at the name Bird, thinks of her old friend Meg Standingwater's brother Bird, who has recently moved to this part of the country. She notices how many died in the late 1880s. An epidemic? Perry Little Elk, Cheyenne 1875-1888; Ollie Walker, Cheyenne 1875-1886;

Maggie Big Fire, Cheyenne, 1869-1887; Joseph Blackbarn, Pawnee1879-1889. She stops. A Joseph. A ten-year-old Joseph. This catches in her throat. The name Joseph and her own 10-year-old Sequoia give her pause. Harry White Wolf, Cheyenne, died 1884, aged 6 months. A six-month-old baby. Someone's child. Charles Edge, Caddo, 1879-1900. The names, the tribes, the dates go on and on. Tribes she's familiar with and some she's never heard of. She crosses herself, says a little prayer. She tastes salt on her lips.

In the battered turquoise truck, Ava drives through campus, past the agricultural and industrial buildings, toward its center. She observes the stately old structures. She parks and walks around, reads the names on the residences. Winona Hall. Sequoyah Hall. Jesse's mother's name, his daughter's name. A group of students come toward her, laughing and talking. One of the young men in his early twenties, the age Jesse was when she met him and just as handsome, asks if they can help her find something. She is looking for the library, she says, she would like to see some Haskell yearbooks. The young man points her in the right direction and adds, "Just watch out for the ghost."

"Ghost?"

With an edge of excitement, a young woman in the group speaks, "Libby, the library ghost. Sometimes you make a stack of books on a table, turn around, and she's thrown them on the floor."

Another adds, "I've seen her long white skirt. I really have. I was working late at night at the library. Nobody else was around. I heard a strange singing sound and I could see her moving behind the bookshelf, next to the wall."

The students have gathered in a tighter group, listening until they become bold enough to share. "I have a friend who came to Haskell to go to school. When she got up in the morning, on her very first morning, she saw a ghost at the foot of her bed. Bird McGuire, wearing the old-timey clothes and all. My friend left the very next day. Couldn't take it."

Ava is curious. "But you didn't leave? You're not scared?"

"If I left every time I got scared at Haskell, I'd have gone a thousand times, starting with the first powwow. We didn't have powwows where I came from, so the loud pounding of the drums scared me big time."

"I kinda like the ghosts. They don't hurt nobody. I think they protect us."

Ava asks if she can take their picture. They pose for her wearing eager young faces, then go on their way, continuing their flirtations and conversations. Ava finds the library and asks for help locating yearbooks. She turns pages for two hours. When she's done, she climbs into the truck and heads toward town. She spends her week's paycheck on a cart full of groceries, then drives to Kaya's house. She knocks on the door and, when she hears Kaya's footsteps, runs to her car, leaving the groceries on the doorstep.

Lawrence

The Grenvilles throw a costume party. Jesse and Ava go as cowboy and Indian. He wears his usual cowboy shirt and jeans plus adds one of Joseph I's bolo ties. Ava wears a sari. They both think this is hysterical.

Emma Jane blows a smoke ring, "So, how long will you be gone on this photographic journey?"

"Late May to August."

"Well, I'll be a monkey's uncle. Raleigh's gonna be in Cyprus fall semester. Starting in August."

"Really?"

"Sabbatical grant. Raleigh?" He comes running. "He's studying some lacemakers somewhere, Lefkara? Lefkarita? Raleigh, did you hear that Ava here is going to her daddy's island? You oughta meet up with her there before you go to Cyprus. It's practically next door, right? How often do you get an entrée to a community like that?" She turns to Ava who is feeling self-conscious in her sari. "Your father came from a little village up in the mountains of Crete, right?"

"I've never been there, but. . . "

"But hell, your father's people are from there. They're gonna welcome you with open arms. Raleigh, this is a golden opportunity."

Raleigh is taking a deep draw on his cherrywood pipe, waiting for Emma Jane to run out of steam. She continues, "Well, I'm the one that makes all of Raleigh's travel plans, so it's settled." Ava sometimes wonders how the Grenville marriage survives. Raleigh knocks his pipe against a piece of furniture like he's rapping on the door and finally utters the sentence he's taken so long to compose.

"Now I don't know if Ava'd want me around for the family reunion, but I have to admit I've always wanted to see Crete." He pauses before going on. "It's the way Greece used to be, they tell me."

"It's settled then. Ava will be an expert tour guide by then, and she can be your photographer for a research excursion to Crete. Then, off you go to talk to them lacemakers." Emma Jane blows out another smoke ring and turns back to Ava, "I wonder if there's someone on campus teaching Greek. He'll need a few words. We'll have to look into that."

The Grenvilles always surprise. Ava stands there in her sari, feeling somewhat more naked than when she walked in and more aware of her own exoticism. She remembers her father's story of her taping pennies onto her fingers and belly dancing. Greece, Turkey, India, everything east of Paris is blending into a mélange of exoticism. She's losing her footing. People are making plans for her, she's flying off to places she knows little about. She's guiding people she's never met. She's meeting up with Professor Grenville on a Greek Island. This last makes her alternately cold and warm, concerned and hungry. She eats several ham-filled biscuits with hummus, a new addition to the Grenville table, along with stuffed grape leaves and baklava. Just when she thinks things had shifted enough in her world, Julie comes up to her, Trent-less.

"Where's my guy Trent?" asks Jesse, even though they've never exactly hung out and pretty much have nothing in common except having been born male.

"Flew the damn coop. No, that's not right. I flew the coop. He flew it metaphorically and then I flew it literally. I am now the proud resident of the Bideaway Motel."

"What?" Ava asks.

Jesse notices the go-away-this-is-girl-talk look in her eyes. He nods to Julie and moves on to meet a rug dealer Grenville has been talking about. Ava stays and repeats, "What?"

"I've only been there a couple of days."

"I've been calling you."

"Sorry. I felt embarrassed." Ava wishes she could put on a sweater or a jacket. Her filmy clothing seems more inappropriate by the moment. Maybe she could wrap herself up in one of that guy's rugs. Julie continues,

"It got to be too much and so I packed my bag and moved out."

"You can't continue to live in a fleabag motel for the rest of your life."

"It's temporary. Really. We're working things out. It's better not living under the same roof for a spell, less tension. We've been meeting for coffee to talk. We'll figure it out."

Ava looks at Julie, who is pale, with blue and purple circles under her eyes, who is thin, so thin now, and somehow looking more beautiful with this haunted look. Ava picks up a biscuit, loads it with ham and hummus and stuffs it into Julie's mouth.

"Eat."

Julie dutifully chews.

"Now wash it down."

Julie obeys.

On the way home, Jesse starts to narrate, like his father: "Once Raven was so hungry and lonely, he made a deal with Whale."

"Ah, a story."

"Raven would fly into Whale's mouth, keep him company and clean his teeth." Jesse seems to smile to himself and she wonders if he didn't just add that bit himself. "In exchange, Raven could eat Whale's blubber."

"Don't you just want to know what that tastes like?"

"You do remember the Makah were whalers. Anyway, Whale ate more and more to satisfy Raven's hunger. Raven grew fatter and fatter on the blubber but continued eating."

"Is this your way of telling me I need to go on a diet?"

"Whale couldn't keep up with Raven's appetite, and Raven started eating more of Whale's insides than just the blubber."

"Oh."

"Eventually, Raven ate Whale's heart."

Ava scrunches up her face with distress.

"Raven struggled with his increased girth but managed to squeeze his way out of Whale's mouth before Whale left this earth. Raven looked down at Whale as he slowly sank, looking like an island, and then disappearing. Raven regretted what he had done and, since then, the sound of his voice has been like crying."

Big Springs

Ava keeps a copy of a fat, old Chicago phone directory in a drawer. About once a year, it comes in handy. She looks in the yellow pages for travel companies and sees the Odyssea Tours ad on the page, complete with the compulsory image of Athena amidst ancient columns. Odys-sea, really? She grits her teeth and dials. She has no contract. Everything in her father's world worked on a handshake, sometimes with a little tip to grease the wheels. Chicago. She pictures the travel posters on the walls as she asks to speak to Spiros. The receptionist—Rhoda, his wife—is eager to help.

"You must be so excited, going to Greece! You and Michalis are going to have such a good time." Michalis? Mickey? "Your father will be smiling down from heaven, so happy he's gonna be watching you two go to the Old Country. He got it all arranged about a year before he left us, God bless his soul." There's some yelling going on in the background. Rhoda pays no attention.

"He got in touch with people, figured it all out. And my Spiros, he is so happy about the photography part. Your daddy was proud of you, always showing us your pictures. My Spiros says someday you're gonna be a big-time *National Geographic* picture taker." The woman can't stop talking. It's amazing they have any customers at all.

"Speaking of which. . . " Ava wedges in her question about adding a week on the tail end to do a photography job for a famous scholar's research project.

"Easy breezy," is the answer.

She immediately calls Mickey.

"MICKEY!!!!"

"Pretty great, huh? I thought we'd gotten the shitty end of the stick inheritance-wise and now look what the old man's gone and done. Gotta love him. You and me, we get to spend two weeks together in the Old

Country. Sweet deal, right?"

"Why didn't you tell me that Dad did this, huh, Mr. Jerkwad?"

"You're excited, I can tell."

Ava admits to being excited, even though she thinks it was rash of her father to do this without asking or telling anyone beforehand. Omigod, she needs to get busy. Gotta sign up for a class in Greek.

"You're gonna take Greek?"

"Maybe. And gotta figure out how to teach tourist photography."

"You can do that part in your sleep."

To herself, she adds: Gotta contact Raleigh about his research plans. That part she's not going to tell Mickey. Her heart is pounding.

Lawrence

One of Raleigh's students is playing banjo at a bar. Ava would have preferred coffee during the daytime at Mo's, but Raleigh said he needed to do it this way, kill two birds with one stone. And no, Emma Jane is not going to come because, let's face it, she certainly did not want to hear another student banjo player. And anyway, he wasn't going to bite her head off, he just wanted to check some dates on the calendar and make a research plan and it'd be good to meet in the evening 'cause the kids were asleep and it was going to be just fine. He reassured her three times that Mrs. G. not only approved but had thought up the plan herself. "It's just drinks."

Ava tries to think of the musician as a chaperone but soon she finds herself enjoying the sound of the old-timey acoustic strumming in the background. Before long, she forgets her hesitation.

In between sets, Raleigh formally, as if they didn't have dinner at each other's houses all the time, and as if their kids didn't hang out constantly, talks about his research aims and how he wants to meet some lyra makers on Crete and hear some performances. Acoustic, like tonight. Gatherings of people in their own context, like they might do if he weren't there. Okay, sounds like he's done a little background research. He needs her to make the introductions and, more importantly, to take photographs to document the research. Yes, he understands that she has a limited knowledge of the language, but she has more than he does and a better understanding of the culture. If he gave her a list of questions to ask in advance, maybe she could learn to ask them? They could tape-record the answers.

His manner is unexpectedly brisk and businesslike, which Ava appreciates. He drinks coffee. She, a mug of craft beer. After the calendar is set, Raleigh closes his date book and orders a Santorini Sunset. The waitress looks puzzled and says she will talk to the bartender. After she's left the table, Raleigh says, "What should we have them put in it?"

"What?"

"I made it up, a drink with a Greek island's name. Now let's think of something to put in it and then they'll mix it up. A month from now, we'll come back and see if they still serve it."

Ava thinks this sounds like wicked fun. Bitter orange. Grenadine. Metaxa. They come up with a few more sunset-colored items before the server comes back with regrets. Off she goes again to the bartender with their list, later returning with two cocktails served in long-stemmed frosted martini glasses, looking very much like a Santorini Sunset. Raleigh raises his glass. "Tell me how to say, 'Bottoms up.'"

"*Ya sou.*"

He repeats. Dutifully. They click glasses. He asks her how to say "Thank you," then "Excuse me." No sign that he has any seductive intent.

Big Springs

At first, Ava doesn't hear words, only a wail. Rage. A voice accusatory and sarcastic, vengeful and in pain. She doesn't even try to decipher the actual words. She distracts herself, distances herself from whatever is flung at her, tells herself that this is what life will be like for the next few years. Xenia will be a teenaged girl any minute, separating from her mother. That is what she tells herself. Xenia will accuse her and push her away. It's natural, it's inevitable. Ava repeats these things over and over as they drive home. But her ears ache and her body starts to tremble. She wants to take her hands off the steering wheel and cover her face to protect herself. She wants to stop up her ears. She is almost afraid. Afraid of this child to whom she gave birth. Whom she nursed and comforted. Starting to decipher actual words, Ava turns into a parking lot. She has an impulse to shoot cannons back. To hurl insults. To protect herself with a counterattack. She stops the car.

They sit for a silent second in the car, in this jail on wheels. Silence oppresses and then Xenia says, "Didn't you hear me? Didn't you hear a word I said? Can't you even have the courtesy to listen to me?" Ava recognizes these phrases, these recriminations, that her daughter hurls but learned at her mother's knee. Ava wishes she had been a kinder, more patient mother. She again thinks: Better off without me.

"Mom? MOM!!!"

"Yes, darling, I'm listening."

"Answer me!"

"Please repeat the question."

"Are you having an affair with Professor Grenville?"

Ava doesn't answer. She's trying to understand why Xenia is calling him Professor Grenville instead of Uncle Raleigh the way she usually does. Ava says, "You mean Uncle Raleigh?"

"He's not my uncle. Now stop avoiding the question. Are you sleeping with him?" The briefest pause, then, "I knew it. I knew it. I knew it."

"What are you talking about?" Ava manages to squeak out, sounding like a guilty thirteen-year-old herself. She is not guilty of sleeping with him, she assures herself, but, at the same time, she flushes red because her Catholic childhood ranks coveting one's neighbor's husband right up there with the actual deed. And covet she has. She has coveted her neighbor's husband. But she should be saying this in a confessional, not to her daughter.

"What are you talking about?"

"Belinda McKenzie's mom saw the two of you at The Patchwork Quilt last night.

"Isn't that the weirdest name? I mean for a coffee house/bar kind of place. I thought it was weird."

"What's weird is that my mother is having an affair with a man my parents make me call Uncle."

192

Ava opens her door and throws up. She heaves the contents of her stomach and even the vomit accuses her with its red and orange Santorini Sunset coloring. She gets out of the truck and paces. Snot trails down below her nose and she licks it off her lips. Then, disgusted with herself, she dry heaves.

"Omigod, are you pregnant?" Xenia stands now, next to her mother.

Ava shakes her head. She tries to think of what to say. "No" is so simple and inadequate, but she says it anyway. "There is no affair, there has been no sleeping with. Raleigh and I had a drink at The Patchwork Quilt, that's all."

"Why would you even do that? Why?"

"We have work to do. I'm going to help him with a project. I do not have to explain this to you. He and I are adults. We're allowed to meet and have coffee, a drink. It was Emma Jane who suggested it."

"Emma Jane thinks you're going to leave Daddy and marry Raleigh." So now he's Raleigh, first name basis.

"That's absurd!" Ava is screeching now. "How can you even think that!"

"I heard them arguing. I was upstairs and they were arguing."

Ava looks at her child, her twelve-year-old child, troubled by the behavior of her adults. Her grown-ups, her role models. She sees them now as flawed. They've fallen off their pedestals. It was inevitable. Painful. Ava observes the narrow shoulders, the long thin legs. Xenia is half bird, half colt. Tears are streaming down her cheeks. Ava shakes her head no. She says quietly and assuredly, "I am not having an affair with Raleigh Grenville, nor have I ever, and I certainly have no plans to leave your father to marry him." At this moment, Ava never wants to see Raleigh Grenville again. She just wants her daughter back. Even though she knows that in a moment's time, she might want to grab Raleigh by his waxed handlebar moustaches, throw him over her shoulder, and take him to her cave. But right now, she only wants to reassure her daughter. To make her believe. She wants to be a woman of character.

Ava opens her arms and leaves it up to Xenia whether she will turn away or walk toward her mother. Xenia wants to believe, too. She looks at her mother's begging eyes and takes a step forward. "C'mere, silly you," Ava says and gives her a hug. In this moment of warmth and reassurance, she tries to think quickly about what to do, what to say next.

"I had a surprise for you, but I guess now's as good a time as any to tell you. You girls can come to Greece with me this summer. For part of the summer, anyway. I can't stand to be away from you so long. So, you and Sequoia and Emma Jane and her girls are coming for the first few weeks. It's what Uncle Raleigh and I were talking about. Then, I'll have to do some work. But it'll be great!" She thinks about how she can make her lie the truth. She will cajole, she will bribe, she will somehow succeed in convincing Emma Jane to bring her daughters. They will become part of the tour group. Everything is going to be all right.

"But Mom, Sequoia and I are going on the powwow circuit with Kaya, remember? We already said yes. Daddy has paid deposits on stuff. And he told his cousins and people on the Makah rez that we're coming. Kaya even ordered new regalia for Sequoia. And I wanted to ask you: could I wear your moose-hide dress? I know it's a little big, but not very much, and it has history and beadwork, and it's gorgeous. It'll make me think of you. Please, please, please?"

Her two girls are drifting away in a boat, waving farewell.

Lawrence

"Am I a bad mother, leaving my kids for weeks?" Ava is asking her women's group, which still meets regularly but has evolved into a more social than political gathering. They've pretty much given up on the Equal Rights Amendment. No more demonstrating on the Capitol steps. Instead, they eat and chat about movies and books about life, home and its challenges.

When Ava puts forth her concerns about leaving her daughters while she goes to Greece, the women burst out with numerous examples of how men seem to have a perfectly fine time being dads and leaving their kids for extended periods. Soldiers. Traveling salesmen.

Ann, a high-school teacher, says, "How about our culture hero, Odysseus? Now, there's one for you. He even had girlfriends along the way, and no one shakes the finger of shame at him."

"Isn't it different for women?" Linda wonders.

"C'mon, that's just residue from the patriarchy, men worrying about whether they were supporting children they actually fathered," a new member named Jasmine adds.

"And why should it be different for women? It's not like you're still nursing them. They don't need your tits anymore." Good old Julie.

"It'll be good for their relationship with their dad. The father-daughter bond will get stronger." Ava is starting to like this Jasmine woman. But she doesn't tell them about Kaya and the powwow circuit. She's ashamed she let it happen.

"Do it now. When they're teenagers, they'll need you to be around so they have something, someone to push away from," adds Carole.

"Doesn't that sound delightful?" Ava responds, not without sarcasm. "I think there's plenty of pushing away already." That much she can say.

In the car on the way home, Julie reassures her. "The girls are going to be fine. I'm more worried about you than the girls. They're discovering who they are. I hope you'll be exploring the world instead of being wracked by parental guilt."

"What do you know about parental guilt?"

"My mom had it bad when she went to work. Think what a great example you are to your daughters. You're pursuing your dream."

"I'm dumping my dad's ashes into the sea!"

"Exactly. Filial piety. Your girls will know to honor you, too."

Ava decides she doesn't want to think about her own death, so she changes the subject. "Do you think I married a boyfriend or a husband?"

"You married a boyfriend AND a husband, lucky you."

"And a gambler."

"And a dancer. And your favorite model."

"Y'know what I want to be when I grow up? A photographer for the *National Geographic.*"

Julie turns quickly to catch the expression on Ava's face and responds, "Perfecto."

"Maybe when the girls go off to college."

"You'll just travel all over the world, taking pictures?"

"I'm so in love with the idea I can barely breathe. Hard job to get, though."

"But Jesse won't get on a plane."

"There is that."

Lawrence

In January, Ava signs up for a class in Conversational Greek. As the teacher begins with the familiar sounds of *"Kali mera,"* Raleigh Grenville lowers his tall frame into a seat in front of her. She whispers, "Thanks for blocking my view." Throughout the class session, she thinks of how vulnerable he is there, in front of her. She could lean forward and kiss his neck or she could strangle him. After their attempts at imitating the teacher's polite and slowly pronounced Greek conversation, Raleigh and Ava pause outside the classroom. Eleni, their teacher, seeing they are people her own age, invites them to go to the student union for a café.

This becomes the ritual over the next weeks.

Life becomes almost routine again, with work, class, the girls' impossible schedule of school activities and sleepovers, and more Grenville parties. After one such event, Ava goes over to help Emma Jane clean up. The Grenvilles may throw extravagant and delicious parties, but they are inclined to leave stacks of dishes, glasses, and sometimes people lingering for days afterward around their living room. Their children forage for food among the leftovers, walking around the hungover. Ava feels compelled to watch out for them, so she finds an excuse to stop over at the house on her way to work. Before knocking, she looks up at the old house with the noble front porch, looking calm and sedate, belying its inhabitants.

No one answers, so she opens the door and calls out Emma Jane's name. She is surprised to find the house clean and sparkling. Emma Jane is in the kitchen, sitting at the table, chain-smoking. There is a cigarette in her hand and another sitting, lit, on the lip of an ashtray. Emma Jane starts talking without so much as a "Hello."

"Kids are gone to church. They've found religion with some local Baptists. Lord knows we never took 'em. I guess we each have our own way of rebelling."

"It happens."

Emma Jane pours a cup of tea for Ava, adding honey and lemon, knowing just how much without asking. "Without them around, I actually felt like cleaning up."

"Looks nice." Ava stubs out the second lit cigarette.

Emma Jane clearly has something on her mind. "Raleigh was down in New Orleans giving a talk at Tulane and he went to see this here fortune teller."

Raleigh had handed out Mardi Gras beads at last night's party, so Ava knew about the trip, but she had heard nothing about a fortune teller. Ava says the obvious, "Part of his research project? Folk belief?"

"My, Ava, you are naïve. Folklorists believe it all, believe everything, don't you know that? Every superstition about olive oil keeping your hair from going gray, every voodoo priest with a cure, every gypsy with a deck of cards. Anyway, he'd heard this fortune teller was really good."

Ava finds Emma Jane Grenville to be a mixture of exhilarating and frightening. Right now, in the middle of the stiffly tidy house, Ava anticipates an earthquake. She concentrates on munching a leftover biscuit while she watches Mrs. G. light up another Marlboro and blow a smoke ring. Ava didn't know people did that anymore until she met Emma Jane. But this house is full of such archaic wonders.

"I suppose you could call it 'research' if you mean research into his own life. Now, just listen, because this does concern you."

Ava struggles trying to swallow the dry biscuit crust. "Me?"

"The fortune teller told him he would marry again and this time it'd be to someone whose birthday is in the summer." Ava swallows. Emma Jane continues, "And I think it's going to be you. I think you're going to be Raleigh's next wife."

Ava does not say, C'mon, I'm happily married OR You're not really going to believe what a stupid fortune teller says! Instead, what she says is, "C'mon, I could never do what you do. This house, the parties, the biscuits."

"Your birthday is in July."

"21ˢᵗ."

"That's what I thought. It's okay. I always knew this wouldn't last. His father was married eight times, did you know that?"

Ava shakes her head uselessly. She's stuck on the notion of what it would be like to have a father who'd been married eight times.

"At least I know he'll be in good hands." Emma Jane exhales another circle of smoke.

"Emma Jane, you even type up his manuscripts for him. He can't leave you."

Big Springs

Spring arrives with its succession of long-awaited colors. The trees sprout tiny leaves and seem hazy with that light, yellowish green that lasts just the briefest time. Ava indulges herself taking photos that capture the emergence of green, the opening of daffodils, then tulips. As the season progresses, Ava pulls lilacs close to her nose so she can breathe in their heady scent. The strong fragrance smacks her with their woozy sensuality.

People keep asking her if she's packed. She only has so many clothes, and she's wearing them. She is trying not to think about getting ready. Okay, she does a little hop-skip dance of delight when her passport arrives. I'm really going, I'm really going, I'm really going. She deliberates for a full hour choosing just the right, new, improved, lightest possible backpack with exactly the necessary number and size of zippered pouches and the most subdued yet earthy forest-green color.

She and Jesse decide to take a long drive to Western Kansas, to Quivira and Cheyenne Bottoms. They can't remember the last time they took an overnight trip together. Maybe they can find each other again. He's been thinking: She's distracted, gone already, and she hasn't even walked out the door. She's been thinking: He's angry, often distant, then suddenly, almost suffocating. They're both thinking: We need this. We've been fighting so much lately. Tomorrow, they will leave the kids with Julie. Everything will be all right. Before Ava takes off for the summer, they need everything to be all right.

On the appointed Friday, they drive west toward the salt flats. Kansas was once a sea and they want to see the fossils that prove it. As they drive through the Flint Hills, Jesse says, "Whoever said Kansas was flat as a pancake never came here."

The rounded, treeless hills look alive, like great comforting shoulders, strong and graceful, stately and inviting. And then, the hills become taller, the shapes more pronounced, like the rounded thighs and breasts of giant odalisques on their sides. Ava keeps asking Jesse to pull over so she can shoot. Neither can remember the last time they did something like this.

They drive by stone outcroppings, cattle ranches, and wide-open spaces. When they stop and venture outside, it is the enveloping and ceaseless sky that strikes them the most. The Kansas sky that they have forgotten to appreciate, the cornflower-blue sky that seems five times bigger than the land, that could almost make you believe in heaven.

Heaven. Sky Blue. Ava recalls her childhood hopscotch games. She would hop on one foot 1, 2, 3 in a row, then 5 and 6 together—a relief to put down both feet—then 6 alone, then 7 and 8 together and then, a rest at "Sky Blue." She understood Sky Blue to be a kind of heaven, the beautiful place you were headed to if you didn't fall while hopping, didn't step on any lines, if you did everything right. She remembers how, before any actual hopscotch game began, her child self would relish doing the elaborate chalk drawing. How she would linger over writing the words "Sky Blue" in her fanciest script and then delight in the embellishment of the background with curlicues and waves, flowers and leaves. The memory is sweet and brief, then she returns to the enormity of the Sky Blue above her. And the quiet. It's not that there are no sounds out here, but that the only sounds are those of living things. No machines mowing or revving up or tunneling into. There is only the occasional sound of birds or wind in the grass. And then, nothing. Total stillness.

They walk toward water. There is a line on the horizon, a white space over the blue water, and they wonder what it could be. Their pant legs swish through the tall grasses and Ava regrets making even this interruption of the quiet. A few disturbed insects fly up, confirming her intrusion. But that does not stop her from continuing onward, toward the water, trying to satisfy her curiosity about the horizon limned with white. As they get closer, the white line becomes white dots become white dabs become white birds, thousands of white sea birds.

Jesse stops. "There," he points. She is the one who lives through her eyes, but he is the one to notice things first. At the far right-hand side of the line of birds, first a few, then all of them begin to take off into the air, into the sky, to become a breathing, flapping cloud of white against the blue, flying to some other, distant part of the salt flats. Snow geese. To behold them is an act of delight and forgetting.

The spell doesn't last. Ava becomes aware of a bit of civilization, a miniature building just this side of the water: a duck blind, the perfect place to take close-ups. She wants to follow this urge, though it would separate her from Jesse. A tug in both directions. Jesse. Photographs. She lets go of his hand, walks into the duck blind, snaps pictures, observes, and wonders: Where is the true home for these migrating birds?

She returns to Jesse, who seems to be searching the ground. He bends over to pick up what he was looking for, a long, white feather. It's been fourteen years since they found the feather of one of the wide-winged creatures in Nebraska on their first cross-country trip. She will pack it in her suitcase, take it with her on the plane. It will bring her luck since her name, after all, means wings.

*

When they feel sufficiently sated with bird-awe, they head back to the truck and start driving toward town. They stop at an inn meant for hunters, check out the one available room with its six single beds lined up against a concrete block wall. The proprietor points out proper areas for disposal of plucked feathers and freezers for carcasses. When at last they are left alone, they jump from bed to bed, threatening to pluck each other, throwing items of their clothes off like they did when they were young. He picks up the solitary crane feather and runs it down the front of her body. She hasn't experienced this kind of need since the loss of her father. Eventually, they slow and find one other, the after-image of white birds taking flight burned into their minds' eyes.

*

The next morning, they head to a more remote area. When they arrive at the water's edge, their shoes sinking in sandy mud, Ava can't help herself. She reaches down and dips her fingers into the water. She licks them, just as she does after eating bacon. Jesse puts on his "Really?" face, followed by his appreciative, "That's my girl!" smile. She is tasting the saline remains of what once was a briny deep.

As if to confirm the marine history, a flotilla of pelicans takes off. Pelicans in Kansas. It's migratory season, and they are following some memory of their species dwelling here when Kansas was a large sea. Hundreds of the long-headed birds, both graceful and clumsy, continue on their journey. Ava mouths the word "Wow" and jumps up and down as the pelicans continue to pass overhead. Maybe this is what the world was like before humans: giant flocks of birds, uninterrupted by silos or buildings, sailing through Sky Blue.

⁕

They want to return home by the "road less travelled," and Jesse finds a small gravel byway. They ride for miles through tall grasses and wild scrub. A cloud of butterflies passes overhead. Monarchs on their way from Mexico swoop down, and a few fly into the slow-moving, open-windowed truck. One lands on Ava's head, another on Jesse's nose. Now that they are headed toward home and seemingly blessed by butterflies, Ava gets up her nerve, "Come with me, come with me to Greece. The girls are taken care of."

Jesse, of course, thinks of Ava's discomfort with the girls' summer arrangement. "Don't be mad at Kaya. She thinks she's helping."

"Come with me."

"You know I can't. We've talked about this a million times. I can't get on a plane. And I don't want you to, either." Then, a deep breath, a smile, "Besides, I wouldn't do you any good over there. Hell, I'm not even sure I can get us out of the damn salt flats and this is Kansas, where I grew up."

"We'll be all right, you and me?"

"Sure. We'll be all right."

Eventually the road turns to dirt and, a few miles further degrades into a series of ruts and puddles. At first, they feel tall and invulnerable in the truck, but then they hit a swampy pit in the middle of the road. Wheels spin. They are officially stuck. Birds and insects, irritated by the sound of grinding, complain and take to the air. Jesse tries again and again but only succeeds in digging in deeper. The majesty of the day is lost. Jesse stops trying.

When he gets out of the truck, his boots sink into the khaki-colored mud. Ava scoots behind the steering wheel and he yells out directions. She guns the engine while he pushes. "Now," he yells. And she tries. Repeatedly, uselessly. When the old turquoise truck finally budges, Jesse hops into the passenger's seat, soaked in mud and swearing under his breath. As Ava drives ahead, they soon realize that they may be saved, but they are still lost. There's no sign of barn or chimney as far as the eye can see. Worse, there is no sign of a sign.

When they've driven through what seems like an endless field of tall marsh grass, they see a route sign, a roadway, an actual paved roadway on which they won't break an axle. Hallelujah. They check the position of the sun and head east.

After miles of static, the radio finally comes through with a recitation of soybean and milo prices, followed by the international news:

A bomb exploded today on Trans World Airlines Flight 840 as it flew over Argos, Greece. **Four American passengers, including an eight-month-old baby, were sucked out of the jet after an explosive** device detonated, blasting a hole under a passenger seat. A terrorist group claims responsibility, saying they were responding to "American Imperialism." The Reagan administration is advising Americans to avoid travel to Greece...

They are both horrified, but Jesse speaks first, "You're not going."

"Of course I'm going."

"You have the children to think about."

Although she is afraid herself, she says, "And a scaredy-cat husband?"

"If that's the way you want to put it, yes! I'm thinking of them and me. You can't go."

"It's the Reagan administration. They're anti-Greek. They're trying to hurt Greece."

He stops the truck. "Please. Don't go."

"They'll cancel the tour anyway, so why bother arguing about it. But if they don't, I'm going."

Angry, he turns up the volume on the radio broadcast: "Three were from the same Greek-American family, believed to have been a grandmother, her daughter, and her granddaughter."

Jesse pounds his fist on the dashboard. "Why can't things be the way they used to be!"

"Used to be? When?" She tries to summon up their traveling honeymoon days, but that's not where he's going.

"Back when the kids were little. Before. . . "

"Before what? Before my job? Before we met the Grenvilles? Before I decided to go to Greece?"

"When things were less complicated. When we were. . . "

"Poor and happy? When I stayed home, wiped noses, and ground up bison? When I had toddlers and cried every day out of sheer loneliness?"

"Don't do this."

"I am doing this!"

⁂

She calls Mickey and Spiros at the travel agency. The reaction is pretty much the same from both: "We're not gonna let those damn terrorists tell us what to do. Sure, some chickenshits will drop out of the trip. We're going. You with us?"

Of course she's with them. Of course, she agrees. If anything, she feels energized.

But numerous times a day, she pictures a baby falling from the sky. She tries to imagine the infant sprouting wings like a cherub, a small angel catching a cloud instead of plummeting to earth at Argos.

She thinks these fantasies will take away the sting, the fear. But one day, downtown, when she is getting ready to go in to talk to her boss, she is so lost in the image of falling she forgets to turn off the truck. She just leaves it running, doesn't even hear its grumbly motor when she climbs out the door. Only when she returns and fumbles for her keys in her pocket does she hear the motor left running. Fortunately, this is Kansas and no one has stolen the old thing.

Big Springs

"You'll move over to our place is what you'll do. You'll stay there while I'm gone. Joseph I, if you can stand him, will be happy for the company." Ava is talking with Julie, who has once again moved into some fleabag motel, money depleted since Trent invested in swampland in Florida, some oil well that never paid off, some cosmetic company that never took off.

Julie skips over the details and answers, "I love Old Joe. But I can't just move in."

"It'd be an enormous help. I've been worried about Jesse. About the house. You're a godsend. Everything is working out perfectly."

"For you, maybe. I don't exactly feel like my life is working out perfectly."

"I'm so sorry, Julie. You must be in terrible pain and here I am just worried about who's gonna feed my horses while I'm gone." Ava thinks about Julie's marriage, distant and bleak, and suddenly values her own, with its highly-charged arguments and bouts of eroticism.

Julie resists. "You're just saying I'm needed so it doesn't seem like I'm a freeloader."

"Listen. You're on Kaya duty while I'm gone. I definitely need you."

"Only if I can stay in the forbidden room. I can't help it. I just like the idea of staying in a forbidden room."

"It's only forbidden to small children."

"Because they might get stolen by some Makah witch deity?"

"Shut your gob. But yeah, there's that. You know it's got the best view."

"And a highchair."

"You cannot touch the highchair." Ava feels like she's violating some trust by even talking about the forbidden room. She bites her tongue. She pinches her own arm to stop being such a bad wife.

"But it won't be necessary, believe me. Trent and I will work things out. We just need a little space is all. We'll have fun dating again. It's crazy, but we always do."

Ava doesn't believe a word Julie is saying but doesn't feel she has the right to judge anyone else's marriage.

In the future, Ava will refer to these months in her marriage as "The Time of War." Anger flashes at the slightest provocation. During a particularly feisty fight, very close to her departure date, and while nursing her ever-present anxiety about Kaya, she says, "Why don't you just do what you want while I'm gone? Go for it. Get it out of your system."

He answers before she can take it back. "Same with you. You can fuck every Greek sailor you meet as far as I'm concerned."

She hates him for saying this. He hates her for not reassuring him. His lip is trembling. She wipes a wet spot off her cheek. They are both too stubborn to take it back. They are acting badly. Soon they will be torn apart and it could turn out like the Nebraska crane feather she once held in her hand: after a section is parted, it can never be mended.

Ava thinks of the open marriages of the hippie era, of the Yeslers she read about in Seattle. No, she's not going to do anything with this so-called permission. She can't imagine. But still, oh yes, if she lets herself, she can.

Jesse distances himself. Angry, he pounds on wood and, sharpening an axe, cuts his hand. With his white-bandaged paw, he pushes Ava away. The children echo his mood. They take permission from him to be angry with their mother. Any enthusiasm for her project has flown away like the pelicans.

She burrows into Greek, jabbering the Hellenic equivalents of: How much for a liter of wine? Where is the nearest doctor? Would you please say that again? She takes refuge in her class, enjoying the adult camaraderie of having after-class coffee with her teacher and Raleigh Grenville. When Eleni learns they will be going to Greece, she tells them she has a vacation house there, in the small village of Petras, near Sitia on the Eastern end of Crete. After the last class, she hands Ava a set of keys and printed directions on how to get to her "little villa," as she calls it. Perhaps she thinks they're a couple. Neither of them disabuse her of this notion.

Ava comes home to a house fragrant with sage smoke. She follows the scent to its source, where she finds Kaya and the girls waving smudging wands, walking the perimeter of the "forbidden room." Julie's easily recognizable baggage stands outside the door. People are moving in before she's even left. She wants to call her mother and ask for advice. She wants to talk to her father, to be reassured that everything is going to be all right. She turns to look at Joseph I, who shrugs his puzzled shoulders, thrumming his fingers anxiously on an armrest.

Another day she finds Kaya and the girls making fans to match their powwow outfits. Sometimes the three of them peruse maps, laughing together like co-conspirators. When they see their mother coming, the girls flash a smile, then quickly turn away. They hide Ava's things and laugh when she can't find them. Ava is more aware of her orphanhood: mother and father dead, husband and children pulling away, maybe forming a new family before she's even left town.

Jesse catches her sleeve as she passes him to go to her darkroom. "What I said the other day—I was angry."

"We were both angry."

"When we first got married. . . "

"We hardly knew each other." They finish each other's sentences, of one mind, yet divided.

"You'd never even been to Kansas, how could I expect. . . ?"

"I knew you never wanted to get on a plane. . . "

They look at each other and know both statements are true. Jesse, determined, speaks first, "It's not that. . . "

Wishing it wasn't going in this direction, Ava continues, "Of course not, we care for each other. . . " She bites her tongue, stops herself from uttering the word, "Right?" She wants to beg him for the assurance but stops.

"I wish it were enough." His words come to her like a sword to her heart, but still she nods her head. He goes on, "What if. . ."

"This time apart could be. . ."

"An opportunity. To see if we're meant to be."

"Meant to be? There's a romantic notion."

"I'm kind of a romantic person, turns out." They both can guess what's coming, but neither of them wants to put it into words. He continues, "Should we give it a test?"

Ava thinks of Julie and Trent. Ava does not want to think of Julie and Trent. But still. She says, "A trial."

"See if what we've been missing, fighting over, is what we need."

She adds, "Or if we need each other more."

Jesse fidgets, pulls up tape from his bandaged hand and sticks it back down until it won't stick any more.

Ava thinks about women's magazine articles that say that 80% of couples who separate never get back together. She says, "Okay, then. When I'm gone, go ahead and have some fun. I won't be here to complain about drinking or gambling or. . . " She doesn't have to fill in the blank.

"Mmmm." He seems to be swallowing gulps of air. "And when you get back, if you come back. . . "

"Of course, I'm coming back." Her voice is rising in volume, she is moving toward heightened anger. He tries to keep his calm, pushes forward to end his sentence already begun.

"You won't have to tell me anything. Just live this time like you want to. Travel, enjoy, it's your time."

Travel. Enjoy. A glimmer of something else enters her emotional landscape, the notion that she might enjoy this trip. A tiny *maybe* leaks into her soul. She still feels the dread but also a teeny tiny release, an exhale, an unexpected anticipation. "It's just a break."

"No rules, no guilt."

And then a gulp of air. She thinks: Omigod, what are we doing?

"Yeah." They both exhale, look away, then turn toward each other again.

She says it first, "The girls?"

"The girls will be fine. They'll be gone all summer."

"Doing Indian things."

"Yeah, well, maybe next summer you can take them to Poland or something."

"I'll miss them terribly."

"You were gonna miss them even if you were home and they were out doing powwows. Maybe this way, if you're doing something too, it won't bother you so much."

She can't imagine. She wants to go. She doesn't want to go. She wants the separation. She doesn't want the separation.

He interrupts her train of thought, of wavering. "Avie?"

"Yes?"

"I don't think I can go to the airport with you."

She knows he can't bear to watch her get on a plane. "Julie will drive me."

He crinkles up his nose like he used to when they were young, when they were just kids, and he says, "If. . . "

"When. . . "

". . . you do come home, please don't take a plane. Take a boat or something. For me."

She tries to answer in the same hopeful tone, "Yeah, sure. Maybe in the meantime they'll dig a giant tunnel or put up a trans-Atlantic bridge and I can just drive home. Now, that might take a while. . . "

He squeezes her shoulder hard with his good hand and walks away.

PART FIVE

Seven days later — May 1986
To Greece

They say *Absence makes the heart grow fonder*. But also, *Out of sight, out of mind*. They say that *Absence sharpens love*. But then again, *Far from the eyes, far from the heart*.

They say *A journey begins with one step*. When Ava is about to take the first step onto the plane, she hesitates, trips, nearly falls. She makes a less-than-dainty entrance, banging into things with her camera, dropping her tape recorder in the aisle, then half-sliding, half-falling into her seat. She waves from the airplane window long after she can see any shapes on the ground.

She photographs the puffy clouds and senses the beginnings of buoyancy, release. She orders herself a glass of wine, reminds herself that she has no one to feed. No one to clean up after. No one.

Big Springs

They're gone. His father is at the library and all the women of the house have left. Ava, on her plane over the sea with her cameras and Dramamine. The girls, in Kaya's camper, filled with preteen excitement, sleeping bags, and beadwork to peddle at powwow stalls. Jesse knows that at some unknown point in the all-too-near future, he will miss them. He shuts up the voice that tells him he is, in fact, already missing them, and listens instead to the blessed silence of the empty house. He cracks open a beer and downs it in one draught. He pulls the phone cord out of the wall. He turns on the cassette player at full volume and sings along, "I can't get no—" plays air guitar, bends his knee in a pretend riff, and lets himself fall onto the bison-hide rug. Any time now Julie will be returning from the airport. Julie with her perky short hair. The music throbs through his body. No, he cannot fantasize about his wife's cousin. He cannot.

Athens, Greece

They've landed. After meeting in the Chicago airport, after the flight delays, the endless snaky lines, the garbled airport instructions announced in several unintelligible languages, the bumpy ride, the sleepless journey, the being scrunched in by multitudes of passengers in long rows, here they are. Mickey and Ava have recited their purposes for travel, been stamped and herded onto a shuttle bus. A loud voice-distorting and headache-producing megaphone shouts out the sights they will see later, when they finally get to Athens. Shut UP!, Ava wants to say. All we see now are acres of barren gray, bleak nothing dotted with multi-story cement buildings. Welcome to Greece. Trigger-finger itchy, Ava starts shooting with her camera anyway.

When they finally do hit civilization, they are gobsmacked by the multitude of vehicles, honking horns, and swarms of people. Ava had pictured parks with ancient temples surrounded by tasteful small hotels. And yes, those high-stepping Greek guards in their pom-pommed shoes.

They get checked in, checked over, and bell-hopped up to their room. Ava and Mickey have made brief calls home to announce their safe arrival to newly-installed answering machines. Ava has rehearsed Greek phrases until her throat hurt and tried, unsuccessfully, to capture the day in her journal. But when a small ivory blossom falls onto the page, she gets the message. Time to smell the night-blooming jasmine. From their wide hotel balcony, glasses of wine in hand, inhaling the opulent scent of the flowers, amazed that they made it alive, Ava and Mickey look up at a view of the Acropolis lit up by night, surely one of the wonders of the world. Mickey, for the first time in his life, is quiet. Dumbstruck by awe or fatigue, he has a stunned look on his face.

Ava breaks the mood with a practical concern, "You did remember to bring 'Dad?'"

"What kind of idiot do you think I am? Of course, I brought him. Packed him in a coffee can."

"Coffee can!" Ava knows this is just a temporary home for her father's ashes, but still.

"He loved coffee. Drank twenty cups a day. Not that you'd know, since you didn't come home all that much."

"I'm gonna forgive you because I know you're tired, but we do have to do something about Dad in the coffee can." She wonders if her father's ashes will smell like Maxwell House.

An exhaustion hits Ava like a door slammed in her face. Suddenly, she wants to sleep for 36 hours. Like a Victorian lady pressing flowers for remembrance, she positions the tiny fragrant trumpet of a petal into her journal and shuts the book.

❧

The next morning, they follow the tour leader's cream-colored umbrella, which she holds high above her head. When she stops, Sofia looks like she is holding up the sky, the folds of her umbrella and her matching outfit contributing to the illusion that she is part of a column. Sofia displays a gentle, indulgent smile as she waits for the group to assemble, some struggling with the Acropolis terrain, others chatting about the inadequate size of their beds or the wonders of the thick yogurt with honey served at breakfast. Sofia speaks about how the Parthenon was built to shelter a forty-foot-tall gold-and-ivory statue of Athena, patron deity of Athens. Ava never made the connection between Athens and Athena, that the ancient city was named, not after some guy in battle gear, but a goddess of wisdom and war, bedecked in snakes, helmet, and lance. The statue is long gone, but her namesake city is spread out below, with its taxis, apartment buildings, and museums.

And then she sees them, the caryatids. A row of tall, noble-looking, dignified women, carved with spirally hair and in sleeveless drapery, each leaning heavily on one foot. Ava straightens her back and stands a little taller as a result. Ava can't show her girls the caryatids right this minute, but what she can do is take a picture. Click. She wants her own daughters to witness this sight, to stand a little taller as a result. "The missing one," Sofia is saying, in her slightly British accent, "is in the British Museum." The listeners contort their faces into a variety of scowls.

When one of the younger travelers suggests they gather for a group photo, someone yells "Jump" and several propel themselves upward like practiced dancers while others lean slightly forward and shrug. The "Odysseans," as they've decided to call themselves.

Ava points out groupings of ancient objects as still-life opportunities;

she makes suggestions about capturing this perfect, clear light; she points out how the fallen columns often sprout wildflowers and cats, and how graffiti was sometimes carved into the ancient blocks of marble. They visit temples, memories of past glory, envisioning lives lived thousands of years ago. At the ancient theatre of Dionysus, they imagine what it might have been like to adore a god devoted to wine, revelry, and drunkenness.

Big Springs

Jesse runs around like a mad man, yanking off his stinky sodden clothes and throwing them in the washer. He jumps into the shower before he remembers that, with the washer running, the temperature will alternate between steaming hot and freezing cold. He dresses quickly, rinses out the sink and tosses away the beer bottles, blots the hopeless bison fur, asks for its forgiveness, and runs out the door. He must not be home when Julie returns. He must arrange his life so that he is away when she is there. At night, when his father is asleep, he'll meet his buddies for a beer, a hand of poker.

Athens

Mickey, quiet for most of the day, comes alive at night. He doesn't sit down with the others in the courtyard of Taverna Plaka, but walks along the stone walls casually, as if he doesn't even see the purple bougainvillea. He ventures into the kitchen, lifts lids off simmering soups, and inspects baking pasticcios. He asks if he can touch the fish. The owner, feigning insult but actually pleased, points out the clear eyes, the gills. Mickey knows this guy. This guy is himself. Standing a foot and a half shorter and weighing 100 pounds less, Demetrios sports the same smile, runs a restaurant not totally unlike the Café Athena back home. Mickey argues for a meal a few steps up from the predictable tourist fare. Demetrios, recognizing a fellow restauranteur who knows what he's talking about even if his Greek is halting and ridiculously outdated, shrugs and says, in clear English, "Why not?" In a short while, Mickey and Demetrios shake hands, slap each other's backs. They've become old friends.

At the tables, bottles of ouzo appear, followed by platters covered with marinated squid, stuffed grape leaves, phyllo stuffed with spinach and cheese, olives of several deep hues. "From the house," says the waiter. Mickey yields a contented sigh as he sits down.

It's a good night to be alive.

Back at the hotel, Ava calls her own Athena, her Auntie Dena.

"We saw your temple today, Auntie Dena."

"I hope you left me an offering!"

Ava is delighted to hear the easy-going voice of the woman who has done her best to replace her own mother in her life.

Dena goes on, "Actually, no, don't go pouring good wine over those old rocks. You'll only make the cats drunk. I prefer you get me a nice bottle of Metaxa on your way home from the duty-free."

Ava is happy she made this call. "We saw the caryatids."

"They hold up the roof, they hold up the world! Like women everywhere."

"I took a few pictures."

"Yeah, but it's hard to fit a bunch of seven-foot-tall stone women in a 3-by-5 picture, right?"

"Right. Thank you, Auntie Dena, for helping me make this trip."

Dena sighs, "Listen, Sweetie. This phone call is costing you all your money. Go, live a little. I want you should come home with good stories to tell."

Ava calls home and leaves a message on the unfamiliar, what-an-invention! answering machine about how she misses them all and how Uncle Mickey is the toast of Athens. Exhausted and elated, she falls into bed.

Big Springs

He lets the phone ring and ring. Phone calls bring bad news. He lets the machine pick it up. Now that the girls are gone, he has vowed only to answer at 9 p.m. each evening, when they are scheduled to call before they head for sleep. They check in with the news of the day, surprised at how different the world looks in various places, how bad or good the food, how homesick or excited they are. He leaves the house each night after their call to play a little poker, have drinks with friends. On his return, he wanders through the house, tucking a blanket around his father, staring at the empty beds of his children. He avoids the forbidden room where Julie sleeps. He tries to get his father fed while she is at work, to be out when she is home. During the days, there are animals to feed, wood to plane and sand. And there is the seed of an idea to nurture. He thinks he may borrow a custom from the Plains Indians since, let's face it, we're all becoming Plains Indians anyway. He considers building a mound. A memorial mound.

Athens

They have only one more day in Athens. Weighted down with hangovers from a long night, the travelers rally reluctantly for yogurt, bread, and thick coffee. Ava gives a brief lecture/demonstration in the hotel lobby on how to photograph objects in a museum, offering tips on how to deal with glass reflections, taking pictures of museum tags.

A bus awaits them at Syntagma Square. A few stragglers have paused at kiosks to buy postcards featuring the cats of Greece. She herself bought several and sent one immediately to Sequoia, of a black shorthair sleeping on a chair at a cafe: "This Greek kitty and I wish you were here. Love, Mom." And one to Xenia of a Persian luxuriating on an ancient column: "Everyone here takes naps. XOXO Mom." On the tour bus, they witness modern Greece, the streets noisy with angry drivers, jackhammers, tourists. Ava thinks of the contrast to the quiet bison ranch at home. She wonders what Jesse is doing, pictures him at his carving bench.

"I have gazed upon the face of Agamemnon." They are face to face with a mask of gold. Nose, eyebrows, chin, lips, cheeks, forehead, all of hammered gold. Sofia is lecturing about the message that Heinrich Schliemann reportedly sent to the Greek king when he found this mask in a grave at Mycenae. She goes on to correct the romantic story, telling them that the mask is at least three hundred years older than the Trojan War, if such a war even happened. As for Schliemann, the story about him is legend only. He never sent the message. But still we hang on to the story. No matter what we know, we can't let go of the golden tale we'd like to believe.

Ava studies the mask and is struck by two things: First, Faux-Agamemnon apparently had a handlebar moustache not unlike that of Raleigh Grenville. And second, what an amazing custom, to memorialize one's dead with a semblance in gold! Ava imagines warming thick sheets of gold and shaping a face. Her father's face. A twinge of guilt rises. They're carrying around her dad's ashes in an aluminum coffee can. She thinks of her dad's smiling face, wants him instantly and forever memorialized in gold—okay, not gonna happen—then after choking up a little, she vows to find something in the gift shop to better house her dad's ashes.

Sofia continues her talk, highlighting handled drinking cups, amber necklaces, crowns, breastplates, whole child-sized golden suits crafted to fit over mummies, molded while still warm.

Ava had been taught in Anthropology 101 that early peoples did everything for purely practical reasons. They painted bison on cave walls because they thought it would increase their chances of a good hunt. She never bought that argument. And even if that was their excuse, the artistry went beyond necessity. And now, seeing amber jewelry, thousands of years old, crafted with care and an eye for beauty, these striking masks, these golden body suits and high crowns, reassures her in her belief that humans have always created, made art, sung the praises of their heroes, and embellished the everyday. People had to do the practical, but they loved doing the beautiful.

Armed with her theory, Ava wanders through the museum with her crew, looking at the sleek sculptural design of the Cycladic pieces, the wavy hippie-like paintings of the Minoans, the depictions of winged and tailed mythological creatures, confirming her theory at every step. There was no need to paint a wavy octopus's arms on a cooking pot. They pass through room after room of magnificent red-and-black vases: Penelope at her loom, feasts, priestesses, Aphrodite. And finally, grave markers memorializing men by depicting them playing with their pet dogs, their widows weeping.

❧

Ava follows the signs to the gift shop. She picks up a few postcards of the gold mask and immediately scribbles one to Julie: "You will, of course, fashion one of these for me when I die."

She walks past the painted reproductions of red-and-black vases with depictions of Achaeans doing battle. Her eye is drawn to something simpler. The tag says it's a copy of one of the lagyoi of the Antikythera shipwreck. Not that she has any idea what that means, but she does understand this: the originals were designed to transport wine. She loves this idea for her dad. She also loves the simple design, the earthy terracotta color. She reaches for one but her hand is stopped by a larger, burlier one. Mickey's. In his other hand, he holds a museum gift shop bag. He's already purchased an imitation red-black-and-gold Greek vase elaborately painted with the design of a Trojan Horse. When she asks him why, he says he's always liked that story. "C'mon, everybody likes that story. Dad liked that story."

"Yeah, that's the story we want—war, trickery, danger—something hiding in a container you don't expect."

"Exactly, you wouldn't expect our dad's ashes in there. Anyway, it's gorgeous. I mean, we need to respect the dead."

"Be practical, Mickey. That vase is gorgeous but there's no way to close up the top."

"Aluminum foil? Yeah, you're right. So, now what do I do with it?"

"Return it."

"I don't return things. That's why I didn't ever really get divorced."

"What?" Ava notices that their voices have become inappropriately loud for the context, but she cannot leave the conversation there.

"We're separated. In the eyes of the church. And me. I'll never

218

remarry."

"And she can't either."

"It's not that we didn't go to court. We did. It's just the church doesn't recognize divorce and neither do I. She can do whatever the hell she wants and I can't believe I'm talking about this with you in a gift shop in Athens."

"Ditto." Having gotten the attention of several customers and clerks, they both lower their voices to a whisper.

"I won't return the vase."

"Keep it. It'll be a good memento. And, what about this for Dad? A wine jug. With a stopper. To get him out of the coffee can."

"Ha!"

They both laugh until Ava's shoulders are shaking and she has tears in her eyes.

Big Springs

Jesse walks into what everyone else calls the "forbidden room," now Julie's. She isn't home and he wants to check on whether the old highchair is still in place, not pushed into a closet or thrown away. He has a rag in his pocket, a piece of an old sweatshirt. He means to dust it, this seat of his brother's, to make him more comfortable, to make him feel less forgotten. Respect for the dead. He wants to oil the wood. He remembers his father doing the same years ago.

When he sees Julie's journal on the dresser, he stops short. She's left it open, like an invitation. He passes, trying not to look, but he catches sight of his name on the page. Perhaps in a complaint she can't bring herself to voice. He picks out a word or two before his eyes blur. Not words of complaint but something else. Private thoughts. He looks away, feels a twinge of guilt for reading. He glances toward her jewelry lying on the night table: slim gold chains, amber beads. He notices a glass with a translucent lipstick stain on the edge and a small, blood-red pool of wine remaining at the bottom, its edges dried. A fly is caught in the glass, hurling itself against the sides when it could just release itself by propelling up. Maybe it's drunk. Jesse sits down on the floor and watches the fly. He thinks about what the fly might have to teach him.

Islands

For this segment, the Odysseans will join others on an excursion boat, stopping at a couple of islands on their way to Crete, the island of their grandparents, the villages of their forebears. Like all good tour boats, the Sirena will stop at Santorini and Mykonos, where pelicans walk the streets and stone windmills stand in rows, looking out to sea.

Elderly women greet them at the first port, veiled in black despite the heat. Some of them hold signs saying domatia—"Rooms"—with pictures of pine beds and gleaming bathrooms. Ava would like to follow one of these women, to stay in her spare room, to let her show how she lives, to share her bread at breakfast. Next time, she tells herself, next time, when I return with the girls, with Jesse, if he'll come.

Ava coaches the travelers on how to shoot in the bright light of the sun glaring off the white and blue of the local architecture. Her own camera seems drawn to recycled olive-oil cans, casually painted in white or bright blue and planted with red geraniums. She loves the informality, the size, the shape, the color, the joy. But even more, her camera loves the brown leathery faces of the people, so clearly relatives of her father and aunts but with deeper grooves, evidence of more life lived in the sun. Old men, fingering worry beads, nod. She searches these faces looking for the one that holds the key to wisdom.

On Santorini, Sofia rounds them all up to witness the famous sunset. They grab bottles of ouzo and honeyed cakes and sprint down the narrow passageways. Ava makes the rounds, helping people adjust their settings and suggesting the best angles to capture the old churches with their tall white bell towers and bright blue rounded rooftops.

When everyone is settled, she hears a haunting, scraping sound that gives her a chill. She turns to see a long-haired young Greek man of about twenty playing a pear-shaped stringed instrument. When he begins to vocalize, Sofia nods, "He's singing the sun down."

"The instrument?"

"A lyra. An older, wiser instrument than the bouzouki and more common here on the islands."

Ava focuses on the young man's face absorbed in his music. When the sky starts to darken, Mickey comes up behind her and says, "Wasn't that spectacular?" Ava realizes she didn't take a single shot of the famous sunset, so intent was she on the changing light and shadows on the young musician's face.

She buys a postcard of an old man wearing a baseball cap, riding sidesaddle on a donkey. She's been told it can take months for a postcard to reach home but still she writes to Joseph I: "I'm getting you one of these side-saddles for Christmas. Love, Ava."

Big Springs

Jesse carries the highchair in one hand, a wine bottle in the other, and heads out to the yard. He has been digging a deep pit for days. He has lined it with shells, arrowheads, cedar mats, the children's discarded toys, anything he can think of that says "Indian" or "childhood." He was impressed by something he saw at the Cahokian Mounds when he and Ava took the children to St. Louis. With white shells, he lays out a pattern in the shape of wings. Within the shape, he lays down the oiled and purified highchair, like a butterfly's body in the middle of the wings. He pours wine over it. He smiles because he knows this is borrowed from Ava. This is for the gods. In the seat of the highchair, Jesse places a Thunderbird he has carved in his wood shop and painted with black, red, and turquoise, with encircled eyes that appear to be both open and closed. For a second he pauses, sorry that no one will see the Thunderbird, then remembers he himself has chosen this time, when no one is home, when his father is sleeping, when everyone else is gone. He knows this is a private act. His goodbye to his brother Theo, whom he has always thought of as Thunderbird.

For years now, he's been trying to find the right goodbye. Sure, there was a funeral all those years ago. A cemetery where his small bones lie. Jesse will not disturb them. That ceremony for young Theo Lightfoot was

221

American. This is for Jesse. And Thunderbird. Their mixed-up, confused bloodline. But that's the way it is now. His children Xenia and Sequoia are off dancing to music more South Dakotan than Northwest Coast or Kansan or Greek. They will be what they will be by choice. They will marry who they marry by choice, as he did. Jesse is choosing, as he did his bride the first moment he laid eyes on her, what he wants from each tradition.

He lifts the spade and throws dirt over the design of shells. He continues to cover the high chair, starting from the bottoms of the legs, until the first dirt hits the small carved Thunderbird, and then he cries out a single syllable of grief. He steps back into the pit and pulls out the Thunderbird. He holds it to his chest. "No witch took you, my little friend, my little brother."

Crete

Mickey and Ava stand at the rail of the ship, the evening lights of Rethymnon visible in the distance. They suspect it's illegal to dump funerary ashes over the rail of a ship, but still they make the sign of the cross and say some clumsy prayers remembered from childhood. They put their four hands on the surface of the vase.

"On the count of three?"

"Together, then. One, two. . . " And Ava pulls the vessel to herself, clutches it to her chest, wailing "Noooooo!" She holds it close, then hands it to her brother. He kisses the vase and sends it flying into the water.

"I thought we were going to scatter. . . "

"We tried. We couldn't." Lit by moonlight, the vase bobs on top of the water. Waves push it about, carry it away, out of sight, to be broken into pieces or to land whole on the beach.

Mickey, large, ample Mickey with his bearlike body, envelops Ava in a hug. After the weepy embrace, it's time for some Metaxa.

Big Springs

Jesse hunts through the liquor cabinet and finds some kind of Greek brandy. He lifts it to his mouth and drinks a big gulp straight from the bottle. When he's had enough, he goes back to the forbidden room and lets his eyes scan a few pages of the journal. Words leap off the page. Mouth. Neck. Hand. How she would like to braid his hair.

White women! He picks up the Metaxa bottle once again and lifts it to his mouth, takes another swallow. He reaches for one of her golden chains, puts it around his neck and looks in the mirror. Amused but unimpressed, he puts it back. He goes back to the journal and reads.

Crete

When they've drunk enough, Ava screws up her nerve and tells Mickey about the separation between her and Jesse.

"You gonna do it? Pick up some Greek sailor and go at it?"

"I don't know. I've been feeling jealous for so many years."

"I always thought you and Cochise were good together. What do I know? I wasn't exactly a success at the marriage thing."

Ava hadn't thought of her situation being at all like Mickey's until now. Both have lost their parents, and both believe their spouses have wandered. "And to top it off, my kids are off with Kaya, dancing at powwows all summer. What would you do in my shoes?"

"My smart kid sister is asking my advice?"

"Who'da thought."

"Y'know, I was always a fuck-up, but you were a hard-working kid, saving up for college, working your way through school. Then you married young. You never got to be a teenager. Yeah, you wanted to eat the hot chili beans, and you were a demonstrating peacenik, but somehow you were always the responsible one. Now you got a free pass. Very tempting." He pauses for effect then smiles. "Just don't let anybody call you a whore."

"You're an asshole."

"You got that right. Seriously, Avie, I've been watching you here.

How your eyes are takin' everything in, like you're here inhaling the experience. Y'know, Dad gave us a chance to learn somethin' here, maybe about what we want outta life. You're a smart cookie, Sis. You'll figure it out. Meanwhile, take it in, enjoy."

Ava is touched that her brother has spoken to her so clearly from the heart, with only the one lapse into snark. "I appreciate your confidence in me. Now, what are we gonna do when we get to this village?"

"Yeah, right. Spiros told me this story about a lady who wanted to visit her family's village on the Peloponnese. Her family had lost touch. Spiros could get her from the airport to a nearby town via the bus. From there, she'd have to take a taxi. She took the plane, the bus, and the taxi to the town and then asked the driver how she could find a family with the name Kostanos. The taxi driver laughed his head off and said, 'Everyone in this town is named Kostanos!'"

"Funny."

"Then, the taxi driver says, 'I'll find you a good one.'"

"A good Kostanos?"

"Yeah, so he drives her to a tall stone house with flowers spilling all over the place. The driver goes to the door and explains what's going on. The woman in the taxi can see he's gesticulating and making faces. The Greek Kostanos woman listens close and then she runs to the car. '*Ela, ela!*' she says and embraces the Greek-American Kostanos in a hug the size of the acropolis. The Greek Kostanos then scolds the taxi driver to hurry up already with the bags. This is a Kostanos from America! A long-awaited guest! The older Greek woman, she strokes the younger woman's face, points out her perfect Kostanos nose and Aunt Irini's famous hair."

Big Springs

Julie calls out for him. Something about a burned-out lightbulb. He's in pajamas. He doesn't wear them ordinarily, but with a guest in the house... He makes his way downstairs, gets a bulb out of the cabinet, drags out the stepstool and takes it to her room, once "the forbidden room." He sees that she's moved what is now her bed directly under the overhead fixture. He climbs up with just a nod of his head in her direction. He can't help noticing she is in her nightclothes, and he tries not to look. He twists the little knob until it is loosened free, then balances carefully as the insect-and-dust-filled glass globe lands in his hands. He takes it, intending to hand it down to Julie. This is the way he and Ava always did it. He'd take it down, she'd go and wash it out and bring it back as he switched out bulbs.

"Julie? Julie? Can you please wash this out in the kitchen sink and bring it back? I'm up here holding all the nuts and bolts." He looks down at her with a smile even he finds false.

"Ew," she says as she peers into the dusty globe with its corpses of moths and wasps from summers past. She holds it away from her body as she walks to the kitchen. He tries not to watch her, but he does think it's funny, the scrunched-up look on her face. The light of the kitchen is behind her, silhouetting her compact body inside the modest but translucent nightgown. He observes the athletic roundness of her backside, then averts his gaze. Turned away, as he puts in the fresh bulb, he sees her journal turned upside down on her nightstand, the pen lying beside it. He bites his lower lip and bends forward to receive the clean, damp globe from her hands. He replaces it, jumps off the bed, and practically runs to his room.

"'Night."

Thronos, Crete

Ava tries to keep the Kostanos story in mind as she and Mickey stand on a scrappy, weedy, barren hill facing a closed door, their bags at their feet. Hungry-looking goats tug at dry wisps of grass growing from under rocks but eye their shoes with interest. It must be 108 degrees. Tall Mickey wipes copious sweat off his brow. They should be knocking but hesitate. Maybe because they saw the sign. Scrawled, the letters red and uneven, as if written by a child, paint drippy, each letter at a different angle and saying only one word: ROOMS. In English. They hear the pastoral clanging of bells as the goats move closer, making a ha-ha-ha-ha! sound. Ava thinks of all the cartoons she's ever seen of people stranded on desert islands, missionaries ending up boiled in pots.

A lizard skitters across the front doorway. All Ava's enthusiasm for homey domatia has faded. She recalls a story about a pioneer family in Kansas who took in roomers only to murder them. The Bloody Benders. Fortunately, before her fantasies take her into more nightmare visions, Mickey speaks.

"This isn't even Dad's village," he says.

"Yeah, I know. Apparently, there are no inns in Petrochori but the guy who runs this place has our last name and might be a relative."

"That taxi sure left in a hurry." Mickey bravely raps his fist against the door. No one answers. He knocks again. The goats skitter away but otherwise, nothing. No answer.

Ava scans the outside of the abandoned-looking building, dust blowing in her face, a half-dead cactus at her feet when, off to the side, she notices a woman sitting in front of what might be a kitchen door, peeling potatoes. She's wearing the kind of housedress and flowery apron women in their old neighborhood might have worn in 1957. The woman lifts her eyes and smiles. Now that Ava has made eye contact, the woman gestures, as if to say with her hands: go in, go right on in. When Mickey tries the door, it creaks loudly but opens.

Shady and welcoming, the inside temperature is 30 degrees cooler. A large restaurant dining room with an even larger terrace faces out onto the mountains and valleys beyond. Ava and Mickey wander, enjoying the cool, letting their eyes get used to the dark. They find what might be a front desk with huge baskets of dried herbs on the counter. Maybe they've arrived at siesta time and everyone is napping. Mickey leans on the desk bell, hitting it repeatedly. He is anxious to know where the hell they are and what proprietor would leave them unattended.

A smiling, middle-aged man appears with his arms extended ahead of him as if he's about to take a familiar face into his hands and start kissing. Which is exactly what he does. First Ava's face, then Mickey's. Then, he says in beautifully accented half-Greek/half-English, "*Ela, Ela. Come, come, I have for you my best room.*" He lifts the suitcases as if they were as light as paper napkins.

They follow him up a wide marble staircase to what seems more like an apartment than a room, with a compact kitchen and two large beds. He flings open the shutters to a large balcony and points high on the horizon and says one word, "Psiloritis." A name they've heard all their lives. The name of the mountain their grandfather climbed in his youth. A name with magical powers. He indicates the location of the shower and toilet then bows out of the room, head inclined in a servile manner.

They guess that he is leaving them to wash up, unpack. They wonder how long they should take before it's all right to go downstairs. They take turns trying to figure out how to use the telephone shower, splattering water on the floor and straight into their faces. They change clothes. They put their feet up on beds and twitch. Then, surprisingly, they both fall asleep. When they awaken, they see the beginnings of sunset. They move the lounge chairs out onto the terrace and enjoy the view. Ava grabs her camera and catches sight of their host setting a table with a view of Psiloritis. They see him gently gesture. They recognize this sideways nod of the head from their father's gestural repertory that says, "When you're ready." They descend the highly polished stairs, their feet clacking in the hushed environment.

"*Ela, ela.* Come, come, sit."

His tone is melodic and inviting. "You must be hungry." On the table are small bowls filled with feta cheese, Kalamata olives, a basket of bread, a carafe of wine. He leaves them for a moment, then comes back with platters lining his arm: stuffed grape leaves and triangles of tiropita and spanakopita. Salads with tomatoes, sliced cucumbers, cheeses, and herbs. A deeply rich rice dish with artichokes and lemon. Marinated green beans. A tender goat stew. Platters covered with lamb chops. Pitchers of red wine and tumblers. Mickey and Ava eat ravenously, drink gratefully.

Their host joins them at the table. When they've had their fill, he addresses Mickey. "Michali, I see you have the handsome Papoutsakis nose. And Ava, the hair from your great-grandmother." All Greeks must read from the same handbook. "They must feed you well in America. You grow so tall. It is a good thing, yes? Your father, he is my cousin. Welcome to the Amari Valley. Homer, do you know him? He called it 'The Land of the Lotus Eaters.' Do you know this in America?"

At a small table in the shade, a pair of grizzled men have taken seats. Dimitri, for that is their cousin's name, brings the men feta, olives, and a bottle of clear liquid. He brings Mickey and Ava a similar bottle and small glasses.

"Ra-shee," he pronounces slowly. "From the house. Do you have it?"

Ava has heard of raki. She realizes that Dimitri is pronouncing both Papoutsakis and raki with a "ch" or "sh" sound where a "k" is written. Island dialect. Something stirs in her, like she's always been waiting to hear Greek pronounced like this. She also realizes that Dimitri's English, like her and Mickey's Greek, is totally in the present tense. They simply don't know how to speak in the past or past perfect. So, they will live in the present tense for now. She likes this idea, holds it to herself like a newborn.

A third man has joined the other two, this one with a huge moustache like those of the men in old depictions of Crete. He is wearing a black mesh kerchief on his head. The three men, fiftyish, hold up their glasses as if to toast them. After they've downed a few glasses, the men take instruments from the wall and start to play. Dimitri himself sings a song dedicated to the drink, raki. "Ra-shee. Ra-a-a-a-a-h-she-e-e-e." His voice climbs and lowers, quivers, lilts and commands, sounding so Middle Eastern it's as if he's calling them to a mosque. His hand invites them to join in.

They do. Dimitri is delighted. He brings out a platter of cookies, each with an almond pressed in the middle. Some fruit, a honeyed cake. More raki. And more raki.

They spend most of the evening listening to the village men playing instruments. Ava recognizes the lyra from the boy playing the sun down on Santorini. There is another, larger stringed instrument as well, with a deeper sound. Mickey and Ava do not know yet that these lyra and loutos are made by a local villager. For now, there is much singing and laughter. They've put aside grief and longing. They have been welcomed.

When they head toward the marbled stairs, Dimitri says, "Tonight you rest. Tomorrow, we go to Petrochori, my home village." He raises his eyebrows like someone with a delicious secret to share. "Holy Spirit Day," he says.

Big Springs

He hears her shriek just as he finishes tucking in his father, who lapses into snoring before Jesse even leaves the room. Jesse makes his way to the "forbidden room" and finds Julie holding her covers up to her chin and pointing at the ceiling. A good-sized spider is slowly making its way across the ceiling above the bed, pausing frequently. He considers what it might be like to be able to walk upside down like that, and then recalls: Ava whacked her own damn spiders. Nevertheless, he grabs a newspaper from the dresser top and climbs up on the bed. He aims but the spider skitters out of reach and then waits, inviting battle.

Julie laughs, then releases the blanket that had earlier shielded her—feeling safe now with a man in the room—then says, "Can you keep a secret?"

He says, "Does it have to do with spiders?"

"I was just thinking how it must be hard for you with Ava gone."

"I'll manage."

"A man has his needs."

"I think I'd better go."

"The spider. The spider!" Looking desperate and afraid, she kneels on the bed now, pointing up at the mobile arachnid.

He relocates to get a better angle on the spider.

"It'd be our little secret. No one would have to know."

"I'd know."

"She told me about your arrangement. That you're free to do what you want." She forks her fingers through her cropped blond hair and her nightgown falls off one shoulder. He hurriedly looks back at the spider. He can't help but remember every time he thought Julie attractive, every glimpse of her legs, her throat, every time he looked then turned away.

She continues, "It won't mean anything. We're both here. We'd be helping each other out really, avoiding other temptations. It'd just be an arrangement." She holds her hands up like she's saying she's not hiding anything, to trust her. He looks back up at the spider, holds himself steady and focused. She says, "Y'know, the very first time I saw you I was so jealous. I thought you were incredibly sexy." He teeters unsteadily but finds his body responding to these words said aloud.

"I'm flattered but. . . "

She whispers something that sounds like "I want to baste you." And then repeats, "I want to taste you." She says this in a quiet voice, like she is almost embarrassed to admit that she likes Brussels sprouts. She says this while he is standing on her bed and she is kneeling, her head at belt height. His body, unwilled by him, seems to become a divining rod. He looks away from her, tries to bite his tongue, tries to focus on the spider, the spider, the spider. When he feels her warm hands on his waistband, unsnapping the one single snap on his pants, he doesn't move, doesn't stop her. He pretends to concentrate on the spider. And then, indeed, he whacks the spider as hard as he can and his pajama pants fall comically to his knees.

He laughs, feeling ridiculous, knowing how Ava would laugh with him. They'd laugh about it for days, for years. But Julie doesn't. Instead, she starts on him with her mouth. He does not stop her. He does not say, "No," nor resist when she pulls him down to a prone position. He does not push her away when she, with expert hand and tongue and lips, brings him to a rather quick ejaculation. It's been weeks since he's had any kind of sex, after all. And then, she mops the center of his body with her short blond hair, rolls her head around his belly, his private parts, clearly enjoying making herself sticky.

Holy shit, he thinks.

He wants to get up. His goal is to pick up the dead spider, throw it away, flush it, but she says, "Unh-unh. My turn. Equal rights." She pulls her nightgown over her head, exposing her upturned white breasts. White skin. The whitest skin he's ever seen. The white of paste and refrigerators. The white of milk. And at that moment, she lowers her white right breast onto his mouth. He does not hesitate to open wide, to circle and partake. His hand does not hesitate to find the other breast to stroke and experience its texture while she moans and shudders. She gives him a gentle push and he willingly turns over, yields control to her completely. She is in charge. This is her show. She started it. She opens her legs to him, moves his head to just there, coaches him where to put thumb and tongue, adds yes, yes, yes, and faster, faster, harder, harder. At last she cries out when her body bucks. He reflects, as much as one can under these circumstances, about how, for the first time in his life, he's had sex without a single kiss or word of endearment. He considers the words: efficient and did the trick.

Jesse pulls on his pants, picks up the dead spider in a tissue, and says, "This must never happen again. Ever."

"Our little secret." She continues to lie on her side like an odalisque in a painting, naked except for a blood-red ribbon tied around her neck.

Petrochori, Crete

Dimitri drives his old red truck up the mountains with speed, shifting forcefully, willing the groaning truck up and up, climbing into herb-scented air. The roadsides become more colorful with wildflowers, the houses spread out, and then suddenly the road narrows into a village. The stone walls surrounding the town are whitewashed, the streets cobbled. As Dimitri leads them to the church, his face assumes a dignified composure. His shirt is starched and pressed and Ava is glad she's wearing her one and only skirt. Mickey turns and says, "Church?" He screws up his face and Ava knows he is remembering the three-hour, incense-laden Orthodox Church services of their childhood. But Dimitri has timed their arrival perfectly for lazy Westerners; they reach the church door just as it opens at the end of the service. Attendees spill out with smiles on their faces and green branches in their hands. A lovely Greek woman hands Ava her branch. Dimitri says it is a custom. "This is called 'philoxenia.' Love of the stranger, hospitality." Everyone is welcoming them with branches. The Greek priest, with his long beard and dark robes, hands each of them a piece of bread. Dimitri nods his head, indicating to go ahead and eat, eat. The home-baked bread tastes of honey.

A large group gathers around them, jostling each other, remarking on how tall they are. They walk together, this group, down the stone cobbles where the purple bougainvillea drops blossoms like giant drops of blood on the street. Dimitri tucks a sprig of rosemary behind his ear. The children run, tagging and teasing each other, watching the American faces, looking for resemblances. They could all be named Papoutsakis.

They enter what looks like a neighborhood store. Outside, a couple of commercial freezers advertise ice-cream confections with bright blue illustrations. Inside, advertising posters adorn the walls, mixed indiscriminately with Cretan folk art: a woolen hanging here, a chocolate-covered caramel bar there. The heady scent in the air, however, has nothing to do with ice cream, but instead conveys the deep pungent smell of lamb. Women wearing flower-printed aprons bustle around, carrying baskets lined with paper napkins and filled with bread. Tables line the length of the room, covered with paper tablecloths clipped on top of oilcloth. Carafes of wine join the bread on the tables.

Mickey and Ava seat themselves across from Dimitri. He now seems an old friend among all these strangers who might be long-lost cousins or newcomers who moved here last week. Mickey is intrigued, anxious, and too big for his chair. Dimitri finds this amusing and brings him a larger one. Mickey laughs his great, hearty laugh.

"Try this, the local wine," Dimitri says. "It is good, I think." And he is right.

Ava is struck by everyone's willingness to be happy, their eagerness to create a party, to put their concerns aside and sing together. She knows they must have woes: illnesses, bad business deals, breaches of trust, adulteries. And yet they come together. A young man of maybe 15 or 16 holds a lyra on his knee, the neck touching his narrow collarbone. His voice is haunting. Stronger, bigger men surround him, requesting this or that song with their booming baritones. One song tells about a hero who led an adventurous and bawdy life. Ava catches an occasional word or phrase: "Those eyes of hers," "And then she saw him," "I want it all." Glasses are raised, bottles emptied, meat gnawed off bones. Arms are slung around shoulders. Ava searches for her father's face among these singing men, and then she sees it; behind another huge Cretan moustache, on a man with rosy cheeks and a hearty laugh. This man has Papa's spirit as well as his face. Grief rises in her again, but she tries to shut it down by imagining this villager balancing a glass on his head. Yet no one does that here.

For hours, the villagers sing, telling tales in song. After they've consumed acres of food, Mickey asks how he can pay back the generosity. Dimitri says *"Tipota, tipota."* Nothing, nothing. They ask again and again. Finally, Dimitri shrugs his shoulders, "Maybe a little ice cream?" Mickey goes out to the bright blue freezers covered with depictions of cartoon characters eating giant ice-cream cones, peers inside. An aproned woman joins him, solicitous, wondering if she can help. He wants to buy the entire contents of the freezers. He knows how to say "All" in Greek and, like the heroes in the songs he's just heard, he says, *"Ta thelo ola."* I want it all. The men are delighted and find another song with that refrain. The lyra is struck with the bow, producing the sound of a past they never knew but now can't help but remember.

Big Springs

Jesse moves earth into giant mounds. He works hard to forget. His children are in Montana. His wife, on some fucking Greek island. He talked to her on the phone yesterday. She sounded happy and full of adventure. If only she were miserable, longing to come home, cutting her trip short to be here, with him. He shovels to forget. He buries to forget. The day is hot and sweat pours down his back. His jeans are soaked. He leans against the shovel to rest and notices Julie's car pull into the shade. He turns away, digs deeper and harder. A stream of icy water hits his back and he jumps before he sees her; Julie, wielding the hose and laughing hard. He throws a shovel of dirt toward her, causing her to drop the hose. He runs to pick it up. He sprays her, dampening her light summer shirt, making it stick to her unbound breasts. "Never again" goes out the window.

What is it that triggers this thrill of illicitness? Why, when we have everything, do we want what can threaten, even destroy? Like candy on a diet, a late-night smoke in the dark with a bummed cigarette after breaking the habit. The desire to throw a stranger against the wall and have at it. To be with someone who sees us not as a husband or father, wife or mother, but lover. To be seen with new appreciative eyes that find some value that has been ignored, taken for granted. To know we're still alive, breathing, and yes, attractive, admired.

Jesse tries to distract himself, to ignore the divining rod between his legs. He thinks of how he's recently felt angry, scared, worried. Old, flaccid, worn. A mirror image of his own father, aged and aging. He wanted a chance to grab again that something fleeting, to feel passion without obligation.

She said, "I want you," uttered in a desperate whisper. He wanted to hear that again and again, wanting to be wanted. He felt himself turning into a magnet, moving toward this voice that was saying "I want you," and he felt younger, stronger, more virile, straighter, taller, desired.

Meronas, Crete

Mickey decides to trek up Psiloritis instead of going to the town of Meronas to meet up with the tour group. "Don't worry, Miss," Dimitri reassures her, "I take good care of him."

Meronas is blessed with mountain spring water, which gushes out of fountains set in a stone wall. She pictures women coming here in old-time embroidered dresses to get pails full to take home. A young woman in jeans edges next to her with a large thermal container and some paper cups. She hands Ava a cupful, urging her to drink, then says in slightly accented English, "Drink. It is good." Cold. Fresh. Good.

The gray-bearded patriarch of the village gives the Chicagoans a tour of the Byzantine Church of the Panagia, set in the side of a steep hill. Inside, dark-hued icons and faded frescoes cover every surface. Saints face forward, hands lifted in blessing, the folds of their clothing accented with gold. Talking about a gilded Madonna and Child, the priest explains that the eyes of the Virgin Mary had been gouged out by invading Turks. The effect is chilling. What would make anyone believe a painting is so powerful one needed to scratch out its eyes?

After the tour, they head to a small terrace outside the church where locals appear, bearing trays of deep red cherries and small glasses of the local brandy. Ava thinks of Nikos Kazantzakis's travels around Crete and how people always fed him before asking his name. As she sips the mellow brandy, she listens to Sofia and the priest discuss ancient customs and obligations of host and guest, the rules of hospitality.

Some of the younger men in the group are having a cherry-pit-spitting contest off the side of the terrace. Laughing loudly and raucously, they are obviously feeling their brandy, spitting sloppily. Flushed with embarrassment, Ava excuses herself and chides the offenders like a stern mother. It is a violation of hospitality to have drunk too much of the liqueur, to spit out what has been given, to spew cherry seeds over the balcony. The gods will be angry.

Big Springs

Joseph I is spending two weeks visiting a friend in a Topeka retirement community, trying it out for himself. Jesse and Julie's vow of "never again" is repeated then ignored often while there are only the two of them in the house. She is infertile, she has told him, so at least that's not an issue. But he already knew that, didn't he, from hearing Ava talk about the disagreements between her and Trent about adoption, surrogacy.

Some days he comes in from work in his carving shed to find her lying naked on the buffalo throw, waiting. He vows every new day to stay away. More nights than he'd like to admit, he violates the promises he made to himself. On the evenings when he insists on "No," when he says he only wants to watch a little TV before bed, he leaves the room for his own bed, fantasizing about what he's just missed. Other nights he avoids the house completely, escapes to the distraction of high-stakes poker games. Even there, he seems to be on a losing streak.

Amari Valley, Crete

Dimitri and Mickey meet up with Ava several days later in a touristy town with lots of cheap souvenirs made in Asian countries. Mickey, suntanned and looking ten pounds thinner, calls out, "I did it!" Ava will be sad to see him leave the next day on a plane back to America. After years of being distant and unfamiliar siblings, they have come to enjoy each other's company.

Ava hugs each tour-group member farewell. They will depart and another group will come. The faces will be different, but the pattern will be the same. For some, a once-in-a-lifetime chance to search for their roots, their people. For most, a surprise at what Greece is really like: modern, bustling cities, some squalid, some smoggy; abundant natural beauty; too many tourists; turquoise and cobalt blue waters; a profusion of flowers; and the ever-welcoming, hospitable Greeks. And yes, pockets of the old life, where the sounds of hand-bowed and plucked instruments can be heard, and the music of voices unamplified, clear and human, singing about passion and error; hunger and war; the need for good will and companionship. For the next seven weeks, this will be her life.

Big Springs

Jesse awakens with his head splitting and a cane knocking against his temple. He looks up from the living room floor to see his father, stern and angry like an Old Testament god. "Wake up, boy, wake up! You seem to think being married to a white woman makes you less of an Indian. You seem to think being an Indian makes you less of a good husband. You're wrong on both counts. Son, you need a medicine man."

Jesse tries to pull himself together despite his throbbing head. He answers his father as if he's still a teenager, "None of your damn business."

"You're becoming a reprobate, son. And now you've gambled away your horses."

He starts to say, "I have not," but then recalls a late-night poker game, a horse trailer coming for Little Joe and Red China. He says what he said to the owner of the trailer, "I'll buy them back. I will. I promise you."

"That's what gamblers always say. Look at you. Your wife is gone, your children are gone, the land is neglected, and now even the horses are gone. Some other woman is living off your life and your father is hungry. Go, get a medicine man."

"I'm sorry, Dad. I'll get you something to eat. I've neglected you."

"Go to your old teacher at Haskell. He'll know what to do. It's time for a shaman. Time for a sweat. Let the heat bake the devils out of you."

Jesse knows his father means it's time for a sweat lodge, a rite of purification, a spiritual cleansing, time for a change. He stumbles around the kitchen, looking for food for his father. Empty beer cans and pizza boxes litter the countertop. Flies buzz around empty, encrusted plates. He opens the fridge and finds only a carryout bag labeled "JULIE" as if this were a college dorm and she had to lay claim to her food. In the freezer, he locates the last package of bison burgers.

The white van of Carlo Spinelli drives onto the gravel driveway. Jesse looks up from cutting his dad's hair and almost cuts his dad's ear off. On purpose. "Now what?"

"A friend in need," his father grumbles.

"You called him?"

"You've got to have somebody, son, who'll tell you the truth."

"And you chose a gender-confused, dope-smoking, ballet-dancing trinket importer to tell me the truth."

"He's your friend, not mine."

Carlo walks into the house without so much as a knock. The dog barely raises his head off the throw rug where he's taken up residence. Homer's gotten mighty skinny lately. Jesse makes a note to get more dog chow. Carlo joins in the conversation as if he's been in the room the whole time. "I think we should go right out to your shed and see what you've got I can take back to sell. I'll pay you in cash so you can buy the horses back."

"Well, maybe. . . "

"Well, maybe you've got some furniture for me to peddle back in the Bay or maybe your horses have been ground up for dog food. C'mon now, don't waste my time."

"A medicine man. The boy needs a medicine man."

"I'm with you, Joe One. I've lined everything up. Tomorrow night, we sweat. No drinking, no gambling, no sex until then."

"What am I, thirteen?"

Joseph I says, "Act like a grown man, we'll start treating you like one."

The sweat wasn't Jesse's idea and he plans to be present in body only, to get it over with. One isn't supposed to be coerced into this kind of thing. Okay, he does find it interesting that Bird Standingwater chose the very spot in the pasture where the bison cows always go to calve. But Jesse isn't sure why this whole thing couldn't have been done somewhere else, on some tribal grounds or the Haskell campus or some fucking dude ranch instead of here, in his own backyard. Then, when Bird goes right smack to that birthing spot, it's a bit eerie. And sure, when they're building the lodge, he can't help but go out and help. It's his land, so he knows where to find the right sapling branches to make the frame, and his house happens to have a lot of buffalo hides to throw over it. And he wouldn't want them to use the wrong kind of rocks. He's heard of white guys using the sort with air pockets that explode when used for the heated grandfather rocks, and he does not want to be injured like some weird New Ager, getting neutered by bits of hot stone exploding in the direction of his testicles. None of that. And he is all for having the sweat lodge so near the creek. They won't have far to haul the water and they can jump in for a cool dip afterwards. That part, at least, he can understand.

On the day of the sweat, Jesse is testy. He'd half-obeyed the rule about no alcohol the day before, thinking: Who made that one up? Firewater didn't come to the Indian until the Invaders arrived so the rule couldn't have been part of an ancient tradition. And anyway, most of the ceremony, if you could call it that, would be conducted in English, their only language in common.

Jesse did fast. He doesn't know why, but he did. And he's pleased that it's good and dark in the lodge. He won't have to look at the other men's naked butts. Every time he does a sweat, he wonders how much of the rigmarole is authentic. Scandinavians had sweats, too.

When Bird starts things off with a chant, Jesse keeps his lips sealed. He'll be in the lodge, but he sure won't participate. Bird starts invoking the four directions and the others chime in, uttering responses like, the North Wind from the North and the sun coming up in the East. When it's Jesse's turn and he's supposed to say something that invokes the West, he snidely says, "Seattle." He can almost see his father's eyes roll in the dark but Bird chuckles and says, "Good one," and lets it be. Bird is Meg Standingwater's brother and those Klallam have a good sense of humor. Jesse tries to sit as spitefully as he can. He is determined not to join in the chorus of song, and his feet certainly will not move in any dancing.

The first round is hot. Very hot. Jesse gasps for air when the flap is opened during the first break. His father would scowl at him, he knows, if he himself wasn't so drained from the heat. Jesse worries about his dad and brings a cup of cool water to Old Joe's lips. His father nods gratefully. During the second round, Jesse can hear the distinct ringing of a telephone. He tries to make a run for it, but Bird hollers him back. Jesse panics: No, don't tell me I'm having auditory hallucinations and we're only in round two!

At the start of the third round, he sees Bird in profile, leaning forward, holding himself perfectly and quietly still, poised in concentration, waiting. Then comes the dancing. Bird is from the Northwest Coast and that's where he got the regalia for Raven and Whale. Raven clacks his beak jaws and Whale seems to swallow him whole. Raven eats his way out and flaps his wings again. The drummers start singing. It sounds like a wail, like they are crying out in a language he doesn't recognize but thinks he can understand; that he can't possibly understand though he desperately wants to. Voices call and respond. The drumbeats resound. He believes he is hearing an ancient song about the pettiness of humans and the wrath of gods.

During the fourth and hottest round, Jesse takes a big draw on the pipe. A loud, wonderful beating makes him forget hunger, fatigue, his fears. Absorbed into the sound, in sympathy with the beat, he feels like he himself is reverberating, like he himself is a kind of drum. He can't help himself when his feet start to move. He always was a dancer. He still is. He is Whale. Then he is Raven. The rhythm of the drum shifts to single, unison beats. The tempo increases. The volume rises. Feathers whirl; sweat gleams; the dancer stomps. His arms extend outward and he cries out, cawing like a bird, "I was Whale. Now I am Raven. I have wings. I was meant to fly. I can fly!"

Crete

Ava wants to call home, which requires finding a little grocery store that has an international phone. She must wait among the buyers of bubble gum and tabloid papers, clutching a bag full of small change. While it rings, she pictures what things would look like at this time of day back in Kansas: the bison and horses grazing, the orange-red sun setting over prairie land, Jesse bronzed from working outside. The phone rings and rings. Not even the answering machine picks up. It's been weeks since she talked to anyone at home. She calls every week but rarely reaches anyone. She recites her phone number to the tune of "Twinkle, Twinkle, Little Star," the way she taught the kids to remember it. She lets it ring and ring. Finally, Julie picks it up. She sounds drowsy, interrupted.

"Oh, did I wake you? Sorry!"

"Ummmm, that's okay. Ava? Wow, it's been so long since I heard your voice."

"How are things? How's it going with Trent?"

"Kaput. We're battling out a divorce agreement. It was the right thing. Oh, Ava, Greece! Tell me everything!"

"I wish I could but I'm standing in a corner grocery story and there's a line of people behind me waiting. It's noisier than hell. But it's been magical, just magical."

"So great! Enjoy! And hey, your kids are back and they're fine and beautiful and terrific. Why didn't anybody tell me how much fun it is to have kids in the house!"

Ava pauses to take in the implications. "But that means Kaya is back, too." Ava expects Julie to speak in code and she does.

"Indeed. And—yes—as expected. Same old, same old."

"Of course."

"Jesse's asleep, actually. Want me to wake him?"

"No, don't bother. I'll call again at a more reasonable time so I can talk to the kids and Jess."

"Sure." Julie says the next line so quietly and conspiratorially, Ava struggles to hear. "Anyway, have fun with Rhett Butler."

"Oh, no, my drachmas are about to run out!"

"Don't worry about anything. Just enjoy! This is a once in a lifetime!"

Ava hangs up the phone and finds herself disappointed to hear that everything is going so well without her. Better off without me.

Heraklion, Crete

Ava stands in the Heraklion Airport, her heart beating wildly as she tries to distract herself by taking photos of the waiting room, focusing especially on the exit signs. She is afraid of herself, of what she might do. When the garbled sound of the flight announcement comes over the blatzy PA, she starts frantically pacing. She tries to put things in perspective. She's said goodbye to all the tour groups. Now she's moving on to the next stage of her work, assisting Professor Grenville in his research. Forget calling him "Raleigh." Professor Grenville, that's what she'll force herself to call him. She's made lists, appointments, and reservations for the next several days to make his research trip as efficient as possible.

It's easy to spot him: his head towering above the other passengers, suited out in white linen, looking every bit the colonialist. She thinks of all the arguments she's had with Jesse through the years over whether anthropology is, by its very nature, a neo-colonialist field. He always insisted "Yes," and let it be damned. She countered that maybe it was a good way for white people to learn about other cultures, that the subjects of the studies could be seen as teachers. But now, spying the tall, lanky, extremely pale, white white white Dr. Grenville, she begins to doubt her earlier position. If she can just keep repeating words like "imperialist" and "expansionist," it will help her keep her critical distance.

But then, oh then, as soon as he spots her in the crowd, his face breaks open like an egg into a gorgeous grin. He is eager and happy to see her. She forgets herself, the public nature of the surroundings, and she runs toward him, like a love-struck ingénue in a Hollywood romantic comedy. And he, the handsome, dashing and, yes, Rhett Butlerish-guy that he is, plays his part by sweeping her up and rubbing his face in her hair. She tells herself this is what old friends do.

Thronos, Crete

Out in the parking lot, they locate the rental Jeep she's arranged for them. It's August and hot, so he sheds his jacket and she wishes she had worn something lighter but yes, she was trying to be modest and stand-offish in a high neck and long sleeves. Imperialist, expansionist, colonialist that he is, he rolls up his sleeves. She blathers on about how they need to go to the town of Rethymnon because of all the craftsmen there and what appointments she's made for the next day. But first up the mountain to Thronos, to the now-familiar Paputsakis Inn.

Dimitri is expecting them and meets them at the door. He bows respectfully and says, "Welcome, Professor." After gifting them with some tasty mezedes and ouzo, he escorts them to their separate rooms on opposite ends of the inn. Good, Ava thinks. Propriety. Decorum. They will be in the public eye until they move to the small house on the far Eastern end of the island. Good, for there is work to be done. But oh, how she wants to be swept up again.

Raleigh suggests they call home. Emma Jane will want to know he's arrived safely, after all, and he happens to know that their two families are assembled at the Grenville house, officially welcoming Xenia and Sequoia home. Ava is eager to talk with her daughters. And calling from a hotel, while they have one, will be far easier than struggling with cranky phones in corner grocery stores. After a few false starts, Dimitri performs all the mechanics and they are connected. They take turns talking, or rather, shouting over the ever-present static.

Jesse says he did a healing sweat. Ava answers, "Yes, it's hot here, too." He asks her if she knew Julie was getting a divorce. She answers that she thinks it's cool Julie's getting her own horse. She tells him about her return to her father's village, the lyra playing and singing. He grasps that there's been a party and tells her he's glad she's having such a good time. When Xenia and Sequoia get on the phone, all giggly over their first trans-Atlantic phone call, they tell her she should expect something from the extra special mailman, meaning but not saying Raleigh. She says, "That's exciting!" but she knows that this is Greece and it can take months for letters to arrive. The conversations are all too brief and unfortunately nonsensical. Finally, everyone sends love and kisses. Afterward, when the phone has been replaced in its cradle, there is a feeling of emptiness and a lost opportunity to say more. Ava reminds herself how tremendous it was to speak with them. Her children. How she loves them.

※

Raleigh and Ava spend the daylight hours visiting the workshops of traditional artisans, evenings listening to local musicians. He quickly gains the trust of the locals, leaning in toward each speaker, maintaining just the right amount of social distance while listening intently. He makes everyone feel like the most important person in the world. His Greek is charmingly primitive, but he quickly picks up the local dialect. When they visit the shops of lyra makers, Ava is enthralled with the instrument-making process and takes numerous photos of tools and half-made instruments as Raleigh inquires about the chain of tradition, at whose feet the craft was learned.

He studies her face over a dinner of grilled lamb chops, lemon-soaked orzo, and a country salad of tomatoes and cucumbers. And there it is, that same absorption in her that he displayed with each craftsperson earlier in the day. He surprises her when he speaks, "We should do a book."

"A what?"

"A book. My text, your photographs. The perfect collaboration. There's plenty of material, an abundance of practitioners. I think we should do it."

Ava thinks of Raleigh's other well-thumbed works, which grace her own bookshelves, splendid tomes, heavily illustrated and written in a language both informative to the scholar and accessible to the ordinary reader. "Let's see how the pictures turn out before we decide. I don't want you to make a deal you might regret."

"I won't. Regret. I make a point of never regretting."

Petras, Crete

They've been driving for hours across the eastern half of Crete, along a highway lined with fifteen-foot hedges covered in thousands of enormous pink blossoms, when Ava announces she's hungry. When isn't she? The flowers, like so many gigantic peonies, remind her of colossal berries and therefore she has an appetite. They decide to stop for lunch along the lakeside of Agios Nicholaos. Ava looks around at the Germans in their sturdy hiking shoes and the English turning their faces up as if they've never seen the sun before and says, "So this is where they put the tourists!" There are numerous restaurants and cafes rimming the lake. Each seems to have an aggressive Greek out front hawking the specials in several languages. Ava hates places like this. She is about to suggest they find some little town where she can peek under the lids of pots simmering on the stove when Raleigh chooses one of the tourist-oriented eateries, following a waiter carrying an aggressively-colored menu encased in plastic with pictures and bad translations. Ava wrinkles up her nose.

Raleigh tells her, "I have no idea what's what in Greek food and here I can point to what I want. Let me order for us, this one time." This is all said with Southern grace and in such a plaintive tone that Ava nods and lets him take the lead. The salad has cabbage grated into it and the fish filet is dry, but Ava makes do. When they lift their glasses, Raleigh flirts a little, and she nods her head coyly in reply. She has an extra glass of wine. She has noticed that he does old-fashioned gentlemanly things like pulling out her chair and opening doors. She's enjoying being taken care of. It makes her feel young and desirable.

When they reach Sitia, they do as their Greek teacher Eleni advised and stop at a grocery store for directions. Besides, they need to provision the house. Milk, meat, vegetables, Band-aids, toilet paper, rice. Raleigh reaches for mysterious powders in boxes that look like they will make pudding. The shopkeeper totals up the bill in his head. He smiles, sizes them up, and tells them there's a place over the hills to the east where tonight there will be music and dancing. The real thing, like the Old Crete. He winks, a gesture that could mean it's not really like the Old Crete, or it could mean it is very much like the old days, just perfect for a couple like them. "It can only be reached by foot," so he draws a map on a grocery bag.

They drive the last mile to Petras, head up the road, and find the whitewashed house with a triangular terrace from which one can see olive groves, goats, mountains, and, most importantly, the sea. The turquoise and cobalt-blue sea. In the dwelling, there is a little sitting room, a kitchen, bath, and two small bedrooms, both with double beds. No television, no radio, no cassette player. Ava throws open the shutters in the room with a sea view, breathes in bliss, and calls out, "Dibs!" Raleigh has no choice but to continue to the other empty bedroom.

After they've had siestas and changed for the evening, they set out with their brown paper map in hand. As soon as they cross over the first hill, they breathe in the scent of hills covered with thyme, sage, and oregano. With every step, they brush against greenery that yields the heady scent of fresh herbs. Along the path, they encounter only one single individual, an ancient man bent under a burden of branches. He appears like a story-book character with his load of sticks. They nod and say, "*Kalyspera*"—"Good evening"—and the old man beckons them to sit on a large flat rock. He reaches into his small cloth sack and pulls out a single tangerine, which he peels and divides into sections, sharing the pieces with the two strangers on the road. Ava explains the Greek ethic of hospitality to Raleigh, who is madly signaling to her that he wants her to photograph this great-grandfather on the road. The old man obliges and smiles, revealing a paucity of teeth and a big heart. Just to make sure they are on the right path, Raleigh mentions the name of the taverna where they are headed. The old man nods and points. "*Kalynichta*"—"Good night"—he says, recalling his own youth.

The taverna is built into the side of a mountain, part cave and part man-made structure. Rows of sheep's heads sit on shelves behind the bar, ready-roasted for eating. Usually one to try any new food, Ava declines this delicacy but delights in recording the sight in photographs. Instead, Ava and Raleigh eat grilled lamb, a Greek country salad, French fries cooked in lamb fat. Ava licks her fingers, pausing, dwelling on the simple pleasure of eating, enjoying the taste of grease on fingers. Maybe even better than bacon.

A small band of musicians take their places and start playing louto and lyra. Electric louto and lyra. Accompanied by drum. So, this is why the grocery man winked, this unexpected electrification out here in this ancient cave. Ava tries to think positively: ancient instruments brought into the present, adapted to current tastes. As her husband once said: Adapt or die.

Young male dancers enter, snaking their way through the taverna, wearing black boots, pants and vests, white shirts. One wears a dagger against his chest. Ava finds this unbelievably alluring, though she'd never admit it back home. The men begin to dance. There is no flailing about, no false moves, no "self-expression." The young men are perfectly poised, dancing in studied unison, in perfect rhythm, yet clearly holding back: passion under restraint.

Raleigh tips the musicians.

In the next piece, the dancers pass a white scarf with tatted edges down the row. The young men take turns setting the pace and step. No one seems to break a sweat. They are beautiful. Ava can look at them openly, admiringly, watching their legs, their shoulders, their faces, their dark hair, their noble noses, their sculpted ears to her heart's content. Here they are, near the top of a mountain, in a cave, music throbbing around them. Ava believes in every earth goddess there ever was. She is ready to copulate in the fields to ensure a great harvest.

She hasn't had the slightest desire for such young men since she was twenty herself. Until now. Watching these boys, desiring them, is sanctioned girl porn. When the dancers finally finish their athletic and passionate display, Ava is ready to take each one of them in turn to her bed. She thinks, to the extent she is capable of thought, that this dancing has probably been responsible for propagating the species for thousands of years. She is so primed that when Raleigh catches her eye, it's as if a bolt of lightning were passing through her. He leans over to whisper in her ear, "I want you." She hears. She pretends not to hear. She hears.

246

With only the gleam of the moon to light their path, it takes a while for their eyes to become accustomed to walking in the dark. When they reach a stream, Ava takes off her sandals and her feet feel the cold of the stones. Raleigh reaches his hand across and the sudden warmth is inviting. She doesn't wait until they reach the other side. There, on the precarious rocks, she turns to him, looks up at him, for he is tall, a tree where there are none. There is asking in her eyes and he's been waiting for such a cue. He leans his head forward to hers. They stand there in a kiss, on the wet shaky rocks, embarrassed, anxious, glad, knowing what will happen if one of them doesn't back down, but mostly feeling an incredible tug, a magnetism. It's been so long since she's been touched, her body responds with a quiver. He smiles, runs his hands up and down her arms, her back, and then he takes a step, almost tumbles into the water, finds his balance, looks around. Is anyone watching? Does anybody care?

He continues to hold her hand as they walk through the herb-covered fields. They might look, from a distance, like a teenaged couple. She in her sundress, barefoot and carrying her sandals; he, tall and lean. They both want to run but, influenced by the dancers and carrying the knowledge of years, they prolong the anticipation, imagine what's to come, linger.

When they reach the little house, Raleigh takes hold of her shoulders and says, "I've waited seven years for you." And then there is the second kiss, the private kiss, the deep longing kiss, the hurry of seeking hands. The warmth of touch, another jolt of lightning through her body. His body feels light to her, ethereal in her arms, almost insubstantial, so she is surprised when she can feel his moustache awakening parts of her. Ridiculous phrases go through her mind: Feather duster. Cookie duster. He is dusting her with the lightest touch. She tells herself to stay in the moment, enjoy what is happening, for it may not happen twice. She tells herself that her desire, if satisfied, will end. She will get it out of her system, this long-awaited collision of bodies. No one will know. As if bewitched, she lets go of reason. All thought is obliterated and there is only sensation. She can barely hear him repeat, "I've waited seven years for you," and she releases.

When they've exhausted themselves, they go up on the flat roof of the little house on the side of the hill. They look up at the sky's spray of stars.

Big Springs

It's almost time for the school year to begin. Julie takes the girls shopping, indulging them in the latest preteen styles, takes them to have their hair permed, whispers to them behind her hand about which boys are cute, helps them repaint their room a moody deep purple. When it's time to register for school, she puts on her most matronly clothes and drives them there. She shakes hands with their teachers.

Petras, Crete

The Petras villagers gather on Sunday to make raki, bake potatoes, and sing. Ava plants herself, elbows on the ground, to get a good shot of the still. A still! The grapes have been pressed for wine and the mast put into this old blackened contraption. The same fire that roasts the potatoes heats and evaporates the liquid. Spirals of coils condense the strong liquor into raki, the stuff her cousin in Thronos sang about. Ava shoots the still from every possible angle.

Between glasses of raki, the villagers sing from a romantic epic called *Erotokritos*. Ava struggles to understand the history they tell. She translates for Raleigh.

"They're saying it's from Vitsentzos Kornaros, who lived in the 1500s."

"Around the time of Shakespeare, then."

"They say he was born right here."

"In Sitia? In Petras?"

"In this house we are standing in front of."

Raleigh surveys the house, which is crumbling and dark. "Shouldn't someone at least put up a plaque?"

She thinks for a second. "I think the singing is the plaque."

The next day, in an antique bookstore, they find a venerable copy of a text by Kornaros. The cover depicts a mermaid, and Ava loves mermaids, so Raleigh reaches into his money belt and buys it for her. She vows to read every word, no matter if it takes the rest of her life to translate. She finds a cassette tape of someone singing from the *Erotokritos* and snatches it up.

They visit a bakery that specializes in elaborately woven Cretan wedding breads. After interviewing the baker, Raleigh says he'd like to buy one. Ava feels dread in the pit of her stomach. She tells herself it's because she was never properly, legally married, but who is she kidding? She tells Raleigh the wedding bread will never last and she'll take a picture instead. Click.

The heat of the day is relieved in the late afternoon by the meltemi wind. Shopkeepers urge them to hurry home so that their purchases are not ruined. Ava explains the nature of the funneling, powerful winds. Raleigh says, "It's not going to rain, though."

"A Northern wind, usually dry. But it is said to make people crazy."

"I'd like to see you crazy."

They head to the roof with a bottle of wine while the breeze is still light. Ava lounges, relaxed, waiting for the wind to bring her insanity to the fore. Unexpectedly, rain starts to fall, and when it does, they both open their mouths to the sky and drink it down. They put out bowls and pots to collect every bit of rainwater they can and when it pours, they dance in the rain, their clothes soaked through and through, before they walk back into the little house to have another tumble together.

Raleigh turns to her with serious intent in his eyes. "I waited for you for seven years. We've loved each other for seven years." Ava feels swoony hearing the declaration, but she also stiffens, anticipating what might come next. "Ava, we work so well together. We're a great team, you and me. I think we could make a go of it."

She bites her tongue but thinks about his words. **We could make a go of it.** His appreciation of her work has restored her faith in its worth, and his attentions have made her feel exceedingly attractive. She thinks of being married to a renowned college professor, living in town, the continued collaboration. She pictures herself in Emma Jane's shoes, making ham biscuits, having a refrigerator the size of a typewriter and children who know no rule. She tries to imagine her own children living in the tall brick house, painting Raleigh's fingernails. As much as she's enjoyed this diversion, this affair, this whatever-it-was, she foresees little joy in its continuation. She already thinks of it as a sweet memory, in the past tense.

When she tells him the truth, that this was wonderful but not a permanent situation, he retreats to the second bedroom. The sound of the torrential rain is almost loud enough to cover the sound of his fists pounding on the wall.

The next morning Raleigh is packed by sunrise, if one can call it a sunrise in a drenching downpour. He pulls out a wad of cash and hands it to her.

She remembers what her brother told her, "I'm not a whore."

"Omigod. It has nothing to do with that. I'm leaving. I'm the sinner. I'm the bad guy. I'm abandoning you here. You'll need cash for food, a taxi. This is for your services."

She slaps his face.

"Your photographic services. Didn't you hear me when I said I love you? For me, this was love. Is love. I've loved you since the moment I laid eyes on you. I did everything I could to make us 'couple friends' so I could be around you. Don't you know what a treasure you are?"

"And now you're leaving."

"You've made it very clear that it's hopeless. If you don't love me by now, I'll have to get over you."

"Where are you going?"

"Cyprus. I'll just go there earlier. I'll work on my study as planned, but now I'll be back home in time for Thanksgiving."

"I've always thought of you as a friend. A very attractive friend. I have sometimes, no, make that often, thought about what it would be like to be with you. But I have a family. You have a wife."

"She's waiting for me to leave her. She told me herself that I would leave her for you."

"She told me, too. I can't do it."

Raleigh searches in the outside pocket of his bag and pulls out a large manila envelope addressed to her with AVA written boldly and with arrows pointing to the word MOM. He says, "Messages from your girls." He pauses, then goes on, "Forgive me for waiting so long to give this to you. I thought if I held it back. . . . I was selfish."

Holding the envelope to her chest in a burst of new anger, Ava turns and walks into her own room. Later, she will find his wad of money stuffed in her backpack.

Once the sound of the car is out of earshot and she's sure he's not coming back, she opens the envelope and finds two smaller ones inside. With the sound of the rain pounding over her head, Ava, still standing, tears open the smaller envelopes and reads.

The Sequoiad

Dear Mommy,

I hope you are having a great time in Greece with Uncle Mickey and whatever Greek relatives you find over there. I am fine.

Remember how when I was little I would lose a tooth and then I would keep putting my tongue where the tooth used to be? You'd tell me not to cuz my tongue would get sore and then I'd complain and not be able to eat spicy food and stuff? But I would keep doing it? That's kinda how it is with you not here. I keep wanting to tell you stuff and you're not here anymore. It wasn't so bad when we were on the road with Auntie Kaya (although I was crazy homesick, I forgot to tell you). But now that we're home, I run to your room to tell you about this goofy joke I heard or ask about homework or can I dye my hair pink? Can I? Please! But you're not here. And remember how I'd say that I kind of liked the taste of my own blood when I lost a tooth and everybody would say "Gross" and "Yuck"??? Well, missing you is kind of like bleeding, too, and sometimes it feels good like I'm all depressed and enjoying feeling sad and I kind of like it and sometimes it just kind of hurts.

I told you that missy stuff and I'm sorry. I'm supposed to be cheerful in this letter, Auntie Emma Jane said.

Dad's made this mound and planted it over with flowers. It's like a memory thing for Grandpa Greek. Xenie and I said the design should be grandpa's head balancing a glass on top. But you know how Dad is, he had to make it like abstract or something. He made a sketch something like this —

Maybe like the very top of grandpa's head and the very bottom of the glass? If you were up in an airplane, I think it would look kind of like lopsided wings. Xenie thinks it's a lot like Dad's boat logo looking in a crazy mirror.

I ate an entire bag of Oreo cookies yesterday.

Love and kisses,

Sequoia.

p.s. Thanks for the postcards. I like the one of the cat lying around sunning on those ancient columns. Grandpa Joe read the postmark and said it took seven weeks to get here. He also said the columns were Corinthian, the fanciest kind.

Love,

Sequins (My new name, do you like it?)

The Xeniad

Hey, Mom,

I hope you and Dr. Grenville are getting lots of work done.

Guess what, I have a boyfriend. I had my first kiss, so I guess I got that out of the way. Under the grandstand. He kept hitting his head on the underside of the aluminum step but otherwise it was okay. His name is Tommy. I call him Tommy the Tomahawk. We make lots of Indian jokes. We're allowed, both being Indian. We kept running into each other since his family was basically on the same powwow tour as us. We'd say, "Bye" and sniffle and a few days later, "It's you again! Hi!" He's more purebred than me. Ojibwe from Minnesota where it snows even more than in Kansas. Tommy says his grandmother doesn't have an indoor toilet. Now that I don't see him anymore (sniffle), we write every day.

Remember Sheila, our old bison cow? The last of the herd? Y'know how she doesn't do much, just stands around on the prairie and you have to practically spoon feed her, she's so old? Well, Dad put me on her back, wearing your old moose-hide dress and carrying my archery stuff. Then, I stood up, right on her back. Dad about keeled over. I posed with my bow and arrow standing on Sheila's back and Dad took a picture with one of your old cameras. I put the picture in here. I hope you like it. I wore your old dress just for you and for nostalgia purposes. Great Grandma Makah made a new dancing dress for me. It's black velvet with rows of cowrie shells hanging all over it, making designs. I learned a few Makah dances when we were out there. Boy, it's far away! Dogs and horses just kinda roam around the town.

Great Grandma Makah took us to this museum with old Makah stuff carved out of whale bone and cedar, kind of like your wedding ring. She told me that Daddy helped dig that old stuff out of the mud. She said he's a furniture carver because it's in his blood, whatever that means.

Daddy's starting up the herd again. He got about a dozen baby bison. Big Sheila was mad for a few days and pushed them away and then we came home one night and found her lying down with the babies cuddled up to her, as if they were her own little piglet litter. Just wanted you to know.

Aunt Julie has settled in. She's pretty cool. She buys me whatever I want, even black lipstick and short short skirts. I hate my new school. The English teacher knows less than Grandpa Joe. I turned in my usual "What I Did During Summer Vacation" essay. I wrote about our powwow competitions and called it "The Xeniad." He didn't even get it. Maybe someday Dad will write a Jessiad and you'll write an Aviad. I really really do want to know what you did on your summer vacation.

Sincerely, (did you know that means "without wax" in Latin?)
Xenia

After reading the letters ten times, Ava climbs into bed and falls asleep, unfed and untoothbrushed, as if she were drugged, to the sound of rain beating on the roof.

The sound of tiny scurrying feet wakens her. She looks down from the bed where she slept and wept to see a rat scuttling across the floor. Two more follow. Then, another. Ava stands up on the bed and yelps a helpless cry before realizing there is no one to hear her. Jesse and the girls are back home, where she left them, thousands of miles away. Raleigh— may he throw himself to the crows—stormed out of the little Greek island house hours ago. Ava summons courage, climbs down, and races for a broom. When she opens the outside door, a wave of rainwater rushes in. Sweeping madly at the accumulating flood, she shoos the tumble of rodents back into the wet. Once outside, she jabs with the broom handle, trying to force open a drain to the road below. She fails. Ava Paputsakis shakes her fist at the pouring sky.

A prolonged screeching tears the air. A great moaning. Ava wants to know what it means. She's afraid to find out what it means. She needs to know what it means. Dropping the broom and grabbing her camera, Ava climbs onto the building's flat roof. What used to be a trickle of a picturesque mountain stream is now a cascade carrying uprooted olive trees and groaning sheep, infant goats and tangled grape vines. She photographs quickly, then wades back inside, hurrying to make a stack of furniture. On top of the pyramid, she puts her beloved camera, her backpack, her suitcase, hoping to keep them above water.

The skies bleed a year's worth of rain in 36 hours. The worst flood in Crete's history. Ava curses every decision she's made that brought her to this place, this time. Agreeing to a trial separation from Jesse. Letting another woman take her young daughters while she followed adventure, camera in hand. Diving into the excitement of an affair. What was she thinking? But didn't she also come to Greece to dispatch her father's ashes into the Aegean? To walk the Cretan mountains of her ancestors? To find long-lost cousins who would teach her to laugh and sing in Greek? The torrent continues. She cannot spend time on regret.

Ava has little food and no vehicle. Raleigh—damn his evil eyes—fled with the rental car. The town of Sitia, the only place to purchase supplies, is more than a mile away.

There is no choice but to go on foot. Ava yanks her backpack off the pile and empties its contents into the suitcase, which she replaces on top of the mound. Soaked to the skin, she takes off down the steep road. Reaching the beach where, only a few days ago, she was basking contentedly on a towel in the sun, she now shivers at the sight of accumulating detritus—olive-oil cans, wine bottles, geraniums, roof tiles—the remnants of civilization. The only bridge to Sitia, where the mountain stream meets the sea, is washed out. Ava ventures out onto what is left of a supporting beam, still holding out the hope that, with some nimble stepping, she can make her way across to town. She surveys the delta of uprooted olive trees, considers trying to make her way across by hopping from log to log, then realizes the senselessness of such a plan.

She turns in defeat back toward the small house, but a loud creak and splitting of wood send her falling. She perceives herself descending as if in slow motion. Her chin glances on something startlingly hard and she detects a sharp object in her mouth, along with the heat of blood. She spits out what she knows to be the better part of a tooth.

A sudden wall of water rushes at her from behind and she is launched in a downward spiral toward the depths of the sea. As her head meets rock, she drinks in the word "concuss." Her body is propelled farther, bumping into planks and pottery as if she herself were an inanimate twig being carried away.

Suddenly all is still. She thinks for a second that she has gone blind but realizes her eyes are tightly shut. She opens them to silvery fish fluttering by, golden sand beneath her feet. Kelp undulates around her—tall, gray green, and ghostly—like seaweedy wraiths. She believes she may have fallen into the realm of the dead.

She sees him then, her father walking toward her along the floor of the sea, oblivious to the lichen on his hair and the octopus riding his shoulder. Of course he would reside here. They'd thrown his ashes into the sea and here he is, restored. She now wonders why she ever thought heaven should be up at all. Why not in the vast depths of the sea?

Her father waves: "Go back. Go back to life, Ava." Seeing him, she chokes up, then notices another materializing beside him, someone she has not seen for decades. Her mother, the young woman she was when she died, there at last to comfort and console, to offer motherly advice and embrace.

Ava reaches to envelop this woman she lost so long ago, but when she extends her arms, her mother warns, "No, you mustn't. If we touch, it will be the end of you. Don't waste your life in weeping and sorrow. Go, Ava, hold onto life."

Her parents start dissolving before her eyes. Ava calls out, "Wait! I have so much to ask you! I need your help! I need you!"

"You'll know what to do," her mother whispers.

"Now, go," the fading image of her father says. "While you can. Go! Grab onto life!"

Despite the compelling desire to clutch on to these, her much-needed parents, to remain in this watery paradise with them, she bends her knees deeply and pushes off with all her might, piloting herself toward a shadow floating on the surface.

***

The next morning, Ava Odesza Paputsakis wakes at dawn, sunshine blasting her eyes. She finds herself lying on a wide board washed up on a beach, being baked by the sun. She is amused to find herself stretched out on what looks like a giant pizza paddle and erupts in a single syllable of laughter. She studies the horizon. Red sky in the morning; sailors, take warning. Thankfully, the heavens are not red but a benevolent blue. She crawls off the board and yawns with ferocity as she stands, only to realize how battered and hungry she is. Carelessly, she steps on the tail of a flailing fish. Maybe, just maybe, the gods are smiling today.

Ava never was a Girl Scout. She hasn't the slightest idea how to make a fire when the world is wet. But she does recognize the empty ache in her belly and the sight of a fish near death's door. She dispatches the fish with a blow to its head and searches for a sharp shell with which to remove its skin and bones. The bits of raw fish she shovels into her mouth seem to melt, welcome and gratifying. Ava surveys the landscape. She recognizes the skyline of Sitia, now far out of reach.

Up. There is no choice but up if she is to find the little house and her meager possessions. Along the way, she takes in her gouged-out surroundings. A sand dune has been excavated bringing to light ancient walls. The crumbling stucco on a cottage where, just a week ago, she was drinking raki with singing villagers, has been washed away to reveal a long-buried Venetian villa. Archaic pieces of pottery, amphora handles, and jug spouts protrude out of what had been a road. The present, excavated, reveals the past.

Ava almost drops to her knees to kiss the flagstone patio of the little vacation house which still stands, though ever more precariously, on the edge of the mountain. Ava knows that, with their olive trees and goats drowned, the villagers' lives are ruined. She counts herself lucky to be alive. Guiltily lucky, for, unlike the people of Petras, she might get away.

Ava pulls her camera from the top of the pyramid and shoots a few photos of the devastated plain below, the unearthed walls of Bronze Age houses, the ravaged village. People lived here once. Early people, ancient people, herself. The skies darken again. She starts to pack. Only the necessities will go into her knapsack, which still clings, wet and empty, to her back. Passport, plane ticket, the letters from her daughters, film, journal, a few changes of underwear. The rest—sundresses, novels, swimsuits—stays behind with an uncertain future.

Standing in ankle-deep water, Ava consumes a chunk of feta and half a bottle of wine, the remnants of a sunlit picnic. She packs the two remaining tins of anchovies and a tangerine in her backpack, along with a few uneaten crackers. She shovels spoonsful of pudding mix directly into her mouth and washes it down with water from one of the pots on the patio. She pours rainwater into the empty wine bottle and does her best to force the cork in. In a vain attempt to wash the salt off her body, she empties another jug of fresh water over her head. Ava changes her clothes and adjusts the strap on her backpack.

She knows she must go up higher for, in Greece, isn't there always a chapel near the top? Inland and up again. Her limbs swollen and torn, she climbs throughout the day, stopping to harvest a floating jar of artichokes, to forage for mountain greens, to photograph the changing terrain. Up she climbs, singing, crying out, pounding her fists on rocks. Bone weary, she spots the wide, whitewashed walls and blue-domed chapel of what she recognizes as a monastery. Like a religious pilgrim of old, she knocks at the gate. Soon a robed monk welcomes her to St. Elias. Recognizing that she is injured, he hurries her into a courtyard, indicating a bench where she is to wait.

The garden seems little affected by the heavy rains. The leaves of the citrus trees, though torn, seem exceptionally green. The oranges appear as minor suns to Ava's tired eyes. She thinks about photographing them, but instead she tears out a page of her journal and draws a quick sketch of the St. Elias courtyard. She's heard it said that St. Elias is a recast version of the ancient god Helios who pulled the sun across the sky each day with his fiery chariot. Light peeks out from behind the clouds.

Brother Raphael greets her with blessings, studies her torn chin, her swollen forehead, her battered limbs. Ava searches her brain for the Greek word for "flood" but manages only to say "rain." He nods and scurries off for salves and gauze, needle and thread. He says something she barely understands about his medical background, then hands her a hefty glass of brandy. Smiling, he gives her the bottoms-up signal and Ava downs the golden liquid.

With clear expertise, he washes her wounds with an herb-scented liquid that has a welcome numbing affect. He burns the end of a needle in the flame of a candle, as her mother used to do, to sterilize. He sews. Time and climbing have caused swelling, but he manages to mend the gash on her chin and the cut on her lip. Raphael reaches into his box of ointments, finding what he needs to soothe and heal.

When he is done, he pours her another tumbler of the monastery's brandy and leads her to one of the small, unadorned guest rooms of the monastery. "Rest, rest," he tells her.

Awakened by the sound of chanting, she smells baking eggplant and melting cheeses. Not sure where to go, cautious not to interrupt the monks or invade a cloistered area, Ava returns to the central garden and waits.

Soon, she is greeted by an elderly stooped Brother Sebastianos, who takes her to a guest dining room.

Olives, grapes, and casseroles of vegetables await her along with just-baked bread, a carafe of wine, and a bowl of giant oranges. She longs to gorge herself but her torn lip and recently repaired chin keep her from eating but the smallest bites. When she shrugs her shoulders, Brother Sebastianos nods and cuts the sweet baklava into tiny bits. He tries to communicate through gestures and buzzing sounds how the honey was harvested from monks' own bees. When she tries to ask him what day it is, she is hushed and told she must sleep. Given more of the golden brandy, she does.

Ava is so happy to be cared for, she could stay forever in this safe place with its glorious potions and baked dishes, but in the morning, with a plan in mind, she asks for a tour of the chapel. An ethereal-looking, young Brother Philippos leads her to an oratory elaborate with gold and candles, where he tells her the stories of the icons in an amalgam of halting English and fluid Greek. St. Katherine with her wheel. Michael the Archangel with his sword. St. Elias surrounded by a ring of flames. Most of the gilded art dates back over a thousand years, but occasionally an original Byzantine piece has been replaced with a poor cardboard copy. Philippos is pointing to one such imposter now; he looks to be in considerable ecstasy as he ponders this cardboard Blessed Virgin. It matters not to him whether the icon is an historic piece of art or a mass-produced cereal box rendition, he is rapturous in the contemplation of holiness. Ava's eyes well up, longing for such bliss.

Ava asks, in what she hopes is a humble voice, to see a calendar. She has a homeward plane to catch. She has lost track of time. Brother Philippos produces an ecclesiastical handbook resplendent with illuminated holy days. He glows at the sight of such opportunities for liturgy and adoration. Ava asks whose feast day they are celebrating this day and he gently indicates a saint whose name she does not recognize and cannot pronounce. She reads the date, puts her hands together in a prayerful pose, and bows her head.

In the cloister garden, Brother Raphael awaits her with his box of liniments and a cup of dittany tea. After receiving his ministrations, she tells him, in carefully rehearsed Greek, that she must find a way to get to Heraklion. Her plane leaves tomorrow night for America, for home. At first, he insists that she needs more rest; he implores her to stay. When she is adamant, he admits that there is a man who minds the windmill who might be willing to drive a car for hire. Like a sudden cloudburst, a longing to embrace her children overtakes her and, even though she long ago gave up the notion of sin, her shoulders shudder like a penitent's and tears appear on her cheeks. Brother Raphael brings her a basin and linen cloth, then turns respectfully away.

When she hears the monks chanting at dawn, Ava rises promptly, checks the Greek spelling of the thank you note she wrote the previous night, and scribbles her initials at the bottom of her drawing of the St. Elias garden. Ava hurries out the gate with the feeling that she is leaving heaven. Her eyes scan the horizon and there, on the next crest, she spots the windmill, its sails plowing the red-streaked sky. She estimates it will take her at least an hour to trek there. Ava grabs one of the walking sticks left at the gate for passing travelers. Later, she will find in her backpack a bundle filled with fig pastries and hearty bread, aged cheeses and bright oranges. A small jar of liniment, a flask of brandy. A strand of worry beads.

She starts walking toward the timeworn windmill. For now, the rain has let up.

PART SIX

Big Springs

Jesse is doing what he needs to do, what he planned to do, so he wonders why he is shaking. He paces again around the outside of the stone building. For the 12th time, he reads the plaque about how the structure was erected by the WPA, then he reads it again, his eyes burning and blurring. He's made lists of pros and cons, column A and column B. He's watched the woolly worms and the flight of birds. He's thought of Raven. This is where it's led him. He straightens up and walks in.

It is an open and airy building, empty except for three parked two-seater planes. Jesse remembers every argument he's had with Ava about her flying and his unwillingness to even get near an airplane. Now, looking at the tall, lanky pilot, he begins to worry again. He tells himself that this worry will keep him safe. He crosses his fingers and makes promises to Jesus, the Great Spirit, and Buddha. Abruptly, he turns toward the exit.

He is almost ready to run when the other man sees him and moves toward him with a big grin on his face and his hand extended for a handshake, "I'm so glad you called."

Crete

By noon, after losing her way twice, Ava reaches the landmark stone windmill and knocks. A middle-aged woman welcomes her into the single-room house with a glass of water and a plate of feta and olives. Ava tells her she is looking to hire a ride to Heraklion. The woman shakes her head but nonetheless fetches her husband. The man says that he is sorry to tell her, but Heraklion has suffered a flood, there are terrible winds. All flights have been cancelled. The power and telephone lines are down. The news seems a confirmation of Jesse's insistence that she not fly home. She will not fly home.

After chewing a Kalamata olive very slowly to disguise her worry, Ava asks if there are any other means of leaving the island, of going north. Oh, yes. The ferry. The big, old-fashioned one. Nothing stops it. She must take the one that goes to Sifnos. It's unclear whether this is an important instruction if Ava wants to leave Crete or if this is a recommendation for travelers, like "You must see the Grand Canyon!" but Ava nods and pulls out a wad of drachmas. The husband modestly chooses a few bills and offers her a bon-voyage glass of wine.

The design of the vessel is low and wide, a great layer cake of a boat, Art Deco that has seen better days, redolent of diesel. Dulled and aged stainless steel wraps the center's giant working parts. She exhales. The old boat makes her feel safe.

Passengers move toward the outdoor deck to wave goodbye, to watch the shore recede as houses, tavernas, and church towers grow smaller and retreat. Seeing the sun go down over Crete, Ava knows she couldn't have a better view from the priciest cruise ship. She recalls another ferry and Jesse reciting Millay:

We were very tired, we were very merry
We had gone back and forth all night on the ferry

Sifnos

She falls instantly in love with the place. White Cycladic houses shaped like giant dice surround an inlet ringed with fish tavernas. Ravenous, Ava sits down at a table. She kicks off her sandals and moves her toes around in the sand while she consumes grilled red mullet and Greek salad. She pours herself the local wine served in a deep blue ceramic pitcher. The waiter is proud to inform her that Sifnos is a potters' island where she can buy a decanter like this one to take home. As much as she'd love to shop, she'll be taking the next ferry to Athens, thank you very much. He laughs, "The next ferry, she won't come to Sifnos for three days. You are, what they say, 'stuck with us.'"

Three days! She locates a phone-call store. She doesn't have many coins, so it'll have to be quick. Once the ringing starts, Ava realizes that it's 2 a.m. back home and she'll undoubtedly be waking someone. The phone clicks and Sequoia's voice is on the other end, frightened. Of course, this is the child subject to nightmares and sleepwalking.

"Sequoia, it's Mommy."

"Mommy! We're gonna get you at the airport tomorrow. In Kansas City."

Ava continues quickly, trying to beat the clock. "That's why I'm calling. I won't be there. My flight was cancelled because of a storm. Daddy doesn't like Mommy flying anyway so I'm going to find another way home. A boat, probably. It'll take a long time. Y'know, just let me talk to Daddy. I love you, Sweetie."

Pause. "Daddy's not here."

"Aunt Julie, then. Let me speak to Aunt Julie."

"She's gone, too. All the grown-ups are at some party. That's sort of why I'm awake. I'm waiting for them to come home."

"Your grandfather?" Time is ticking away. "Just repeat after me: Mommy will not be on the plane. She'll find another way." Then she remembers the promise jokingly made to Jesse. "I may drive home on the Trans-Atlantic Highway. Tell Daddy that. It may take a very long time."

"A very long time. Like your postcards."

"Yes! Like my postcards! I love you and Xenia so much. Someday, it'll all be. . . " A Greek operator interrupts with an indecipherable message. A flush of acid hits Ava's belly but she tries to shut off her mind and heart. She shouts "I love you" into the receiver.

Ava boards a local bus full of old men, chickens, and raucous teenagers. On the way to the far side of the island, she notices narrow stone structures about two stories tall with triangular cutouts near the top. One of the teens informs her that they are dovecotes, where pigeons were housed back in the 16th century. Homing pigeons. Ava takes this as a good sign.

Getting off the bus, she recognizes the hand-scrawled signs for domatia and takes one for $8 a night, a clean and airy room with bright blue shutters that open onto the sea. She drops herself onto the white, starched linen of the bed and falls asleep instantly, feeling safe and well guarded by the landlady with a gap-toothed smile.

The next morning, Ava walks ancient stone paths, climbing up to the center of the island, where she visits a tiny chapel no bigger than a bedroom, filled with silver-framed icons and an over-sized chandelier. She lights a candle as thanksgiving for her survival.

The medieval pedestrian town of Kastro is whitewashed and festooned with fuschia-colored bougainvillea. Ava feels like she is walking through a piece of sculpture, enjoys the sensation of being inside of something larger than herself. She stops for lunch in a taverna with a view of the terraced hills and delights in the sprigs of greenery in her peasant salad of tomatoes and cucumbers. She asks what they are. The waiter points to a nearby bush and says, *"Caperi."* Caper leaves.

When she finds the potters' quarters, Ava chooses a bowl with a blue-on-blue pattern for Sequoia, one in earth tones for Xenia.

Kansas City

Jesse drives the girls to the Kansas City airport despite Sequoia's protests. The child, after all, is subject to nightmares. Jesse holds a bouquet in his hand as they wait at the gate but there is no sign of Ava. Jesse hushes Sequoia, who insists that her mother will arrive on a boat. When he inquires, the airline reports that Ava never left Europe. And yes, they will certainly check on her connecting flight from Heraklion.

Sequoia keeps saying, "Why doesn't anybody believe me?"

He would hate to admit it but part of him is relieved. He doesn't know how they would face each other, what they would say to one another.

Leaving Sifnos

The ferry to Piraeus looks sleek, modern, and tiny compared to the giant lumbering vessel Ava had taken to Sifnos, and she hesitates before boarding. Soon, they are out in open waters and the winds are strong. Venturesome young men hold fast to the ship's rails, letting the breezes take their bodies, which unfurl horizontally like sails. No longer young or daring, Ava contents herself to record in photos. But the sight of the boys' feats makes her consider her own attraction to the unknown, to chance-taking, to the exotic. She thinks of her childhood self with pennies taped to her fingers, dancing. Or her youthful self, looking out to the sea from that long-ago Seattle breakfast, eager to board a boat, to travel, to go. She could be that woman or she could stand tall like a caryatid, stable, strong, reliable, holding up the great edifice of family. Is she more like Odysseus the wanderer or the Odysseus who yearns to return home to his family on an island good for raising goats?

Big Springs

The next day, Jesse and Julie get in the car to shop for groceries. On the empty country road, she moves her hand to his lap, onto his fly.

"I'm trying to drive."

"Then pull over." He does. It's been a long time. A very long time. And the situation has changed. Ava is missing.

But when Julie's hand unzips, he pushes her hand away. "I can't do this."

She answers, "You know Ava is never coming home."

Leaving Piraeus

From Piraeus, Ava takes a bus to where the baby fell from the sky, out of the bottom of a plane. She leaves flowers, whispers a prayer for the child, the mother, the grandmother. Not wanting to forget, she lifts her camera and shoots.

From the bus window, she sees road signs with the venerable names of Mycenae and Corinth, then boards a ferry from Igoumenitsa to Ancona, Italy. From there, a train west. If she just keeps moving north and west, she'll get home.

Spello, Italy

When it gets to be late afternoon in Umbria, she disembarks at a walled town on a hill. A sign says Spello. Her girls would be amused by the name, like taking the English word "spell" and adding an "o" in a kind of fake Italian. I'ma gonna spello your name in Italiano. She might admonish them for such a simplistic idea of how language works, but inside, she'd be amused.

A shuttle takes visitors up the hill to the town center and Ava asks the driver how she might find a room. He tells her to ask Vittoria behind the bar around the corner. The senora looks Ava up and down, then utters a stream of words in Italian. Vittoria rents rooms for quiet women who don't make noise. Ava points to herself and says, "*Americana. Esposata. Tranquilla.*" She points to her wedding ring. She's not sure if "esposata" is Italian or Spanish but Vittoria nods and gives her a key off a ring hanging from her belt. She points to her eye, indicating Ava should look at room number 10. She writes down a lofty price, shrugs her shoulders and says, "*Festa, festa.*" Ava understands that the high price has something to do with a local festival, pulls dollars from her money belt, and takes the room, sight unseen. Vittoria gives her a glass of local wine and a piece of bread slathered in truffle butter. Ava sips, chews, appreciates.

When Vittoria observes her obvious pleasure, she pushes another plate her way. Grilled vegetables drenched in garlicky olive oil and some warm-from-the-oven bread to soak it up. She takes away key #10 and gives her #7 instead and sends her grandson up with Ava's backpack. After serving Ava five delectable dishes, Vittoria takes her by the hand and points to the stone-paved pedestrian path. She mimes sleeping and then walking up the path, she says the word *infiorata* multiple times. Ava wonders if it means anger or fire but she does as she's told. She sinks into a nap. When she wakes, she splashes water on her face and heads up the road.

A corkscrew pattern winds up the narrowing hill. Alongside the pedestrian path, the doors of houses and storerooms open onto villagers sorting through bins and bowls of flower petals and herb leaves. The scent is intoxicating. Large outlines cover the ground of the small piazzas of the town. Here and there, locals have taken to them with tweezers, placing the petals one by one onto the patterns with great care. Further up the hill, a few flower paintings are more complete. Many are abstract, with marvelous designs, like stained glass windows done in flowers. Others are religious depictions of the Madonna and child or saints with their symbols. Children work on one of St. Francis feeding the birds.

She reaches the main piazza outside the cathedral, where a dozen or more groups work fervently: men, women, teenagers, children together in small groups. Sometimes they consult each other, but no one argues or raises their voice. Ava orders herself a small dinner at an outdoor café under a pergola, scrambled eggs and a glass of local wine. Again, the unmistakable scent and taste of truffles. The diligent, busy bee villagers continue to create the flower installations, and she's glad to have her camera with her.

An English woman at the next table says, "The *infiorata*. I come every year. They stay up all night installing these paintings with flowers and herbs."

"Really?" Ava wants to know more.

"They start gathering the wildflowers a month beforehand. They use some dry, some fresh. It's a friendly competition entered by each district of the town. In the morning, there'll be—well, you'll see. My name is Cecily, by the way."

"I'm Ava."

"Ava. What a lovely name. Latin for wings, isn't it? You sound American but you certainly don't look it."

Ava considers how deep her skin has tanned with all the time outdoors in Greece. "Greek and Polish-American."

"Your hair is glorious, if you don't mind the compliment. Are you enjoying the tartufi, the local truffles? It's the season here in Umbria."

"Do pigs really dig them up, the truffles?" Ava wants to know.

"The locals are terribly secretive about the process, but that's what I've heard."

"Does that mean when we eat truffles, we've turned ourselves into pigs?"

Cecily finds this highly amusing and endearingly American. "Love that. You'll notice they also serve roast boar. It's on all the menus from here to Florence. Perhaps when a truffle boar is retired, we eat them, too."

Ava turns to photograph the villagers.

"*Ciao*," says Cecily as she leaves the café.

"*Ciao*." Infiorata. En-flowering. Much better than fury or fire. After she finishes a dark chocolate éclair, Ava wanders the rest of town. The sun has set and electric lights illuminate the locals who, indeed, stay up all night to work with great diligence and finesse on the infiorata. Ava envisages what it would be like to do an infiorata on the streets of Topeka or Lawrence. Unfortunately, the Kansas winds would blow it all away.

Back at the hotel, Ava puts a five-dollar bill on the counter and asks Vittoria to put through an international call. The phone rings. And rings. When the answering machine picks up, Vittoria shakes her head and hangs up.

Big Springs

There are meetings with the airline and police. Information comes in about the flood, the cancelled flights from Heraklion. Ava is missing. Officers say, "In these cases, what we often see is that the person wanted to disappear. Unless, of course, the worst has happened." Jesse chooses to believe she is alive and well. He quakes when he considers the alternative.

Sequoia insists her mom is on her way home. If not on a boat, then on what she carefully enunciates as, "The Trans-Atlantic Highway." What had been something of a joke in a desperate conversation now gives Jesse hope. Ava is on her way home. The long way home.

Spello

When dawn comes, Ava orders the same scrambled eggs with tartufo nero, the seductive and delicious black truffles. She's stayed up all night to watch the enflowering of Spello. Along with the coming of the light is the sound of the cathedral bells. Locals have scurried off to attend mass, leaving the streets nearly empty, providing Ava with a chance to purchase film and take photos of the finished products. Ava decides she'll just stay for the judging and then catch the northbound train.

After mass, the large doors of the cathedral swing open and a formal procession emerges. Altar boys heft huge candles and swing censers. A brocade canopy held up on golden poles shelters someone, perhaps a dignitary. Ava wants to see this up close. She edges herself forward through the crowd, between T-shirts and handbags. She wedges herself between bodies to get a better view. Then, she sees him, the bishop. With his high hat, perhaps he is even a cardinal. Ava quickly moves forward with her camera.

The bishop and his entourage walk directly toward the infiorata, then onto and through the carefully arranged designs. With every step, they ruffle the flower petals and herb leaves, which take to the air. The gorgeous installations are disturbed, undone, fly in the breeze. Ava wants to cry out, "No! Stop!" but, of course, she understands this is intentional, that the patterns are designed to be destroyed. Ava thinks about the inevitability of change at the same time she is regretting the loss of the art. She is filled with sadness and elation. The people of Spello follow the bishop, walk in his footsteps, further disrupt the infiorata with every step. Ava can't bring herself to step onto these carpets of flowers, so she walks along the edges, pressing herself against buildings. She photographs the disturbance, the mussed-up pictures, the de-flowering.

Cecily spots her, waves, and says, "It took me three years of watching before I stepped into the fray."

"I'm not sure I can do it."

"There'll be new ones next year. They'll start drawing the sketches tomorrow."

Ava nods.

Cecily continues, "It's like life, though, isn't it? We're always dying but also always being born."

Ava tries to smile.

Cecily adds, "Do be careful of the food here. It's addictive. The best in Italy. Sometimes I think I'll just stay here and eat tartufi for the rest of my days. Care for lunch?"

Big Springs

He reprimands himself for all his failings. He married a woman who rode with wild horses, then tried to contain her. He wasn't attentive enough, too consumed with his own concerns. Next time, he'll fly with her to Greece. Or Poland. To see her people. And maybe his.

Spello

"Where are you going next?" Cecily asks, in a café with a view of the gold and green Umbrian hills.

Ava stabs a piece of fennel that's been cooked with the *porcetta* they're devouring. "I was going straight home though I wish I could go to Poland. Now that I've seen the ancestral homeland on one side of the family, I want to do the other. My mother's people."

"Poland. I imagine great forests of white birch. I've never been there, of course. It's very difficult to get in, isn't it?"

"It is?"

"What with communist rule, you have to be invited by someone living there months in advance, exchange money before you arrive. I'm no expert, of course. I've just heard from people."

Ava vows to return to Europe, to look up her distant cousins in Poland.

"It must be an important search, finding one's roots. For Americans, that is, who seem to come from everywhere, don't they?"

"Except for people like my husband, who's Native."

Cecily executes a rapid intake of breath, like she's just met the Wizard. "You know someone who's a Native American? No, no, you say you're married to him!"

"Kind of."

"Terribly naïve of me but does he still, I mean, does he ever wear any, you know, the feathers and all?"

"Not usually. I mean he's every bit a modern man, but sometimes he does wear traditional regalia when he's dancing. He performs traditional dances at powwows." Every word she is saying sounds out of place in this medieval town where she's eating truffles shaved on everything as if tartufi were as common as radishes.

"You said, 'kind of' married?"

"We were taking a break from each other but now I'm about to head home."

Ava clearly is uncomfortable with the topic and Cecily seizes the opportunity. "I know exactly what we must do then. We'll go to Florence. You can't have come all the way across The Pond without visiting Florence."

"I couldn't?"

"You mustn't."

A private car seems to appear magically. Ava suddenly feels ill-dressed and under-cultured. Cecily, on the other hand, seems full of delight at having discovered a new pet. Ava reminds herself what Sequoia said about all the adults being off at a party. Better off without her.

Florence

At Cecily's apartment in Florence, Ava asks to use the phone to call home. Cecily closes the French doors behind her. Ava might actually be able to hear people speak.

Julie answers, "You're alive!"

"Oh, yes! I did talk to Sequoia, didn't she tell anybody?"

"We thought she'd had a dream. But you're alive!"

"I'm in Florence and I'm trying to get home without taking a plane."

"Ah yeah. Jesse's phobia."

Ava paces around the high-ceilinged room with its hand-crafted furniture. She might have to tell Cecily about Jesse's work. Maybe she'd be interested. . .

"Ava, still there? Not to worry. The kids are fine. They're at school, of course. But don't worry about them. Y'know, it's like they've got three mothers now with me and Emma Jane and Kaya. A lot of people to look after them. The girls are amazing."

My girls, my girls, my girls. Ava tries to push away thoughts of her girls having three mothers. Her fingers play nervously with an ornamental tassel. She needs to speak to Jesse. She's afraid to speak to Jesse. "Is Jesse there?"

"Sorry, honey, he's in Lawrence. He's been going there a lot lately. Maybe something to do with Haskell but what do I know?"

"Lawrence. Of course." Ava's heart sinks. Lawrence, where Kaya lives. She struggles to ask, "Julie? Is Jesse. . . Is Jesse seeing. . . someone?"

The long silence answers her question. Finally, Julie replies, "You know how Jesse and Kaya were always close. And then you had your arrangement. What can I say? I guess he—succumbed?"

Ava does not want to hear any more. Her husband has "succumbed." The family's reconfigured. Her children might not even think of her anymore. Maybe they are better off without her. "Julie, I want you to tell the girls I love them so much and I'm on my way home."

"On your way home. Got it. Ava, listen: you've got a once in a lifetime opportunity, so you may as well enjoy the trip! *Ciao.*"

"*Ciao.*"

※

Cecily sees to Ava's art history education. They walk into a museum with a special wave as if Cecily herself was surnamed Uffizi. With her thirteen years of Catholic schooling, Ava can pick out a martyr's iconography, like the Catherine Wheel or Saint Agatha's eyes, but still she finds herself breathless taking in the gold of the altarpieces, the translucence of the Botticellis. When they visit Michelangelo's *David,* Ava falls in love. She wants to touch his furrowed brow, press herself against his marble torso.

Feet aching, head spinning, faint from heat, they sit down for an afternoon lunch. Cecily encourages Ava to eat heartily. "We're going to eat like pigs, my dear, and find ourselves beautiful Italian boys to flirt with."

Ava lets the flirtation comment pass and concentrates on the culinary one. "Can pigs eat pigs?"

"Pigs will eat anything, my dear, even shit."

Ava laughs. I won't be eating like a pig then."

They do consume sautéed zucchini blossoms stuffed with creamy cheese; platters of eggplant and peppers, thinly sliced and marinated in oil and garlic; risotto with porcinis and, of course, black truffles. And they drink. Wine flows from bottomless carafes.

Ava's head is spinning when they go shopping. Cecily buys her a short red dress to show off her long legs. And then there's the shoes. Italian shoes. Ava's been wondering how the local women could walk on the cobblestones in such high heels, and she is just about to find out because Cecily treats her to a stunning pair. And, sure enough, as they stroll through the artisan section of town, dark handsome strangers ogle and catcall. They walk on.

But when a blond Florentine man pauses, smiles gently at her, and says *"Ciao,"* Ava says *"Ciao"* back. She continues walking, but something prompts her to look back, and when she does, the handsome young man is looking back toward her, still smiling with a gentle, vulnerable look. He reminds her of Carlo.

Cecily beckons to him and says, "Let's all go for a drink." When Cecily asks him something in very fast Italian, he nods and leaves the table. Minutes later, he reappears with another young Italian man, this one dark and mysterious.

Ava mulls over what Julie said about Jesse. He's succumbed. She remembers a phrase her mother used to say, "What's good for the goose is good for the gander." Her brother said she'd always been the responsible one, missed being a carefree teenager. Ava is emboldened. Once in a lifetime, she tells herself, once in a lifetime. She notices that, like Michelangelo's *David*, Marco has hands that are large for his frame, working hands. She remembers having read that the artist used a Florentine artisan as his model for his *David* and she wonders what Marco makes or paints. Ava surveys his clothing for a stray paint fleck. What she does notice is how young he is, in his late twenties perhaps. Italian men marry late.

When the waiter comes, Marco turns to her and inquires, *"Ceci?"* Ava has no idea what he's talking about, and the word sounds uncomfortably like the Polish word for "children," so she's puzzled. He pinches his own cheek to demonstrate. *"Ceci."* She assumes this is bar food and nods. A platter of marinated garbanzo beans arrives with crusty peasant bread. He repeats his Italian lesson, only this time he pinches her cheek. He does so with tenderness, lingering, then strokes her cheek and touches her mouth, urging her to say the word. *Ceci.* He continues gently with a few more Italian words for her to learn. *"Prego"* and *"Grazie."* He dips the bread into the *ceci* and puts it into her mouth. She says, "Mmmmmm," then realizes she must say the word, so she blurts it out: *"Grazie."* He applauds and moves his hand to her thigh. She shoves it away. He continues his meal, catching her eye often and saying, *"Che bella!"* exclaiming over her beauty. What's good for the goose.

Marco's arm is around her, slowly rubbing her shoulder, and she starts to fantasize about him unzipping, unhooking. The adults are having a party. Once in a lifetime. Taking a break. He puts his hand in front of her ear as if he were about to tell her a secret, but when he whispers, his lips touch her earlobe.

After the bitter taste of Campari in her mouth—looks like Koolaid but tastes like Novocain—Ava staggers down the street with Cecily and the two Italians, more inebriated than she's ever been. They make their way through an ancient door into a workshop where imitation classical and Renaissance sculptures are made for the tourist trade. Marco is, indeed, an artisan. Plaster of Paris Della Robbia-like wreaths lie in profusion. Decorative plates in various stages of completion, some with only their blue rims painted, others with blue rims plus yellow and red flowers. An artisanal assembly line. This is how the hand-painted plates in souvenir shops come to be. Marco leads her by the hand, giving a tour, but when he makes a quick turn and leans in for a kiss, she doesn't resist. She succumbs. And succumbs.

For several mornings, Ava pays homage to Michelangelo's *David*, then meets Marco in the evening. She reminds herself hourly that this is what separated people do. She thinks of the Amish custom of letting the teenagers run free. She claims her missed teenagerhood, her fun in the sun, her just desserts. She spends her days visiting baptistry doors and cathedral towers, nights in flirting and eating. *Carpe diem,* Cecily reminds her, and she does indeed *carpe* the *diem.*

One lazy afternoon, as they sit in a sun-stricken piazza sipping drinks, Ava notices an Italian couple with two children. The smiling mother and father are tossing a neon-bright plastic ring, a smaller version of a hula hoop, back and forth. The two girls, around four and six years of age, run between them trying to catch the ring, giggling. Ava rises, kisses Marco on both cheeks and says, "*Ciao*." The same word for hi and bye. She heads for the train station. Trains, buses, and ferries. North and West. North and West.

Topeka

"I won't regret. I make a point of never regretting." Jesse says this to the tall pilot even though he feels like he is about to burst.

"You've gotten over the hardest part, you know. Getting yourself over here. Touching a plane, sitting inside one. This week, we'll drive around the tarmac in this baby. I promise we won't lift off. You're doing well. Really well."

Wales

The road is flanked by high hedges and 300-year-old inns. Looking out the bus window, she reads signs pointing in various directions. To Shepton Mallet and Farrington Gurney, Peasedown St. John's, Chew, Midsomer Norton and Chipping Norton as well as Chipping Sodbury, Thornbury, and The Horringtons, both East and West. She thinks they might be nearing the sea when they pass a sign for Weston Super-Mare and Avonmouth. But then, there is a jolt. The bus driver slams on the brakes and Ava falls to the floor. She lands on her wrist, twisting it oddly. She helps an elderly couple to their feet. The 90-something-year-old man remarks, "I always wanted to fly."

As they stand, awaiting a replacement bus, two men smile at Ava. Her wrist is throbbing and she's happy for the distraction. One of them asks if she can guess what they do for a living. The other points to his eyes.

"Can't you tell?" When she looks at their eyes, which look to be heavily blackened with eyeliner, all she can think of is "drag queen." She doesn't want to offend, so she shrugs, "I give up."

"Coal miners."

The other, impatient, suggests, "Why wait for the bus? Are you off to Cardiff? We're but three miles from town." As they stroll in the refreshing drizzle, the miners tell her how they are in a men's chorus. Going to sing that very night in the cathedral.

"We're called The Mermen, our group. Ah, there we go, there's the sign for the show." As if on cue, a sign adorned with tritons and waves is just ahead. When they get closer, she can see a group picture of 50 or so men. Handsome and rugged, of various ages, posing in woolly suits.

"Seven o'clock," says the dark, handsome one, making it sound like an invitation.

The other adds, with twinkle in his eye, "We sing so beautifully you're going to have to stuff cotton in your ears or you'll stay here forever."

The men retreat into the church to rehearse and Ava finds herself a pharmacy to get some aspirin to alleviate the ache in her wrist, then a fish-and-chips place to eat. Then it's back to the cathedral where The Mermen perform. They sing in both English and Welsh, and she is enchanted. When the singing comes to an end, she stands and applauds, hoping for an encore.

Ava congratulates her bus mates on their performance. The blonde nods but goes off to greet his young wife and two lads. Smiling, the dark-haired one shifts from foot to foot.

"So, what'd ya really think?"

"Everyone else was stuffing Kleenex in their ears since it was too beautiful to have been the voices of mere mortals. But I was brave and listened. Did you hear me clamoring for more?"

"Thank you for that." And then, with tongue firmly in cheek, "It's traditional, you know, to treat one of the boys to a pint."

When they've found a seat in a low-ceiling Elizabethan-feeling pub, he says, "I'm famished." He orders roast, potatoes, and peas for both. Ever hungry, she eats again. And picks up the check.

When drinkers start singing in the pub and Owain joins in, she lifts her camera. He mugs, pretending to show off his coal-worker's muscles. She notices the lines of coal in the creases of his wrists. She is enjoying the sound of the men's voices and the damp heat of the room.

She teeters when she gets to her feet. They walk down a narrow mews, past an old wall painted with a mural of a mermaid. Ava staggers, bumps her injured wrist on an iron gate, cringes. Owain takes her hand in his to investigate. "We'd best have that looked at."

In the waiting room of an all-night clinic, he sings to her quietly to pass the time and keep her calm.

Big Springs

He watches Julie walk across the room. He observes her closely as she sits down slowly, crosses her legs, smiles at him. There is a martini in front of her with five olives. She says it's her favorite part, the olives soaked in martini juice, so that's what he's given her. She pops an olive in her mouth. "Mmmmmm."

He says, "You were going to tell me?"

"Raleigh Grenville, have you heard? He's leaving Emma Jane and marrying some grad student. Emma Jane says she always knew he would leave her. The girl's name is July."

Wales

The sky is streaky with red. Ava's wrist is immobilized by what looks like a convention of tongue depressors, bandaged tight. In the growing daylight, she can see the coal dust around Owain's eyes more clearly.

"The Welsh national anthem was composed in my hometown." He pulls himself up straight and tall. She does the same, in honor. After singing, he adds, "You have a home to go to, I know. But I thank you for the evening. You'll be leaving from Cardiff airport, I imagine."

"I can't take a plane. My husband made me promise."

"There are ships from Cardiff going to the Azores. Freighters. That's how a lot of my countrymen make it to the U.S. First, to the Azores, find another boat there. It's not too bad on the price."

"I've never heard of the Azores."

"The Hawaii of the Atlantic, some say. Others say, so what if there's palm trees if the wind blows like that?"

"I'm from Kansas. Known for its wind."

"It's halfway home and that's something."

He walks her to the shipyard. She takes his picture repeatedly along the way. Crinkly dark-lined eyes. Black-as-coal hair. Dressed in a suit jacket and a now-crumpled shirt. A worker's cap on his head. He makes inquiries, speaking Welsh, its many consonants musical on his lips.

"Keep safe," he says to her. Then, something he's clearly been rehearsing, "Except for adverts with 49 other blokes, there aren't many photos of this mug of mine so, please kindly send me a photo, will you?" Shyly, he hands her a piece of paper with his address carefully block-printed on it.

Topeka

Jesse nods. The pilot smiles. They taxi and lift off. Jesse holds on with all his might. Surely, he is going to die but nonetheless he opens his eyes. Sky. Clouds. He looks below at the miniaturized barns and houses, the people shrunken to paper dolls. The pilot tells him to hang on. He gives a brief instruction. Jesse wasn't expecting this. He is flying.

A Freighter

Ava boards the boat that will take her halfway to the States. She will have time on this freighter, to think, reflect. About herself and Jesse. She fantasizes about a possible future together in which they drive around the country, rediscovering their early days in the turquoise pick-up. She smiles so broadly other passengers decide to avoid sitting near the crazy lady. Then, Julie's words ring again: "You know how Jesse and Kaya were always close. What can I say, I guess he succumbed."

On the ship, day-to-day life is slow and unchanging except for the color and temper of the sea. The food is a dull gray-brown but filling. Ava occasionally chats with the captain, whose main message is: "On the sea you learn the pettiness of your own worries. You can't control the weather nor the waves so you learn to live with them, to bend, or to take cover."

The captain sets up an area for archery on an aisle where no one will get hit by an errant arrow. Maybe she will surprise her girls by improving her skills. She shoots an hour each day.

Penny, an older woman who wears her white-streaked hair tucked in a practical bun, spends her days practicing calligraphy at one of the pink-and-gray Formica tables. She travels with a huge supply of rag stock paper on which she carefully repeats the shapes of S and K. While pretending to read a mystery, Ava studies the older woman's progress. Today, Penny looks directly into Ava's eyes with her piercing blue gaze, "Try it already. You're not going to learn a thing just watching." Penny moves a stack of paper to Ava's side of the table, pushes the inkwell between them. "Start with a T or an L. Give it a nice slant."

Ava decides to make a book. She shows Penny the herbs and flowers she pressed into her journal—night-blooming jasmine, philoxenia, wild oregano, and thyme from the Greek hills. While Ava secures the fragile dried petals and leaves to the pages and letters the names of the plants, Penny talks about her marriage, "We take a break from each other for a month each year, Odie and I do. People turn up their noses at us, but it's worked for us for forty-two years so who's to say. You should find your own way, create your own marriage, you know. Don't let other people rule you. What works for them works for them. Now, I'm wondering how we're going to bind up this book. Maybe Captain will give us some nautical rope and we can untwine it, use a strand to sew it up. It'll be a handsome book for your handsome husband."

Big Springs

Jesse now pilots in earnest, with his teacher at his side. It'll take a while for him to get a license. He wonders, though, if he'll ever be able to board a plane that someone else is going to pilot, ever trust someone that much again.

The Azores

A sound, like the gods are scraping their swords against their shields in anger. Ava runs out on deck, barefoot. The fog is so dense, she can't see her hand before her eyes. On both sides of the ship, she can barely make out the walls of craggy rock. She is surprised to hear the captain's voice so close to her, "Guess we're caught between a rock and a hard place." Gallows humor.

Sailors are bailing water. Others are pulling down lifeboats and jackets. The captain continues, "Now if we just had a few tons of Vaseline." Then, "Believe it or not, we're very close to our destination. That way," he points, "we'll get you out of here." In the anxious run down the gangplank, Ava falls.

She opens her eyes to a tropical hospital decorated with twinkling lights and a giant cardboard Santa. She squeaks out a few words though no one is listening. Pulling herself up on wobbly legs, she totters to where her clothes hang on a peg. Ava will take the next plane off this blasted island and head home. Jesse will just have to live with it.

Big Springs

Jesse tries to make the most of Christmas and fails. He invited Ava's Aunt Dena down from Chicago, and of course Mickey and Carlo, Emma Jane Grenville and her children. The food is tasteless and so are the jokes. Everyone is trying too hard. Carlo reminds everyone about how Ava would always forget to serve one dish and it would sit forgotten in the fridge. The girls are disconsolate. A shipment arrived the day before: a long trunk of a red oak tree from Chicago. They believe their father will use this wood to carve a boat, knowing this is his version of a casket. They believe he has lost hope.

What he says contradicts what he has done. "Your mother is just a little lost, like that time Xenia got confused in the grocery store."

"I was, like, three!"

"Maybe she's got amnesia, like a soap opera character." Sequoia tries to cheer people up, and everyone laughs dutifully. Carlo turns on the radio. "Y'know, there's always so many carols on the radio at Christmas, we'll find something. We'll sing along." Instead, they hear:

> An emergency descent was initiated immediately but the hand grenade in the cockpit exploded, control was lost, and the aircraft crash-landed, broke in two, and caught fire.

Carlo almost rips the dial off the radio and suggests they take a nice, long winter walk. Everyone goes except Aunt Dena, who pleads old age and creaky knees.

Jesse trails behind the rest of the group, kicking over clods, throwing stones toward fence posts. He wonders if his letter ever got to Ava. What a fool he was to entrust it to a white man, someone obviously smitten with his wife! He hasn't told the others about the suitcase that arrived last week with Ava's clothing inside gone moldy, and a letter in half English, half Greek saying something about how this baggage had been found in the post-flood rubble. It's getting harder to believe she'll return.

Dena hears the phone ring but she won't pick it up, not wanting to invade the family's privacy. In her old age, she's become less daring and more respectful. She startles when she hears a click followed by the girls singing some song about leaving a message and giggling, followed by a lot of static. She hears a voice, maybe her niece's voice, if Ava were swallowed up by a gravel pit. Whoever it is sounds like she's got a mouth full of marbles. Something about lubbing. "Loving," that's it. And how she's going to "fry to cat a blane." Blane, plane? And, "You're jut gwanna hatta git ober it, Jethie." Jethie could mean Jesse. And then there's a mechanical sound cutting her off. Only then, too late, does Dena pick up the phone. She holds it uselessly in her hand, listening to the irritating tone. She speaks her niece's name louder and louder but there's only the dial tone answering her back. "Ava? AVA!!!!" Dena presses all the buttons on the frustrating machine, but there's only the reply, "Bleeeeeeeeeeeeeee."

When everyone returns home, stomping the snow off their boots, she signals for Jesse to come to her but he says, "Gotta go and feed the stock. Tell me later, okay?" But Julie, ever curious Julie, comes to her and sits close. Aunt Dena never cared for Julie. She didn't like Julie's expensive shoes and how she drank martinis just for show, even though she didn't really like them. That wasn't the worst thing, but it said something about her. Always reaching, climbing. Even in childhood, Julie always trailed behind Ava, imitating everything she did. She had to have the same Mary Janes, and later the same dentist. She even had her straight hair curled to look more like her cousin's.

"Dena?"

"Nothing. Just a message on the phone. The machine got it. For Jesse. Let him know, okay?"

"Of course. Thanks."

Dena thinks back to the dinner and how Julie sat next to Jesse, where Ava used to. How she seemed to be the boss lady of the house now, straightening the children's collars and squeezing Jesse's arm. Dena's eyes roam around the living room, disapproving of the modern, angular painting in red and black, the white couch chosen more for style than comfort. Dena decides to head back to Chicago first thing in the morning.

Julie turns the answering machine switch to OFF.

PART SEVEN

Boston

She's gotten this far, but Ava doesn't have enough cash to buy herself a plane ticket to Kansas City. She paces the sidewalk outside the terminal, looking for an omen. Cars whiz by, picking up recent arrivals. She recognizes a young woman from the plane, sitting on the curb, tearing up a large cardboard box. The woman pulls a marker from her pocket. She letters in a large and careful hand:

FROM EUROPE TO INDIANAPOLIS!!!!

Ava smiles at this younger version of herself and asks, "May I join you? I'm going further, Kansas."

"That'd be great! Safer, right? I'm Cary."

"Ava."

Drivers are intrigued by the sign and they instantly find a ride. Then another and another. Cary entertains the drivers with her tales of Florence and Amsterdam and the rocky ride from the Azores, tarting up her stories, embellishing them as they ride, developing an epic account. Ava is eager to see her children.

In Ohio, they are stuck. An evening snow has fallen and hitchhiking rules are strict in the state. Cary points to her sleeping bag and says, "If we're in it together, we might just stay alive." It is a roomy down sleeping bag, and Ava is grateful. What a story this will be, she thinks: sleeping in the snow on the median of the interstate.

At dawn, Ava is awake first, half-surprised to be alive. On the first ride of the day, she catches herself in the rearview mirror. She's lost her Greek tan. Her eyes are sunken. There are purple circles beneath them, like bruises. She tries to yank her fingers through the thicket of her matted hair but fails. Cary parts company in Indianapolis.

On the Road

In the dark, Ava has little hope of getting a ride but then she sees a car with a single headlight slow down. She thinks of the word "padiddle" that was used for such cars when she was a child and laughs to herself. There was also a kissing game that involved single-head-lamped cars, but she can no longer remember the rules.

"Hop in," the driver says and she does, grateful. "I noticed the camera around your neck, figured you wouldn't murder me," he continues. She tries to laugh at the bad joke but just a little squeak comes out where her voice should be. "Do you take a lot of pictures?"

"I am a photographer by trade, I guess you might say."

"Anything I'd know of? Am I giving a ride to the star of the *National Geographic?*"

"Not a chance. I'm a nobody."

"Well hi, Nobody, I'm Paulie. I was glad to see you on the side of the road. Relieves the boredom, you know. Only so long you can count sheep without going to sleep." Paulie. A grown man who wants to be called Paulie.

"Sheep?" She looks around the roadside and sees mostly corn. Flat land and corn. Some wilder wooded places here and there.

He notices her visual surveying and adds, "Not literal sheep. Though I do like these sheepskin seat covers."

Ava feels silly to have even considered literal sheep. "They are cozy and warm. Welcome on a cold night like this."

Paulie puts on the radio and she dozes off without meaning to. Who knows how long she's been asleep when the car pulls to a stop in the middle of nowhere. "Sorry, but I gotta take a whiz."

Ava leaves the car to stretch her legs. She tries to face away from the driver and hums as loudly as she can. She stretches, leans over to touch her toes. She is singing so loudly she doesn't hear Paulie's return. Doesn't know he's behind her until he pushes himself against her hard and she falls against the car. She screams, or tries to, but she's not sure anything comes out of her mouth. He fells her like a tree and she is on the ground. He covers her mouth with one hand as he tries to dry hump her angrily and hurriedly. He keeps saying, "You're NOBODY!!! NOBODY!!!!"

She tries but fails to bite his hand. She pounds on him as hard as she can. "NOOOO!" she can hear herself saying louder and louder, "STOP! STOP!" Then, for some reason she will never understand, she takes a breath, points at the sky and says, "Paulie, LOOK!" In the millisecond of distraction, an image from a self-defense circular handed out at her women's group flashes through her mind. She jams the palm of her hand into his nose, then knees him in the groin with all she's got. He grunts and she manages to push free and run. From the side of the road, she hefts a large rock which she throws with all her might at the one lit headlamp and cries out, "NOBODY!!!" When the man struggles up and comes toward her, she picks up the rock again and throws it directly at him. She scoops up her camera and runs.

Running is struggle and running is exuberance. She slides, falls, picks herself up. She finds a side road and takes it, hides in a barn, waits until she knows Paulie can't be following her any longer. She breathes a sigh of relief and of accomplishment. Yes, she had been unwise. Yes, she had gone off her guard. But she fought him off. When it came right down to it, she fought him off. Ava flexes her muscles like a Popeye cartoon and smiles. Though she is certainly worn out from her journey, maybe even a little ill, she is strong, as in courageous, as in undaunted, as in "I can face anything now." She knows, not just thinks but knows, that whatever awaits her at home, she can handle it. She can speak up for herself. She can create her own life, whatever that might mean.

But meanwhile, she has a long, cold road ahead of her.

Suburban St. Louis

With a quarter in her hand, Ava stands before a phone. A phone above a shelf, surrounded by acoustical tiles of the kind that used to cover the ceilings of basement rec rooms when she was little. Off-white with an abundance of small holes punched in them, the tiles look like they're made of painted compressed cardboard.

She is in the USA. She can phone now. She will speak to Jesse or one of the girls or maybe Julie. She intends to drop the quarter into the slot. She lifts the coin but has trouble managing the simple journey with her hand. The dots in the tiles are moving, swimming before her eyes. It's not just that she's crying. It's that her heart is beating wildly and in random spurts. Everything in her body hurts, especially her stomach and whatever organs may help it do its work. Her belly is bloated; she is woozy and unable to think clearly. She is frayed beyond words. She is sick, damn it. It takes both of her hands to steady the quarter enough to drop it in the slot. But she fumbles with the dial and gets a wrong number, an immigrant voice. Hallo? Who there? Over and over. Then a slamming.

Ava drops to the floor. She thinks she will faint but manages to stay conscious. She counts out the money in her wallet. She weaves her way toward the golden arches of a McDonald's. She swallows a burger in great gobbles, then something comes up in her throat. She runs into the bathroom and retches. She sits down on the toilet. She does not want to move ever again. She dozes off. When she awakens, it is too late for hitchhiking. Shit. She can't stay here all night. She needs advice. Aunt Dena. She finds another quarter in the bottom of her backpack. She concentrates and makes sure each number is correct as she dials.

Dena answers on the first ring, as if she was expecting the call. "Avie? Is that you? What's wrong, Honey? What happened?!"

Ava tells her in a rush of words that she is back in the USA, on her way home, to Jesse. When she says Jesse's name, she breaks down. The dam breaks and she is shaking with a convulsion of tears and snot.

"That's all right, Honey, get it all out. It's gonna be okay. You're on your way home. It's gonna be okay. I know it. I just know it."

"Auntie Dena, I was hitchhiking and. . . "

"A man? Did he hurt you?"

"He tried but I fought him off."

"Damn wolf, trying to have his way with you." Even in the emergency nature of the phone call, Ava is amused by the old-fashioned, indirect language of her aunt.

"He was a wolf. And I was a lamb. Until I became a lion." Ava's breathing is labored. She gasps between sentences.

"Good for you. I always knew you had it in you. Now you can do anything. You're sure you're not hurt?"

"Not hurt." Ava tries not to communicate how sick and tired she feels. How spent.

"You are all powerful. Do you hear me? Where are you?"

"Outside of St. Louis."

"Do you want to come here, to Chicago?"

"I want to go home, see my babies."

"Of course. They miss you, Honey. They need you, they really need you."

Ava decides not to ask for money or a plane ticket. It's only a six-hour drive from where she is now. She can do this. Didn't her Aunt Athena tell her she was all powerful? "I think I can make it there by New Year's. But I've run out of money for a motel."

"Tell me what you see out the window of the phone booth."

"I'm on a suburban street, just off the highway. Small houses. Some oldish apartment buildings. A couple of Italian-looking restaurants."

"Good. Walk west in a straight line. Walk until you see a strip mall. There'll be a laundromat there. Aunt Dena always knows these things."

"A laundromat?"

"Where there are small houses and apartments, there are laundromats. Laundromats are warm and they stay open all night. There'll be one nearby with water in the name. Suds'n'Rinse or Rain'n'Dry. Something like that. Go inside, get warm. Wash your dirty clothes. Relax and let life be kind to you. I promise you, life will be good again. And you will find a magazine there."

Ava pictures a stack of dog-eared copies of *Auto World* and *Good Housekeeping*. "Sure."

When she does see a strip mall ahead, she tries to conjure up a laundromat, as if she can bring it into existence by wishing. Shivering, her teeth clattering, she's ready to give up when the Rain-Bo Lawn-dro-mat appears as a mecca before her eyes. She practically runs to get inside. The floors are covered in AstroTurf carpeting—easy to hose down?—and the walls are painted in rainbow-hued murals interrupted by dozens of instructions and warnings. Stacks of fan magazines litter the floor. Ava fumbles for change, puts a load in, and claims an empty blue plastic bucket chair. She keeps the camera strapped across her chest and the backpack between her feet, held tight. The proprietor has mounted a sign that makes Ava smile: WOULD THE LAST CUSTOMER PLEASE PULL DOOR FIRMLY SHUT and she nods off, thinking of the billboard back in Seattle and soothed by the lulling sound of dryers spinning.

"Excuse me, I'm so sorry." Someone has tripped over her feet. She apologizes for her outstretched legs and the man in a crisp pin stripe shirt apologizes again, adding, "Wife got the washer and dryer. Ex-wife, I mean. And I haven't the slightest idea how to go about buying new ones."

She has the urge to tell him that she can go shopping with him first thing tomorrow. Surely there's a Sears. Her Kenmore has lasted her over fifteen years. But she needs to get her clothes dried and get on the road, so she just nods. Giant snowflakes drift outside the window. After a few minutes, Mr. Crisp asks her about the camera. Oh, no, not again.

"I used to work for a newspaper."

"But then, you got sick of the routine and decided to hitchhike around Europe?"

Is it that obvious? "I used to work for a newspaper and then a travel agency. Long story."

The gentleman in the pinstripes looks overwhelmed. "Do you know how to work these things? I'm growing to appreciate what my wife, ex-wife, did. I try to read the directions, but I keep getting stuck on the syntax and forget the content. Occupational hazard, I'm an editor."

"Ah."

"Magazine. *Nomads.* Never heard of it, right? Think of *National Geographic* without the subscribers. When I saw your camera, not exactly an Instamatic, I thought maybe you might be, y'know, anybody who's hitchhiked around Europe taking pictures is always somebody I want to talk with. Don't worry, I'm not hitting on you. Not that you're not perfectly attractive, it's just that I've finally come out as gay. Probably contributed a bit to the end of the marriage. You'd think I'd know how to use a washer and dryer." Mr. Crisp points to one of the signs: QUARTER ONLY FOR WASH. DIME ONLY FOR DRY. NO CANADIANS, PLEASE!

She laughs. "I don't think they're prejudiced against our Northern neighbors, they just don't like their coinage." She guides him through sorting and acquiring detergent, loading and putting the coins in. PLEASE NOT TO TAMPER WITH THE COIN BOXES—THEY ARE WIRED TO AN ALARM SYSTEM!! DO NOT OVERLODE!!!

He chooses a red bucket seat, fiddles with his briefcase. Open, close. Open, close. Open. Ava runs this over in her mind: The man brought a briefcase to a laundromat? He pulls out a couple of issues of *Nomads* and a pile of paperwork. He sorts through piles, thrums his fingers on the briefcase edge, looks over at Ava. Finally, he gets up his nerve.

"I hate to disturb you again, but I'd appreciate your professional opinion."

It's something to do. "Sure." She puts down the stained and tattered celebrity magazine she was pretending to read.

"I'm Howard," he says.

"Hi, Howard." She doesn't offer her name.

He hands her some photos for an article.

She asks about the magazine's needs, goals. She makes observations about purpose, depth of field, and sharpness. The conversation continues through the drying cycle—PLEASE REMOVE DRY CLOTHES IMMEDIATELY TO AVOID SPONTANEOUS COMBUSTION!!!—and Ava starts perking up talking to the stranger. She tells him about her trips to Sifnos and Wales. Outside, the wind is howling and snow is falling heavily. A blizzard. Ava considers the possibility of sleeping on the AstroTurf flooring.

"I know this is audacious of me, but it's awfully late and I'd hate to think of you spending the night in one of these plastic chairs when I have a perfectly good guest room in a perfectly boring 3-bedroom house just a few blocks away." He continues, "I have a selfish interest. I want to hear more of your stories about those Greek islands. Please? And I could use your advice on the journal. Magazine. You'd be helping me out and making a boring night interesting."

She considers every warning in news articles about disappearing women, but she feels like she's known Mr. Crisp for years.

"Just a minute," she says. She points to the restroom and then a copy of *Nomads*. "Mind if I take this with me?"

"I'd be flattered."

She pages through the issue as she pees. She looks for the masthead and sure enough, finds Howard Rodenberg listed as an editor. She could die here or she could die in his house. She chooses to believe in this kind person. He might have an elaborate ruse to get victims to his lair, but in her gut, she thinks not. She quickly reads an article on Morocco so she has something to say to Howard when she comes out. She immediately bumps into a short Asian man emerging from a back room with a vacuum cleaner saying, "Big storm. Out, out!" That seals the deal.

Once at his house—and yes, it is a boring brick ranch with feeble

Christmas lights hanging around the edges—he escorts her to a study/guest room. He points out the closet with his ex-wife's clothes—well okay, her discarded, unwanted clothes—and tells her she can take her pick. She's tired of the threadbare duds she's been wearing, so she showers and finds some bland going-to-the-mall clothes that almost fit her.

In the mirror, she looks like a stranger. Her face is raw from cold and wind; her hair, wild and untamed. Her frame is spare, her lips chapped. Her eyelashes and brows have gone missing, as if the wind swept them away. In the Junior League suburban clothes, she is even more a stranger. Ava looked like a tramp before. Now she looks like a tramp who was given clothes by the Salvation Army. She sleeps heavily on the fold-out couch. In the morning, she wakens to the compelling aroma of eggs and bacon. Bacon. She eats like a lumberjack.

Outside, the snow is still falling.

"We're trapped," says Howard. He has the radio tuned to the weather station. He asks her if she'd like to call home. She lets it ring a dozen times, but no one answers.

She passes the time telling him about Cretan wedding breads and Sifnian dovecotes. He's eager to see her photos and convinces her they should develop a roll or two in his dark room in the basement. She ignores the stories of women trapped for years in dank cellars and follows Howard to his tidy basement and well-equipped dark room. She chooses the rolls from Crete. Craftsmen in their workshops putting strings on traditional instruments. Women in flowered aprons smiling over casseroles of artichokes and rice. Young men in black boots dancing. Howard delights in seeing the photos come to light. He comments on her composition.

They are snowed in for three days. Ava asks Howard if she can develop a few more photos. She wants to make a small album for her family, using photos from the places where she especially thought of them. Seeing the caryatids. Her cousin toasting on Holy Spirit Day. A cat, a mermaid. Willie Nelson's "You Were Always on My Mind" is running though her brain repeatedly and that's what she wants to call the little album, but she decides it's too much, too heart-baring. Maybe

Greekscapes? Too cold. She begs some heavy paper, adhesive, and black felt marker from Howard, who is delighted to help. When the images are arranged, she outlines each photo in black and prints "Glimpses of Greece" across the top of the first page.

Ava calls home again. On the second ring, Joe I answers, saying, "No answer machine." He is speaking loudly.

She finds herself shouting in response. "Joe! Hello, this is Ava!"

"Ava?" Joe says her name Ah-vah.

"I'm in Saint Louis. I'm on my way home."

"Ava come home."

She wonders why he is speaking like E.T. but finds herself echoing him. "Yes, Ava come home. Is Jesse there?"

"No, Jesse at store. With girls."

"Please tell him I'm on my way. I'll be home for New Year's."

"Ava come home."

"Yes, Ava come home." The receiver clicks off and she's left wondering if she's misremembering how aged Joe was when she left or whether there's been some deterioration in her absence.

☙

On the fourth day, Howard and Ava shovel themselves out. He refuses to take her to the highway to hitchhike. "I'll take you to the train, I'll take you to the plane. Hell, I'll buy you a ticket to fly home." They compromise with his buying her a Greyhound ticket as far as Kansas City. When everything is packed in his hatchback, including more of his wife's clothes than she really wants, they begin the drive, only to stop in front of an old downtown office building.

"I lied," he says, "I want you to meet the gang."

They trundle through the snow and into the building, onto an ancient elevator and up to the 3rd floor, where the door opens onto the compact offices of *Nomad*. The walls are covered in colorful travel photos. Gus, the one staff member there, greets Howard with sighs of relief. Howard insists she show off her photos of the young men dancing in the mountain village.

"I love this one. They're leaping so high, they look like they're flying,"

And then it starts. "Tell him about. . . " And the rest of the morning is spent with her relating stories of her travels. Howard and Gus smile at each other, genuinely pleased. They insist she write down short accounts of what she experienced. When the day is done, Howard drives her back to his house.

"You tricked me."

"Wasn't it fun? The buses weren't leaving anyway. Roads are still blocked."

"You tricked me!"

"I'll have a check cut for you. We don't pay much but it'll be something. And please send me more. More photos, more stories. You're a nomad."

"I'm very tired."

"I know. Just one more question: It looks to me like you're not totally sure if you want to go home."

"I feel like I have to. . ."

"Face the music?"

"I have to face the music."

When he drives her to the bus station the next day, he looks her straight in the eye and says, "Keep in touch. Please." He hands her a corned beef sandwich wrapped in aluminum foil. He waits until the bus leaves the station, waving until she is out of sight.

Lawrence

She walks down Massachusetts Street, the main drag of this college town, both familiar and strange. It seems wider than she remembers, almost painfully sunny. Incredibly fatigued, Ava bumps into lampposts and the corners of buildings, as if she were drunk. She must sit down before she falls down, so she plops herself on a bench next to a homeless person guarding a shopping cart. Her bench-mate appears to have more possessions than Ava. Except for home, of course, if that is still hers.

Two women pass by. She thinks she recognizes the voices. "This is going to be the best New Year's Eve ever. . ."

Ava calls out, "Julie. . ." Her cousin's eyes quickly and

uncomfortably sweep over her on the homeless bench, then move on without recognition. Julie and the other woman enter a shop with flapper and hippie-style dresses in the store windows, theatrical outfits and lacy items worn in the twenties or seventies. Is that style coming back?, Ava wonders, as if it matters.

Ava catches her own reflection. Her hair is tangled, belly distended, complexion sallow, frame skinny and bent. She does look like an unfortunate beggar. She must get a move on. Hitchhike, taxi, bus, whatever. She needs to get home while Julie is out. She needs to see if her home is still home.

Big Springs

Her ride, a student driving home to Topeka, takes her as far as the mailbox by the road. Out of habit or curiosity, she opens it. Fliers and junk mail fall out, a few bills addressed to Jesse or herself or both, a few envelopes addressed to Julie. Ava carries the mail toward the kitchen door. Then she spots Kaya's car. Uh-oh. She shouts out but no one comes except Homer the dog, prancing on the ice in the late December cold. He runs up to her, tail wagging. Ava leans over to pet him and he licks her face enthusiastically. Finally, somebody! She opens the door to let Homer and the mail in and takes a quick surveying glance. The home she lived in, that she created, is gone. Julie's things have been added to it. Red and black geometric paintings. White couch. It even smells different. Ava can't yet bear to walk into this altered world, so she steps back outside. She takes a deep breath and tries to take in the sight of the new hills. Jesse's mounds.

She calls up her strength and nerve and calls out again, "Helloooooooooo!!!!! Jesse??????"

Kaya's voice answers from Jesse's workshop.

Face the music, face the music, Ava tells herself. Why didn't Jesse and I truly, legally get married, go to the courthouse, do the thing you're supposed to do. Her thoughts spin in circles. And then she sees Kaya, a kind smile on Kaya's face. And she feels an embrace. A warm, welcoming, maternal embrace.

Kaya says, "You're alive! You're home!" Ava finds herself weeping on Kaya's shoulder, clutching on to her. Kaya continues, "He's gone to do some chores. Julie's in town. They'll all be back soon. Come with me. I'll explain everything. I'm just so glad you're alive!!"

✦

Kaya drives like she's leaving a fire toward her own Lawrence street, taking pains to avoid passing the tall Grenville home. She looks around and then signals Ava in, hurrying her into the kitchen. Pulling food out of the cupboards and refrigerator, Kaya warns, "Eat slowly or you'll throw up."

"I'll try."

"Don't try to talk. While you eat, I'll catch you up on the things you need to know. Don't worry, I'll listen to your story someday over a campfire."

"I'll sing it to you."

"Shut up and eat."

Ava nibbles on cubes of cheese, drinks a carton of chocolate milk, consumes a leftover bison burger. Kaya nods her head and Ava knows this is Sheila, the last bison of the herd. Probably died of old age. She mentally thanks Sheila for giving her nourishment in this life and starts chowing down on some coleslaw and potato chips.

Kaya breaks the silence. "He tried. For as long as he could. He believed. I think he still believes. Evidence to the contrary."

"Evidence to the contrary?"

"Shut up and eat."

Ava slowly chews on some wonderfully salty cashews.

"You didn't arrive. Then, Jesse found out you never got on the plane. Something about a flood. Raleigh told Jesse about the terrible flood you were in."

"A terrible flood that he left me in. Asshole."

"Agreed. By the way, he's left Emma Jane and married one of his students in a big hurry. Somebody named July, for chrissake."

"That was quick!"

"Enough talking. We've got to clean you up. I don't want nits in my house."

"Nits?" asks an incredulous Ava.

298

Kaya none too gently scrubs her hair with a vile-smelling soap and, while Ava's hair is wet, she tortures it with a fine-tooth comb. She sighs discontentedly and gets her scissors.

"No!"

"Yes! You don't want to give lice to Jesse, much less to your girls. You're taking a bath in lye soap as well. We're getting every strand of hair off your body."

"I do not have lice!"

"Stop being a child. An adult does what's necessary. She stops playing and indulging herself and does what is necessary."

Ava looks down sheepishly and submits. Wearing plastic gloves, Kaya cuts off Ava's long tangled tresses into a mess on the newspaper-covered floor. She cuts close to the scalp and Ava thinks about the days when Haskell was an Indian boarding school, when all the Indian children had their precious hair cut off to enter the white world. They cried losing their hair, native clothes, language, amulets.

When Kaya takes out her Lady Schick razor, Ava must bite her tongue to stop from screaming NO! While she cuts and shaves, Kaya tells her how Julie's affection for Jesse became more obvious. How she encouraged him to believe Ava had died and was washed away somewhere in Greece. How she flirted with him. How Julie said she would be good for the family. She was Ava's first cousin, after all, and the girls have known her all their lives. She would do everything to make their lives good and serve the memory of their mother.

"But Jesse kept putting her off with one project or another. I think he always knew you'd come back. So, he did an earth-moving project, like the old Indians around these parts did. He built a mound for his brother. Then he planted it with herbs and flowers for the spring. Y'know, hyacinths, tulips, snowdrops. He promised her that when he was done planting, he would be with her." Ava spits up some of her food and Kaya wipes her mouth like a mother does a child's. "Let's just say, he took his time about it."

"He believed I was coming back."

"Meanwhile, she was busy making sure your girls liked her. Took them shopping, splurged on fancy clothes."

"Indulged them."

"Bought them. But then Jesse told her a whopper. He said, she knew, didn't she, that he was obligated to carve a canoe in your honor. It was a necessary tradition of the Makah people."

"Bullshit." Ava says.

"Bullshit, indeed, but still, it sounded real, like a great memorial. He compared it to a headstone. He had to make this vessel for his deceased wife. To push her off into eternity in a boat."

"Huh. I like that. Not that I want to be dead."

"She bought it. It wouldn't be a terribly large one, he promised. He'd carve Raven and Whale. Paint it red inside. That part is real Makah, the red part."

"I know." Ava remembers one of the first times she saw Jesse. How he was showing off a Makah-carved boat to his friends. That boat was painted red inside. Those friends were Kaya and Carlo. He had carved that boat, too. It's what he does. He crafts wood.

Kaya continues, "And maybe some other animals from the story of your life together. Frog and—I don't know. Well, you get the idea. He carved but mostly he stalled and took his sweet time about it. She grew impatient. He whittled and sanded. She complained and he finally started painting. Every day he painted. Turquoise and black and red. Raven flying into the mouth of Whale. Whale opening to Raven."

"Raven eating out the insides of the whale. In that story, Raven does not exactly come across as the good guy."

"You don't want to be Whale, do you? Think of it this way: if you didn't come home, you would have eaten him out from the inside, right down to his heart. And that's what he was living."

Ava tries to understand. She holds the notion like a fragile house of cards in her tired brain, but then it collapses.

"In any case, every day he painted and every night after she fell asleep, he went out and sanded off some of the paint."

"Sneaky poker player, as always."

"That's another story. Anyhow, he stalled and, of course, she grew suspicious. One night she caught him red-handed. So to speak."

"Ha."

"But last week, your suitcase came, and it seemed like a sign that you really had died."

"My suitcase?"

"After all this time, someone dug it out of the flood debris and sent it to the address on the luggage tag. It got here full of moldy clothes. We all lost faith."

"I left it back in Crete because I couldn't carry it."

"Well, you're alive—thank the wind that brought you here—but you're not a very good listener. You keep interrupting my story."

"Sorry." Despite the reprimand, Ava goes on. "I saw her downtown shopping. She was trying on a fancy dress."

"Don't jump to conclusions. New Year's Eve."

Ava looks away from Kaya, toward a corner of the wall where there is a small dusty cobweb, and asks the hardest question, "Have I been replaced?"

"Give me a break. You know what they say, 'The show ain't over until the fat lady sings.'"

After the shaving and the lye soap scrub, Kaya runs a second bath, a bubble bath. The reward. After Ava soaks, she emerges in the clothing Kaya has put out for her, a turquoise sweater dress, gift from Auntie Dena.

Ava says, "Wasn't this my dress?"

"Yeah, I stole it from you and, well, I'm giving it back. I hope you'll forgive me."

"What's to forgive?"

Kaya takes a deep breath and lets all the air out in a big stream of words. "I let you believe your husband was unfaithful to you. I wanted you to believe it. I did everything to make you believe it. He was my old friend from way back and I didn't want to lose him to you. I stole from you. There is a lot to forgive."

Ava runs her hand over her shaved head. "We'll get through it. We'll talk it out, but right now. . . "

"Right now, you have to have a nap. Gonna be a long night. You'll need it."

Ava starts to ask questions, tries to understand how she was so turned upside down about everything she knew, but when she starts to ask, Kaya puts a finger to her lips and points her to the couch. She covers Ava with a hand-crocheted coverlet and sings a lullaby to her. Within seconds, Ava drops off.

She awakens with a start. She knows she must go to the house, to confront Julie, to be with her children before she sees Jesse. The children.

"When will the girls get home?"

"Go back to sleep. You need your rest."

"I can't sleep. When?"

"Less than a half hour."

"Let's go."

She tries to stand nonchalantly, adopting the pose of the other parents, leaning against Kaya's car. The girls walk, unseeing, complaining about their strict teacher and a troublesome boy who teases them. And then they see her. It takes a few seconds for them to understand who she is without her hair, to compute this unexpected appearance. But when they figure it out, they run and cry out, "Mommy," as if they were still three and five. They wrap themselves around her meager body, squeezing hard. She pulls them even closer. Kaya shoos them into the car. Too much of a scene. The three of them climb into the backseat, with Ava in the middle. Kaya, like a chauffeur, glances at them in the mirror. The high-pitched excited voices overlap with screaming and questions. Many questions.

"What happened to your hair?!" Sequoia wants to know.

"I think she looks elegant, like Sinead O'Connor."

"You're alive! Our mommy's alive!"

"You're home!" Xenia says and then, "Why were you gone so long?"

"I didn't want to take a plane so it took a long time."

"I told you she called about the Trans-Atlantic Highway!"

"No such thing," snaps the erudite Xenia.

Sequoia, ever direct, says, "You made us worry so much! Why did you make us worry?"

"I know. And I'm sorry. I don't know if I can ever make it up to you."

A sudden silence acknowledges the long road ahead, with a lot of explaining to do. Explaining that will involve tears and spitting anger but also, hopefully, peace, a coming together. But for now, just for now, to get through this night, they'll make a joke of it. Like in the old days. Isn't that what they used to do?

Sequoia: "With enough ice cream and nail polish, maybe."

Xenia: "And no curfews for the rest of our lives."

Sequoia: "And buying us everything we want."

Ava: "I'm still your mother, you know."

Sequoia: "Did you get our letters? Did you figure out the 'iad' part?"

Ava: "I adored them, and I'm sure you have lots more stories to tell. I want to hear everything. Every word." She tries to hold back the tears.

Xenia: "Aunt Julie has lots of parties."

Ava: "Well, that sounds fun." There is a silence that satisfies Ava that it is not fun.

Sequoia: "Daddy thinks you're dead." This is so blunt Ava starts laughing.

Xenia: "No, he doesn't. He's just pretending."

Sequoia: "He wouldn'ta married her, really, Mom. He'd've thoughta something.He always does."

Big Springs

Ava tells the girls they have their whole lives to sort things through, but right now she must go talk with Julie and their daddy.

Xenia expresses her disappointment. "Oh, no! An 'adult conversation?' Already? You just got back."

And Sequoia agrees, "No fair."

"They don't know I'm back yet."

Kaya herds the girls into her house and hands Ava her car keys. Ava says, "Wait. I have a couple of things I want to give the girls." Ava searches the contents of her backpack for the little gifts she has brought them. Miniature replicas of ancient toys, goddess statues, pottery bowls. The girls sit close to her. Sequoia pets her arm as if Ava needs reassurance. Kaya brings out cookies and hot chocolate.

Xenia speaks up. "Why didn't you call us? I know we were gone at the beginning of your trip, but then later. . . "

Sequoia is irritated. "She did call. Remember? Nobody believed me."

"Sometimes I called and you were asleep or at school. And sometimes it was just too hard to call. For a while, I was in a one-street village and the only place to call from was a teensy store a mile and half away where ten people were waiting in line and I couldn't wait. Sometimes I left a message on the answering machine." She looks at the faces of her stricken-looking daughters and knows this is insufficient. "But that's no excuse, really. I missed you terribly but I was so far away. I don't know if you'll ever understand."

Sequoia tries, "You were on your own adventure. Like we were on an adventure with Auntie Kaya. Sometimes I even forgot about you, Mommy, for hours at a time, because there was so much happening."

And then Xenia, "It's our fault you left, isn't it? We left you and so you left us."

"No! Don't ever think that!" Decades of therapy may be necessary to undo thoughts like that. "We'll talk about it, though. We'll talk about everything. I'll show you pictures of my trip and we'll talk."

"Pictures? Now. Show us the pictures NOW!"

Ava reaches for her bedraggled backpack and pulls out the little album. The girls sit next to their mother as close as they can get, leaning on her shoulders and knees. Sequoia is eager to know about the Minoan lady and her 4,000-year-old jewelry. Xenia laughs at the cat next to the Coca-Cola case and wants to ride in the carriage by the sea. They both listen dutifully as their mother explains how the caryatids, like all women, carry the weight of the world. They don't know yet that they will grow into travelers themselves. Xenia will become a dancer on the West Coast who tours the world with her dance company. Sequoia will take her Smith junior year abroad and later settle in Paris. Sequoia will favor hydro-therapy and give birth to her children in a tub. Xenia will go into analysis.

But right now, their eyelids and limbs grow heavy. Ava extracts herself from their dozing bodies. Kaya covers them with the crocheted coverlet and Ava kisses their foreheads.

❧

When Ava pulls into the familiar driveway, she pictures Jesse's earth mound covered in spring flowers. Spring. If she's still here then. Her stomach is doing flips on a tightrope.

She walks into the living room and turns on a light. White linen couch on a bison ranch. Really? The abstract painting in angry angles. The bison throw on the floor, serving as a rug. Ava takes off her shoes and walks on the thick fur. It does little to make her feel more at home. The room smells of Spanish olives and Lysol. Christmas decorations have already been taken down, except for a forlorn elf on the mantel.

Ava calls the Eldridge Hotel and makes a room reservation. She takes a deep breath, steels herself, and walks into the "forbidden room." A hammer and a box of nails have been left casually on a side table, as if someone were about to hang a picture and was interrupted. Or just finished hanging one. There it is, a new painting recently hung on the wall, a casually painted red heart against a black background. Below are her husband's jeans crumpled on the floor. She grits her teeth, picks up the hammer, and extracts three nails from the box. She nails the jeans to the wooden floor.

She lies down on the bed, as if she wants to imagine what happened there, to feel it in her body. Springing up quickly, Ava yanks the sheets and pillows off. She carries them outside and stuffs them in the metal trash bin. When she gets back in the house, she pulls an overnight bag from under Julie's bed and starts packing it. A thin nightgown that won't keep her warm on a winter's eve. A change of underwear. She opens the right-hand closet door. Her children's bows and arrows are stored here. Their powwow dresses. Her husband's regalia. She catches the smell of feathers and sweat. She closes it swiftly and opens the other side. Julie's clothes hang neatly. A slinky cocktail dress is pushed to one side waiting to be worn, a sequined New Year's Eve dress in a dry cleaner's bag. Ava strikes a match from the pack next to the bedside candle and with it she slowly melts the cleaning bag plastic onto the dress. When a small fire starts, she stomps the dress beneath her feet, then drops the ruined frock into the overnight bag along with a pair of clumsy, mismatched shoes.

Ava fingers items in her cousin's jewelry box. She finds a few of her own pieces there, undoubtedly borrowed from her room. Ava retrieves these and puts them on. A pair of clip-on rhinestone earrings that were her mother's, a choker necklace, a few bangles. She looks in the mirror to catch the effect. And then, she sees herself. With her shaved head, she looks like a victim at a. . . She stops her self-torture mid-sentence. No. No more thoughts of victimhood. She locates Xenia's bow and arrow in the storage closet, pulls the bow taught and sends the arrow sailing into the heart of the new painting.

Ava walks into the kitchen and opens the freezer. Vodka, good. She looks in the cabinet where liquor used to be stored, but there's cat food there now. She opens several other cupboards and finally finds vermouth in a high cabinet above the fridge. She takes out a pair of cocktail glasses, an anniversary gift from Carlo. Carlo. She could use clever and witty Carlo right about now. She runs water over the glasses and puts them in the freezer. She finds the jar of Spanish olives she knew would be there. The cocktail shaker Jesse and Ava never used, but now lives here on the counter, within easy reach. She pulls some blue cheese from the fridge drawer and locates crackers. She readies everything as if for a party.

Ava has to pee. She's been holding it far too long. Her whole body feels pulled in, contracted, held back. Ava sits on the toilet with the door open. She empties herself and wishes she could just stay there, seated, her head on her hands, pissing hot pee, holding her bald head in her own hands. No, she really wants other hands to hold her.

She stands up quickly, re-assembles herself. She rummages through the tiny drawers of the bathroom and finds remnants of make-up there. She forces herself to look only at the rims of her eyes as she draws a pencil across, then adds the slightest bit of turquoise shadow, mascara, eyebrow pencil. She never wore that kind of makeup before, but her usually thick eyebrows and lashes look like they've been gnawed away by giant insects. Peachy blush. Mascara, applied a second time. Lipstick, darker than what she's used to, but it'll do. She stands back and surveys herself. She has to feel generous about herself if she's going to do this. Time for a pep talk. I'm not skinny, just slim like a model. Svelte. From the right angle, my head does look a little like Sinead O'Connor's. Maybe. With make-up and the right jewelry, gauntness can come off as stylish. Yeah, right.

There is no time to rehearse. No time to compose lines. Already there is the sound of tires on gravel. Ava quickly mixes two dirty martinis with extra olives and places them on a tray, next to the cheese, bread, and cocktail napkins she arranged earlier. She leaves the room.

The door creaks familiarly as it has for years.

"Kaya? Kaya, you here? I saw your car outside so I know you're here.

306

Kaya?" Julie spots the martinis on the coffee table and picks up a stray bit of blue cheese to put in her mouth. "Ah, Jesse, are you being sneaky? Jess? Are you trying to surprise me for New Year's Eve, you naughty boy?"

Ava stands in the doorway of the "forbidden room" and says, "I thought we could do this in a civilized manner. Please, have a drink!"

"Ava! You look like death warmed over, Kitten."

"And we're off to a good start."

"What the hell happened to you?" Julie picks up one of the martinis and takes a gulp, as if the potion could heal whatever ailment has caused her to see wraiths.

"Not much. A stretch of hitchhiking in the snow, bit of a flood, hint of a shipwreck."

Julie's face re-configures into what looks like worry. "Did you say shipwreck? Omigod, I'm sorry that happened to you."

To Ava's dismay, Julie's concern sounds genuine. This is not what she expected. Something akin to regret wells up inside. She chews and swallows a martini-marinated olive which makes her cough. She takes a giant swallow of the cocktail to wash it down, decides to be direct. "Julia, I'm home now. I'm ready to take my house back. I'm ready to take my husband back."

"I don't think you're the one who gets to make that decision. You went off and abandoned your husband."

"You don't know the first thing about it. He and I had an agreement, an understanding."

"And how did that work out for you?" She doesn't wait for an answer. "Meanwhile, I was here by his side, taking his children to school, ballet lessons, picking out their clothes. . . "

Ava can't help but interrupt. "MY children."

"You abandoned them, too."

"I'll handle that with them, thank you very much."

"They hate you."

"I don't think so."

"They will. You know it. They'll never forgive you." This is, of course, the worst possible outcome in Ava's mind. The children will resent her so much that they will want to live without her. Sure, they welcomed her, but once they think about it. . .

"Ava, do what's best for them, for a change. Let them have a fresh start with me. You can travel all over the fucking world, take pictures of Zulus or whatever. I'm happy here on this farm. I don't want anything else. I don't need anything else. He is all I want."

Ava's curiosity kicks in. She swallows another gulp of liquid courage and asks, "How long. . .?"

". . . have I wanted him? Since the first time I saw him." Ava tries to think back, to remember when that was. Chicago. The wedding. A long time ago.

Julie continues, "And there you are, furrowing your brow, about to complain again. You have no right to complain. You had your share. The perfect life, the perfect man, hell, even the perfect wet dreams. Your life was perfect and all you could do was complain and run away." Ava wonders for a second if that, indeed, was the truth. Julie goes on, "You left your life behind and I picked up the pieces."

This is not the way Ava wanted things to go. "We'll see what he has to say about it."

"Ha! You'll let a man decide your fate? What happened to feminist Ava?"

Ava thinks back to her plan, now woefully derailed. She needs to tell Julie the pertinent information before this goes any further. She takes a deep breath, looks right into Julie's eyes, and speaks in the calmest voice she can muster. "I've booked a room at the Eldridge. I've packed an overnight bag for you. I'll talk with Jesse tonight. If he wants to be with you, he'll follow you there. If he decides to stay with me, you'll be on your own."

Julie replies as if Ava has said something entirely different. Something more like how much she loved and appreciated this cousin of hers. "We had some good times, Ava, didn't we?"

"This isn't the way this was supposed to go."

"Scott-free, is that what you expected? Scott-free? You bat your eyelashes and it's all yours again? Look at you. You look like a sick baby bird that fell out of the nest and broke its neck. No feathers, pale and scrawny, miserable."

Ava tries not to let the statement in. A dead baby bird. She shifts gears, "You didn't tell him when I called, did you? When I called on Christmas and the other times, you didn't even tell him."

"As if that matters. You left your life. Possession is nine-tenths of the law and I've got that on my side. You left behind everyone you supposedly loved and, guess what. They've learned to live without you."

This is more than Ava can bear. "Get your own damn house! Get your own damn life!"

Julie seems unfazed. "You had Jesse. You had Raleigh, too, I hear. Ava, you attracted and tormented the men in your life. But they've moved on. We've all moved on. Me, Jesse, the kids."

Ava is standing now, towering over Julie. She picks up the overnight bag and heaves it toward the door. Her voice is clear and determined. "Get out of my house. Leave! Now!"

Julie practically skips to the door. "Thanks for the night at the Eldridge. Jesse and I are gonna enjoy the fucking hell out of it."

⁂

After the car door slams and Julie's tires push away on the gravel, Ava lifts the cocktail shaker to her mouth and drinks the remaining mixture as if it were a glass of lemonade on a hot summer's day. She knows martinis have never done her any favors. She doesn't even like the taste. She shouldn't gulp. Yet, gulp she does. She needn't weep. Yet weep she does. Mascara-blackened tears pour down her cheeks and she wipes at them with the palm of her hand, turning the droplets into dark smears.

Grabbing a pack of matches from "the forbidden room," Ava stomps a few more times on the nailed-down jeans and walks out into the yard. Fortunately, the night has turned relatively mild. Kansas is different from the Chicago of her youth, where several feet of snow could stay on the ground all winter. Here, the occasional winter day in the 60s lets you air out your bedclothes. And that is what she is here for: bedclothes. She picks up a few dried twigs and places them around the sheets and pillows. She delights in the fast-yellow flame of the match. She experiences a minor pyromaniacal thrill lighting the twigs. When the sheets catch fire, she practically dances. But then comes the awful putrid odor of burning feathers. Damn. She's burning her own treasured goose-down pillows, beloved and then abandoned to Julie. She slams the cover on the galvanized trash bin and turns away.

The revenge of the martinis causes her to skid on a patch of ice, but she manages to open the door to her darkroom. She runs her fingers over the practical gear, now coated with layers of dust. She takes in the skull-and-cross-bone warnings on containers she placed high, out of the reach of children. She mouths the names of the toxic chemicals, her developing aids. When she is about to leave, when she is reaching up to turn out the light, her fingers graze a stack of mail and several envelopes fall to the ground, in her path. She picks them up and smiles to see the names of old friends written on red or green or white Christmas card envelopes, greetings from college or Seattle friends who don't know about her trip away or her delayed return. There is one larger, more recent envelope from *Nomads.* She smiles even wider now. I can always move to St. Louis, she assures herself. These are tipsy thoughts. The martinis have done their job of turning her brain into a field of radishes. She walks a little unsteadily on her way to Jesse's carving shed.

She can't miss it. It's in the middle of the room, the long canoe, painted red inside and carved with animal heads and legs. Frog is prominent. Her muddled brain searches through its dusty file cabinets of information to recall some shared experience of frogs. Only that silly story Joe I would tell about harvesting frozen frog legs. The sides of the canoe are deep, and if she peers over the edge she can see pillows softening the flat bottom. She turns away quickly. The idea of Jesse making and arranging this for her body, her dead body, sends quakes through her shoulders. No. No. No.

She forces herself to breathe deeply and walk around the room, to get her bearings. She walks as purposefully as she can to Jesse's cork board, where he's always kept his orders, photos torn out of magazines, notes to himself. And then she sees it, a gorgeous photograph of his work, his own carved furniture in a high-end design magazine. And yes, there is his name in the bold-faced title of the article. **Jesse Lightfoot Speaks and the World Listens.** Something about the Native voice in his carving work. Ava doesn't like the metaphor but does recognize the Makah carving techniques in the headboards. Pink order slips for coffee tables, bookshelves, couch frames, picture frames, side tables, beds are piled high. Many for beds, his beautiful beds.

For a second Ava is jubilant over the news of his success, but then she is hit with a terrible weariness, like the plummet on a roller coaster after the highest climb. He is doing all right. She is happy for him. This is good. Ava walks to the painted canoe and sees that on the other side there is a small step stool. She walks up the two steps and puts a foot into the canoe. It rocks for a second but then steadies and she does the next thing that pops into her head: she tries it on for size. Ava first kneels and then turns so she can lie prone on top of the satiny pillows waiting to receive her. She can't help but recall their first married mating, in a similar boat, one he may also have carved. She remembers the urgency, the need they had for each other.

Something is wrong. This boat is too long. He misremembered her height. Just then, Homer the elderly Samoyed trots in. "Where have you been, buddy?" Homer steps up the little ladder as if it were made for his old arthritic legs, and maybe it was. He hops with unexpectedly youthful grace into the canoe, licks her face, wags his tail, turns around three times, and plops himself at her feet. She thinks of the carved monuments to medieval saints and lords, their faithful dogs carved at their feet. Jesse wasn't really thinking of knocking off old Homer and burying him with me, was he? She knows her radish brain is sending her down ridiculous aisles of woeful thoughts. It's just the martinis. She just needs to close her eyes a minute. A bit of rest before Jesse arrives. She crosses her arms across her chest like a medieval lady and wishes for a lily to hold in her hand, her lady hand, her lily-laden lady hand. She pictures the lily. She conjures the lily. She embraces the lily. Someone is placing coins on her eyelids, she is sure of it. She will have a good journey and travel to where she needs to travel. Good night, sweet prince. The dog is snoring. She surrenders.

Ava senses more than sees that she is being lifted. She knows she is being carried, like when she was a small child and fell asleep in her parents' car. She'd be lifted but push consciousness away, hang on to her dream state, at that moment a world more credible than the real.

Steps, doors, hallways, and then she is gently lowered, tucked in. She sleeps in the half-drowsed pleasant state of near-oblivion. She feels a warm wetness on her cheek. She hopes it is the wetness of kisses, even dog kisses would do, but she knows that it is unfleshly cloth that touches her cheeks. She is being washed. She must be dead. Truly dead and someone is washing her for burial. If she were dead, would she be this aware of being washed? Perhaps her spirit would stay with her long enough to witness ministrations and grief. Ava concludes that she has no way of knowing and this gives her permission to keep her eyes sealed shut, to dream for a while longer.

When she does experiment with opening her eyes, it is only for a second, and then she closes them tightly again. She grasps that she is in a room with a roaring fire and that she is not alone. A scent wafts toward her. Pipe smoke. Someone is smoking in the room. This could be her wake. Her funeral. When she next opens her eyes, it is as the tiniest of slits so as not to be noticed. But once again a victim of her own over-developed sense of curiosity, she opens her eyes for a few seconds longer. And then she sees him. Jesse. She sees him in profile, leaning forward, concentrating, waiting. Wearing a buffalo headdress, he stands incredibly still, just to the left of the fireplace fire. She thinks: Omigod, he's so. . .

And then, the sound begins. The loud, wonderful beating. Her attention goes sharply to the right where the sound is coming from. A familiar sound. A recording from long ago. The sound is strong. It makes her forget hunger, fatigue, her fears. She is absorbed into the sound, as if she herself were a drum.

He begins to dance. She wants to see this. She is eager to see this. She must see this. She watches as he strikes the floor with bare feet. As he steps from side to side, the buffalo head trembles, the horns vibrate.

Unaware of her open eyes, Jesse turns from profile to face toward the fire. She sees a buffalo tail hanging down the middle of his back. When he moves his head sharply to the left, the pelt and tail move to his shoulder, revealing his own skin, and there, gracing his back an elaborate tattoo of feathered wings. Wings!

"Omigod!" she says, sitting up all too quickly, like a jack-in-the-box.

He stops, shuts off the music, and turns toward her. "Ava! Are you all right?"

"You have wings on your back!"

He answers quietly, almost sheepishly. "Oh, yeah, I learned to fly."

For a wild second, she believes she has entered an afterlife peopled with buffalo angels. But then he speaks: "You're back! You're alive, breathing!"

"I guess so. But the dance? The buffalo headdress?"

She waits, as she knows she must, for him to put away the regalia. He carefully, prayerfully, reverently places each of the pieces into a small trunk next to the fireplace. He waits to answer while he handles the objects, and then says, "It's part of a Buffalo-Calling Ceremony. I thought it'd be a good idea, since the ceremony is about renewal, circle of life, that kind of thing."

"I get it. I think." A tiny sprig of hope pushes up through the fog.

"It's an old dance. A very old dance."

She observes that without the buffalo headdress, she can see his familiar black shiny hair, except now there is also a streak of white framing his face with dignity. A white streak that came from age or worry or her own misdeeds.

"Bird Standingwater learned it from a Sioux medicine man, and he's been teaching it to me." He closes the lid of the trunk but remains standing. He is wearing jeans and seems to be surveying the room, trying to remember where he put his shirt.

Ava's questions come out in a quick stream, "Are you becoming a shaman? Were you just bringing me back to life? Not ready to ship me off to eternity in that boat so you danced me back to life, something like that?"

"What are you talking about?"

"The dance. You just brought me back. From something. Unconsciousness or something."

"Ah. So maybe it works." He smiles his old wry unreadable smile. "Actually, I'm learning the dance for my father."

"Your father?"

"Same thing with the canoe you were—trying out." Ava's stomach lurches at the mention of the boat. "It's a dance to call upon the spirits to help him, so that he makes the journey in a good way."

"What journey?"

"Dad had another stroke. I just came home from the hospital. Ava, we can talk about it later."

"I have to go see him." Ava moves her feet to the ground, tries to stand. Too unsteady, she instantly and inelegantly plops back down.

"It's too late."

"No!" A wallop of guilt hits her. She's been gone so long her father-in-law has died.

"Ava, oh god, I just meant that visiting hours are over." He takes a breath. "I'm going to perform the buffalo dance for him tomorrow, in his hospital room. It's okay. He's ready. It's a good thing."

"Nobody told me! Nobody told me about your father!" How dare the world not stand still while she was gone! How dare the people in her life be mortal!

"I just did tell you. Avie, you've been gone seven months."

"About that. . ." She tries to stand again, to take the floor, to explain herself but she teeters again and must sit.

"Ava, are you sure you're all right? You seem a little unsteady on your feet."

"I drank a pitcher of martinis is all."

He laughs a little. "You and martinis never did mix." His face reassembles into a more concerned expression. "You need to eat." He mentally surveys the contents of the refrigerator. "BLT?"

"On rye. No L." She loves that they are having an ordinary conversation after this extraordinary moment. It reminds her of their life together. Filaments of the ineffable woven in with the quotidian.

"Without the L, as if I could forget."

"About that, the seven months. . ."

"Let's wait. We can have that conversation when we're done eating." He is foraging in the fridge, pulling out something wrapped in old time butcher paper. "At least we have good bacon."

"From Steinkuehler's down the road?"

"Mmmm-hmm." Jesse turns the gas on under the heavy iron skillet. Ava understands that he is living up to his tribe's reputation. People Generous with Food. Something that fit so perfectly with Greek and Polish customs of hospitality, it had always been common ground. Feed the guest before you even ask their name. And she is a guest now, whatever that might mean. Jesse looks up at her from his task and says, "I see you're sporting a new hairdo. Going for a Sinead O'Connor kinda thing?" He misses her gorgeous mane, thinks, how could she have done this?, but is not about to say so.

"I've been told I look like a dead baby bird."

"More like a newborn chick."

"Y'mean, like a chicken chick?" It sounds so much like "chicken shit," they both burst out laughing.

"Maybe a crane chick. A little wobbly on its feet. Did you know they grow an inch a day?"

"Wow. But about the wobbly part, you do remember that I drank a shaker of martinis. Before I—went to sleep."

"Passed out."

Damn, she thinks. Moderation, moderation, I must learn moderation. When the strong scent of bacon comes to her happy nostrils, she breathes in deeply and swears off moderation once again. "Bacon. Who doesn't love bacon?"

⚜

They eat appreciatively, familiarly, chatting in détente about meaningless things like the weather and the goodness of the bacon. They are waiting to be finished with this formality before the real event of the night. After Jesse puts the last dish into the dishwasher, he turns to Ava and looks her straight in the eye. "You nailed my jeans to the floor."

"You did have sex with her, didn't you?"

He doesn't answer immediately, but when he does it's more honest than she can bear. "I did. And the sex was great." Her heart descends into her belly.

"Are you sorry?"

"No."

She manages to sigh out a single syllable. "Oh."

"It was great because I never kissed her, never said one word of endearment. Didn't have to. It was functional, quick, and over with."

Well, at least there's that, she thinks. "Are you in love with her?"

"In love with her? She may be your blood, but that woman is . . ." He can't bring himself, even now, to insult her relative to her face. Crazy cousin. Loony toons.

"What?"

"It was just a few times, the sex."

"Is that supposed to make me feel better?" She is bouncing the heel of her left foot up and down nervously and loudly.

"And then, I did a sweat. My dad insisted that I do a sweat. I had gone

315

into a deep funk after you and the girls left. I gambled. A lot."

"You gambled."

"I gambled your horses away."

"Red China and Little Joe? No!" She yells out more loudly about this than she had about the sex with her cousin Julie.

"Like I was saying, I did this sweat. I had to get my head screwed back on right. 'Screwed' is a bad choice of words."

"My horses!"

"I got them back. Had to pay through the nose, but I got them back. I stopped things with Julie then, too. But she still hung around. I couldn't throw her out. She's your kin. Then, she started helping out with the kids."

Ava's thinking about the limits of the rules of hospitality. Why didn't he throw her out? "Your jeans on her floor? Today?"

"She borrowed them. The washer's broken. She was re-painting the room, hanging up another goddam painting, and she asked to borrow an old pair. They never fit me right. Too damn tight." He recites this elaborately, unconvincingly, perhaps not even wanting her to believe him, wanting to get caught in the lie.

"You're telling me Julie left them on the floor. Julie. You expect me to believe that?"

"Ava, a week ago, a package arrived with your suitcase in it. I had been holding onto the belief that you were alive until that package came." He pauses for emphasis. "Seven months."

"So, you were finding consolation in my cousin's twat? And then you lie to me about it? Aren't you just a little bit sorry? Are you?"

"You left on an extremely long trip. Are you sorry?"

"No." This may not be the most healing thing to say, but it is the truth. Ava loves that she has ventured forth, seen something of the world. She waits to see a reaction on Jesse's face. Omigod, what have I done?

But he just nods his head and says, "Good."

What does she do with that? What the hell does she do with that answer? She has the unexpected urge to share something of her experiences, so she says, "Oh, Jesse, I saw the caryatids and giant pelicans and I heard old men playing music in my father's village! I walked in the footsteps of my ancestors." She hopes that he will stop her here, say something understanding about finding one's ancestors, but he does not. Perhaps everything she's ever believed about Native Americans is false.

Maybe she's learned nothing in all this time. Ava looks over at him to see that his eyes are downcast, but he is clearly listening. "I went to this village in Italy where they create images on the ground out of flower blossoms and herbs. And then the pictures blow away."

This makes him look up. "Really?"

"I thought of you and the girls every single day. I wanted you with me to see what I was seeing."

"You slept with Christopher-Robin Raleigh whatever-the-fuck, though, didn't you?"

"Yes."

"Are you sorry?"

She struggles with this. "No." She wants to be sorry. Everything she knows tells her she should be sorry, must be sorry, better be shamefully sorry.

"Good. You were headed in that direction for a long time. Besides, we had agreed." He pauses here to catch his breath. He is trying so hard to be understanding and fair, but something about this conversation is making him short of breath. He thinks about how he is aging. They used to fight with such gusto.

She interrupts his train of thought. "Now that I think about it, I am sorry. He turned out to be an asshole." She pauses for effect. "He left in the middle of a flood. A flood. I had to forage for food." This isn't producing the desired effect, so she adds, "He wanted me to marry him and I said 'No.'"

Jesse ignores the bait, sucks in more air and says, "You slept with other men, too, am I right? You enjoyed your freedom."

"One other. And yes."

"Good." He's not going to be able to be restrained much longer.

"I can tell you. . . "

"God, spare me the details. You did what you had to do. I did what I had to do."

"You can't really be pleased."

He struggles to begin the next words and finally says, "No. I'm not. I hate everything about it, but you had the right. We agreed and you had the right." He struggles to begin again, to say the words he has been rehearsing in his head for months and then, just lets it all cascade out, "I meant what I wrote in that letter to you about how, all those years ago, I had been drawn to you because you had such hungry, curious eyes. Because you ran with wild horses, for chrissake, and then I tried to squash that very thing that I loved. I even used Kaya to make you jealous, hoping I could keep you. I tried to keep you to myself. For that I am sorry. For years of that, years—I am deeply sorry." He looks at her for a reply. When she doesn't answer, he turns his gaze to the floor until she gathers her words.

"What letter? What are you talking about?"

"The letter I gave to Raleigh to take to you. Oh. Oh, no. He didn't give it to you."

Puzzled and curious, Ava watches as Jesse opens the roll top desk and starts throwing papers, envelopes, bills, and stamps to the floor. Finally, he digs into a small drawer that has a place for a key, now long lost. There, in a metal fireproof box that contains birth certificates and a life-insurance policy, he finds what he is looking for. He straightens and flattens the crumpled pages, then hands them over to her.

"I did keep a draft."

Dear Ava,

The 2nd thing I loved about you was your hair. Your gorgeous ~~spirally~~ hair. I thought of you as The Girl with the Pre-Raphaelite Hair. ~~I wanted to bury my face in your hair.~~

But the 1st thing I loved about you were your searching, eager-to-learn-everything eyes. Even before you told me the story of how you rode on that beach in Chile, I thought of you as a wild horse with an amazing appetite for life, galloping with your mane flying. You wanted to eat life, dance life, shout life, and I wanted that close to me. Who wouldn't want you?

I took a woman who had ridden with wild horses and brought her home to a sick father and a herd of bison. I wanted to take that ~~zest,~~ eagerness and contain it, jar it, put it up for winter.

What was I thinking? If I tamed you, you would no longer be the woman I fell in love with. You'd be a more ordinary breed. Hair pinned up, eyes steady on the embroidery in your lap. Why couldn't I see that? Of course, when the opportunity came, your eye for the open road, your hunger for life ~~and its experiences~~ was awakened.

I brought you home and tried to domesticate you. I am so sorry.

And now, what can I offer but a willingness to go back to the drawing board. Please come back.

When Jesse sees her eyes lift from the page, he says, "Sorry, I think the final version was better, shorter, less gushy. Damn him for not giving it to you."

Ava stands, dumbstruck, scans the letter again. "I love this letter and right now, this very minute, I do so appreciate the apology. That must have been hard to do. I am moved." She smiles, then, remembering the girl's letters and their names for the letters. "The Jessiad."

"But?"

"But, I was a grown-up. I could have been more direct, more forthcoming, I could have asked for what I really wanted. I didn't. And then, when I had this chance, this chance to. . . " She thinks the word "wander,"4 she thinks the word "travel," but can't say another syllable. She's swallowed a gigantic toad and can't croak another word out. It should be simpler. This should be simpler.

He's thought about this conversation a million times. He's rehearsed these words a thousand times. "I thought you were leaving me forever. I didn't want to be the one left, so I did the so-called 'manly' thing and pushed you away."

They pause here, as if by agreement. Jesse adds another log to the fire. Ava picks up a striped dish towel and wipes her face. They both know somewhere in the recesses of their brains that they can't settle everything in one night of talk. That doesn't stop them. Ava is aware of tears making tracks down her cheeks again. She speaks, but quietly.

"I couldn't be everything you wanted me to be, I couldn't."

"I know."

"I'll never be Kaya."

"You know what 'Kaya' means? It's Hopi for 'Elder Sister.' I don't need another big sister."

"I'll never be one of you, I'll never be Indian."

"And I'll never be Greek. Or Polish. Oh, Ava, I chose you. You chose me. We will never be each other. We will never have each other's history or moods or thumbprints. We may never even understand each other."

"That sounds like a fatal flaw."

Silence.

She thinks back to those days when they decided to try out a separation. What a mixture of sorrow and celebration it felt like. "When this trip began, I felt so free. But when I saw each new thing, I thought of you, I thought of you every day. Like I said, I wanted you there."

"Then why, tell me why didn't you come home?"

"It must be so hard to understand. First, there was a problem with the flooded airport, the cancelled flight, but I didn't even hang around to see if I could take another plane. I left. To this day, I'm not sure I understand why." She takes in a deep breath. "But no, I kind of do. It's just hard for me to admit." She exhales so hard, she almost spits. "Sure, there was the thing about you not wanting me to fly. But there was something else." She swallows. "I just felt there was more to me. I wanted to experience more of me. My full life. I felt a hunger for more of my own life. I felt a hunger to at least try."

"You put me through hell, Ava! The girls and me. We thought you were dead. We thought we had lost you."

"I tried to call you. I did call you. I left messages."

"You could have tried harder!"

"Julie didn't give you the messages."

"You know better than to rely on Julie or a machine. You knew better. We, your husband, your children, we were waiting. Missing you. The kids—they were suffering without you. I thought maybe you were lying somewhere, injured or dead. Or maybe somebody hurt you and you were alone and . . . "

"I—oh, god—I see that now. But then, back then, I didn't even know if you wanted me anymore. And the girls. Hell, they went off with Kaya on that trip. I didn't think anyone needed me anymore. I thought you'd all be better off without me."

"Better off without you?" A quake starts low in his body and rises until his shoulders are shaking. He tries to hold down tears and is not successful. "Ava, you were everything to me." He turns away to hide this outburst of emotion.

Were? Were everything? Why the past tense? Why the tears? She finds her legs. She stands and goes to him. "I'm not sure what to—I'm struggling right now to even say . . . " She closes her eyes tight and tries to go on, to recall the words she'd composed on a ship, in a laundromat, on the side of a road. Simple words. An apology. "I'm sorry I caused you such pain." He doesn't answer. She puts her hands on his shoulders. She does what she's wanted to do since her first glimpse of the tattoo. With her fingers, she traces the wings on his back. She leans her head against him.

He turns around. Quickly. And when he turns around, it is not to embrace but to examine, to take a good look at her scars, one on her lip, one on her chin. He noticed the raised white line on her jaw when he was washing the black smear off her cheeks and now he needs to take another look. There it is, white, long, and thickened. He was worried about her lying injured somewhere. And there's the smaller scar on her lip and the chipped tooth he saw when she smiled. He scrutinizes it now. "You were hurt, weren't you?"

She is silent and her silence is his answer.

"Damn it, I should have gone with you. You begged me to go. What was I thinking?"

"You mean you could have been there to protect me? Jesse, I needed to do this on my own. Hey, I took a few bumps, but I survived!"

He notices again how thin she is. She weighs less than a bag of potato chips. She has no hair. "What happened to you?"

"Jesse, I lived through some shit and I did it, I survived, on my own. I am stronger. Maybe I have more to give. To our girls." He hears an unfamiliar conviction in her voice. She speaks with a new confidence and he believes her. "Y'know, mister, I did learn some stuff on the road."

He realizes that something has changed in her. Maybe it is a sinewy inner strength or the maturity of age that makes her less naïve, or maybe it's a smidgeon of wisdom earned, but it's there and he can't ignore it. "You're going to want to do this again, aren't you?"

"I'm going to want to travel again, if that's what you mean. Maybe not like I did this last time, but I want to do more photography, to capture the ways humans live and create. Out there, in the world. I have to."

The old wry smile creeps onto his face and this surprises her. He thinks maybe, just maybe, this is it. This is the time to tell her about what he's been up to. "My so-called pain and misery did lead to one good thing. I learned to fly."

"You mean like in some Raven dance? Have you been initiated into some secret society?" She wishes she knew more, she should have tried to learn more about the rituals, the dances. "See, this is when I feel stupid."

"You are anything but stupid." He takes a breath and almost laughs. His anger, his fury evaporate when he starts to tell her. "I went to the old airport in Topeka and took flying lessons."

"You learned to fly? A plane?" Stunned, she can do nothing but stare at his beautiful face.

"I did it so I wouldn't be afraid. To fly. With you."

They are standing a foot apart. Struck dumb, she runs her hand slowly over her bald head. He wants to touch that head of hers, to rub it, as if that would bring them luck. She looks at him, his slightly open lips. She wants to put her thumb in his mouth. She wonders what it all means; she doesn't care what it means; she very much wants to know what it all means.

It doesn't matter who speaks first because they are both thinking the same thing. They don't know if they'll ever forgive each other, be able to go on together.

Caution.

Caution.

To HELL with caution.

"Ava, you are my life."

She steps closer; he leans forward. She closes her eyes, feels warmth. Was that a kiss? Or a feather grazing her lips? Then another kiss and she remembers this oozy feeling of being turned into chocolate that has melted into a glob in the sun.

He lifts her dress gently over her hips, her shoulders, her newborn head. She unbuttons him slowly, slowly.

This may be the last time. Or maybe it is the first time. Perhaps they are together for old time's sake. Perhaps they will never be together again. They want to know what is new about each other. They want to know what is familiar. They want to know what they've forgotten, forgiven. They explore each other looking for cues, looking for answers, looking for questions.

Afterward, she gives him the book she's made for him and he, impressed, dances his fingers over the pressed leaves. He's always wanted to make her a garden of herbs. Sage. Oregano. Thyme. He attempts a toast with a long-forgotten Ukrainian rhyme and she, smiling, raises her glass, as if she could understand. They lean on their elbows, embarrassed and peaceful.

But then, there is something, something beyond them, something in the very earth making a vibration, yielding a sound. They stop and listen.

Somewhere, someone is singing a familiar song.

Somewhere, someone is counting out twelve grapes.

Somewhere, someone is blowing a cardboard horn.

They look at each other and their eyes agree. They know what to do. They will do what they have always done on this night, this mark on the calendar, this one night of oneness. They ignore the underwear tangled on the ground. He pulls up his jeans, she tugs down her dress. They run up the stairs to the treehouse room where, looking out the huge windows, they can see two counties and, in the distance, discern flashes of light and curls of smoke.

Somewhere, someone is setting off Chinese fireworks.

Somewhere, someone dressed in yellow, is drinking chicha.

Somewhere, someone is painting a front door red.

She turns to see the other, unwindowed wall covered in photographs. He follows her, taking in the images of powwows and Polish Easters, children dancing, Christmases past. They pause at the sight of themselves, people who've known each other a long time, people who've been friends, for that is what they are.

Somewhere, someone is cooking Hoppin' John.

Somewhere, someone is reading tarot cards.

Somewhere, someone is pounding a pot with a wooden spoon.

And then, they do what they must do. They turn to face the bed. This bed he built from a living tree grown from a West Coast twig torn from a tipi pole, carried in a plastic bucket across the country, and pushed into the Kansas soil; this bed he augmented these past seven months with Polish white birch and Ukrainian cherry, with English walnut and driftwood olive; this bed incised with the outline of a boat, the shape of a raven and that of a whale, and carved with the faces of their children and the initials of lovers, for that is what they are.

Somewhere, someone is uncorking champagne.

Somewhere, someone is breaking plates.

Somewhere, someone is beating a drum.

Somewhat clumsily, they climb onto the bed and help each other stand up. They are still for a moment, facing one another as they listen to each other breathe. So many breaths they've heard from each other in this room.

Somewhere, someone is counting down.

Somewhere, someone is jumping twelve times.

Somewhere, temple bells are ringing.

Between photographs and windows, they stand on the handmade bed together, teetering on the unevenness. And then they begin. They start to jump and bounce and shout and howl. They spring, leap, laugh, and bound.

They roar and bellow and jump some more. They jump higher and higher, closer and closer to the edge, until they are on the verge of falling.

But then, just then, they reach out and catch each other.

Mid-air.

.

.

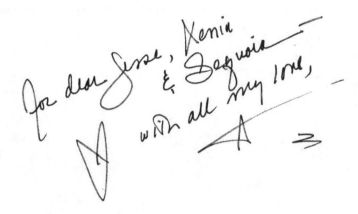

For dear Jesse, Xenia
& Sequoia —
with all my love,

GLIMPSES OF GREECE

329

ACKNOWLEDGEMENTS

My lasting gratitude to a certain young dancer (Makah) who performed barefoot on the streets of Seattle. Through my relationship with him during those intense months of racial conflict surrounding indigenous rights, I learned about the politics of dance, the beauty of otherness, and the cost of driving while Indian. We parted ways after that summer, but the memories and lessons of those days are always with me. And thanks to the Makah people, known to be "generous with food," who fed me salmon on their beaches and, despite my foolish naivete, welcomed me.

A novel which spans decades and cultures rests on the expertise of generous consultants. My copious thanks to Marilyn Russell (Ojibwe), Native art historian, and Gloria Graves (Mississippi Choctaw), library technician, both of whom gave hours of their time telling their personal stories and educating me on the evolution of Haskell Indian Nations University from a traditional Indian boarding school to a full-fledged university. Gloria also provided me with theses and yearbooks to peruse and tales of Libby the library ghost. Heartfelt thanks to my nephew David Posthumus, anthropologist at the University of South Dakota, for sharing his expertise on Native spirituality. His insights on the Lakota buffalo ceremony were invaluable.

Abundant appreciation to Lampros Paputsakis who, over the course of many summers, invited my husband and me to remote villages on Crete for celebrations of Holy Spirit Day, where I learned about the custom of philoxenia, literally the love of the stranger, when otherness is celebrated through gathering, feasting, and epic song. When Lampros learned I was writing this book, he told me how his beloved Amari Valley was memorialized in the *Odyssey* as the Land of the Lotus Eaters, a place one never wants to leave.

Love and hugs to our other Greek and Greek-American friends who helped me understand the culture of hospitality as we shared long evenings of food, drink, and stories. Velissarios Karacostas, Tina Bucuvalas and Michalis Fotiadis, thanks for your companionship. A special thanks to Tracey Cullen, archeologist of pre-historical Greece and dear friend for decades, who read multiple drafts and made meaningful and helpful suggestions on text and design, always with her ever-gentle, encouraging words.

Deep thanks to my late Polish-American grandmother who taught me to carve lambs out of butter and other endearing customs of hospitality. And fond gratitude to my beloved cousins who continue to be supportive and honorable (as opposed to their fictional counterpart in this book). And to my family in Poland, who replace every spoonful of food eaten with three spoons more, my appreciation.

I am fortunate in having friends and family who read my amateurish drafts, who were generous with their time and thoughtful. I'm talking about you, Emily Kofron, Jeffrey Ann Goudie, Cecil Wooten, Ben Lerner, Ann Palmer, Marion Cott, Susan Zuber, Emily Nicholas Posthumus, and Bonnie Nicholas. Special shout-outs to the generosity of Tom Averill for his careful editing and to Harriet Lerner for the copious energy she spent supporting the novel.

Appreciation goes out to listeners at readings from captive audiences in Topeka living rooms to the Mediterranean Studies Conference in Rethymnon, Crete. And to Grant Tracey for boosting my faith in this work by publishing an early excerpt, "Horseradish," in *The North American Review.*

Enormous bouquets of thanks to Thea Rademacher of Flint Hills Publishing for taking on this project and for her positive energy, her generous and adventurous spirit, and her lifesaving sense of humor. And grateful applause to Barbara Waterman-Peters for her extraordinary artistry and collaborative openness on the cover painting.

Love and appreciation to my daughter, Inge Hansen, who sat with me at an outdoor café in Ghent, eating Belgian waffles covered in strawberries, whipped cream, and advocaat, while asking pointed textual questions in her gentlest voice. When later I had doubts about the profusion of cultures represented in the book, she answered, "This is who we are."

A special thanks to my fellow traveler in life and art, Tom Prasch, who trekked around Greece several times with me, visiting islands that claimed that Odysseus had slept there. And more thanks to him for accompanying me to the U.S. Northwest Coast, where we stayed on the Makah reservation so I could revisit my enchantment. And yet more thanks for his patient reading and unsurpassed editing, which made *Watching Men Dance* a far more engaging read.

I find myself writing these acknowledgements in the pandemic era of sheltering at home and social distancing, when it is hard to even imagine hitting the road again. Yet it is the travelers and the wanderers I am thinking of, those who wish to engage with the stranger, to learn from difference, and to see the world. I thank you all for reading my book. I hope that the travels within these covers will help relieve the ache of wanderlust and keep you content under your very own covers for now. Be patient. Soon, we will be on the road again.

ABOUT THE AUTHOR

Marcia Cebulska grew up in Chicago and has spent most of her career writing for the stage and screen. Her critically acclaimed plays have been produced at thousands of venues worldwide and her screenwriting aired on PBS. She has received the Jane Chambers International Award, the Dorothy Silver Award, several Master Artist Fellowships, and a National Endowment for the Arts commission. Marcia's guided journal SKYWRITING was released in 2019. WATCHING MEN DANCE is her first novel. Marcia lives in Topeka, Kansas with her husband, historian Tom Prasch.

9 781733 203562